The Investor's Guide to Economic Fundamentals

Wiley Finance Series

The Investor's Guide to Economic Fundamentals

John Calverley

JOHN WILEY & SONS, LTD

Other Wiley Editorial Offices

John Wiley & Sons Inc., 111 River Street, Hoboken, NJ 07030, USA

Jossey-Bass, 989 Market Street, San Francisco, CA 94103-1741, USA

Wiley-VCH Verlag GmbH, Boschstr. 12, D-69469 Weinheim, Germany

John Wiley & Sons Australia Ltd, 33 Park Road, Milton, Queensland 4064, Australia

John Wiley & Sons (Asia) Pte Ltd, 2 Clementi Loop #02-01, Jin Xing Distripark, Singapore 129809

John Wiley & Sons Canada Ltd, 22 Worcester Road, Etobicoke, Ontario, Canada M9W 1L1

Library of Congress Cataloging-in-Publication Data

Calverley, John.
    Investors guide to economic fundamentals / John Calverley.
      p.   cm.—(Wiley finance series)
    Includes index.
    ISBN 0-470-84690-9 (cased : alk. paper)
    1. Investments—Handbooks, manuals, etc.   I. Title.   II. Series.

    HG4527 .C258   2002
    330—dc21   2002028093

British Library Cataloguing in Publication Data

A catalogue record for this book is available from the British Library

ISBN 0-470-84690-9

Typeset in 10/12pt Times by TechBooks, New Delhi, India
Printed and bound in Great Britain by Antony Rowe, Chippenham, Wiltshire
This book is printed on acid-free paper responsibly manufactured from sustainable forestry
in which at least two trees are planted for each one used for paper production.

To Aileen

Contents

Figures

Tables

Preface

Why does the stock market rise dramatically one year and fall sharply the next? Which way will interest rates go next? Why are bond yields at today's level? Are bonds cheap? Why is the dollar so strong? What do property yields say about the property market? What caused the Asian crisis? Will fiscal expansion work? These are some of the questions this book tries to address by looking at the economic fundamentals driving markets. It is aimed at all those engaged in investment, both market practitioners and private investors.

As a practising business economist, my job is to make sense of market levels and movements and then advise management and clients on future opportunities and risks. These pages represent an accumulated view, derived from 25 years of close observation of markets, experiencing the investment process, talking to other analysts and practitioners as well as academic study. The book aims, above all, to be a practical guide, easy to read, explaining fundamental relationships in a concise and easily digestible form.

With a good knowledge of fundamentals readers can approach any given market environment with tools that are not only timeless, but provide a guide to what is happening in a long-term and cyclical framework and contribute to a sound investment decision, with full appreciation of the risks. Even investors who use approaches that make little use of fundamental analysis — for example, indexed funds or technical analysts — can benefit from a background understanding.

Of course understanding market fundamentals does not mean that making money is easy, but it does mean that investors can recognise the recurring patterns and comprehend the risks involved. Ultimately the only way to earn more than the risk-free investment (in other words, government paper, preferably index-linked) is to take on some kind of risk, whether it be market risk or credit risk. After you read this book I hope you will have a better understanding of how to incorporate fundamentals into the investment process and how to assess these risks.

HOW TO USE THIS BOOK

This book can be read from beginning to end of course, but it is also designed to allow the reader to dip into any chapter as desired. For example, the reader interested in the fundamentals of stock markets can go straight to Chapter 13. Or if the immediate interest is in understanding monetary policy, the reader can go directly to Chapter 5. Also, in the glossary the reader will find most of the jargon that is commonly used in the markets, from arbitrage investing to yield curve. A section on websites lists some of the most useful resources, noting especially sites with good links.

The book is structured as follows. Part I (Chapters 1–10) looks at economic fundamentals for investors, to explain how economic forces combine with monetary and fiscal policy to determine interest rates, economic growth and inflation. The chapters start with economic growth and the cycle, moving through inflation, deflation and unemployment to monetary and fiscal policy. In Chapter 4 an assessment of the so-called 'new economy' is made. Chapter 7 discusses the feedback from asset prices to the economy and policy, an increasing area of interest to policymakers and the markets. Chapters 8–10 look at international aspects including the exchange rate, trade and globalisation and emerging markets.

Part II (Chapters 11–17) then takes each of the major asset classes in turn and explains how they are assessed using fundamental techniques. Individual chapters cover money markets, bonds, stocks, currencies, property, emerging markets and commodities.

Part III concludes with three chapters. Chapter 18 provides a summary of the main body of the book with a table showing the typical response of each asset class to economic events. Chapter 19 looks at different approaches to investment, from market timing to hedge funds and discusses how economic fundamentals are used in each case. Chapter 20 looks at how the fundamentals have changed over the last 10 years and hazards some guesses about future developments.

Although it is very much the author's contention that the fundamentals are just that, fundamental, in practice there are substantial shifts over time, sometimes caused by changing policy approaches and sometimes due to changes in the economy. Over the last 10 years the most significant changes have been the widespread adoption of inflation targeting, the emergence of deflation, the collapse of the 'Asian miracle' and the emergence of historically high stock market valuations.

Throughout the book the reader will find sections focusing on a market over a specific period, for example a profile of the last US business cycle or an explanation of the Asia crisis, explaining what happened and why. Naturally, considerable attention is paid to the US economy, but the reader will also find detailed discussions of Japan, Euroland, the UK and emerging economies.

I have also included forecasts or alternative scenarios of where I think markets are going at the time of writing (April 2002). When you read this book you will be able to test these against what has actually happened. Doubtless, since markets are always full of surprises you will find plenty of differences! In a way this should be taken as a health warning of the difficulties of forecasting markets. Not only are markets frequently hit by unexpected 'shocks', but there are always many different forces working at the same time.

I have thoroughly enjoyed writing this book. Markets provide an endless source of interest and excitement because of the continuous process of change and evolution, and the fundamentals are always being tested by new events and new policy approaches. I hope you enjoy reading it.

Acknowledgements

I would like to thank American Express Bank for encouraging me to pursue this project. I would also like to thank my colleagues in the Global Economics Unit for their support while I was immersed in drafts as well as for their ideas and suggestions from which I have borrowed liberally. I would especially like to thank Kevin Grice for reading the manuscript and providing detailed comments, and also Sharon Thornton for patiently helping me with the charts, tables and corrections. Naturally all remaining errors and omissions are mine.

Part I
Economics for Investors

1

Why Economic Growth Matters

Changes in economic growth are crucial for investors. Not only do the phases of the economic cycle bring attendant moves in interest rates, bond yields, stock valuations, etc., but a faster or slower trend growth rate directly influences profits and therefore long-term stock market returns.

More fundamentally, economic growth is what distinguishes investment from gambling. Games of pure chance such as roulette, as well as games that incorporate skills such as poker or backing horses, suffer from the limitation that each person's winnings are offset by someone else's losses. In economics jargon, they are 'zero-sum games', i.e. the sum of everybody's gains and losses is zero. Investment is different. With investment, everyone can gain, but this is true only as long as the economy continues to grow.

TREND VERSUS CYCLE

For as long as economics has been a subject of study economic growth has moved in cycles, with periods of fast growth interspersed with periods of slow growth or decline. Economists like to separate this cycle from the 'trend' or 'underlying' growth of the economy. The advantage of this approach is that it divides the study of economic growth into two disciplines: an analysis of the cycle and an analysis of the trend (the subject of this chapter). Chapter 2 looks at business cycles.

However, while it is convenient to split growth into two components, it should not be assumed that the trend is completely independent of the cycle. Some economists argue that a long period of recession may actually depress the trend rate of growth and vice versa. Figure 1.1 shows GDP growth for the US economy over the last 40 years and includes a 10-year moving average to indicate the long-term trend. From the early 1970s through to the mid-1990s the cycle became more pronounced while trend growth declined. More recently, however, there is evidence of faster trend economic growth in the USA, with reduced volatility, notwithstanding the sharp drop in GDP growth in 2001.

MEASURES OF GROWTH

Economists assess the output or production of an economy with a variety of measures but gross domestic product (GDP) is the one most commonly used. GDP measures the total value of goods and services produced in an economy, i.e. everything produced for sale to the final user. While GDP is always the most important ultimate measure, the data are usually released too late to be of value for the investor. Other data releases that give partial clues to the direction of the economy are often watched more closely because they give an earlier indication of trends.

One indicator that is scrutinised particularly closely is Purchasing Managers' indices, re-named Supply Managers' indices in the USA from January 2001. The US Institute of Supply Managers' Index has been available for decades and provides a very good indicator of business

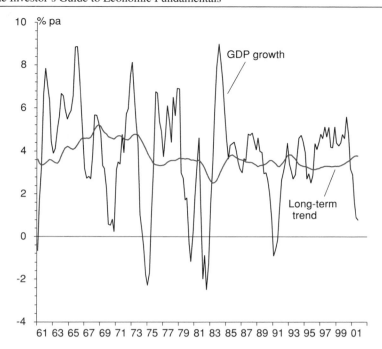

Figure 1.1   The US economic cycle and trend
Source: Thomson Datastream

confidence in the production sector. More recently a 'non-manufacturing' survey has also been available. Purchasing managers' surveys have also been instituted in Euroland and the UK over the last 10 years but they are treated with more caution by analysts because they are relatively new and have not been calibrated over several cycles. All these indices are based on a survey of 'purchasing managers' in companies, asking each a series of questions on his or her company's situation, including orders, inventories, hiring plans, prices paid, etc.

Industrial production is another key indicator. Although industry accounts for only around 20–25% of GDP in most OECD countries (the main industrial countries), its output tends to be more volatile than the rest of the economy and therefore provides a good signal of overall trends. When the economy is expanding producers will often increase output faster than sales in anticipation of future sales (not wanting to miss out and confident of not being left with unsold inventory). When the economy is contracting, industrial production will usually decline much more than GDP because producers are trying to clear excess inventories. Other useful indicators of GDP are leading indicators, employment and retail sales.

For investors there are four different ways that GDP can be analysed which provide useful insights.

1. *Nominal versus real GDP.* The difference between the two is inflation, in this case as measured by the GDP price deflator. Real GDP is what counts and what can be compared across countries and across time.
2. *The demand components approach.* This looks at the various components of GDP, e.g. consumer spending, investment, government spending, net exports, etc. Each of these

components responds in different ways to changes in variables such as interest rates and exchange rates, and so economists use this breakdown as a way of analysing the likely changes in the economy. This approach is sometimes called 'Keynesian' after the British economist J.M. Keynes.[1]

3. *Investment versus productivity.* How much of the increase in output is due to new machines (i.e. new investment) that can create more output and how much is due to better use of the existing machines (i.e. greater productivity)?

4. *Supply-side components of growth.* Growth is broken down into changes in employment and hours worked and changes in labour productivity.

These four approaches are analysed in detail later in this chapter. Note, however, that there are other approaches to GDP: for example, GDP can be broken down on the income side, so that gross domestic income is equal to wages, profits, rent and interest. Another way to cut GDP is by dividing it between agriculture, industry and services.

EXPANDING ECONOMIES

Why do some countries grow faster than others? The simplest way to answer this question is in terms of the third approach to GDP discussed above, namely investment and productivity, i.e. output per hour. The fast-growing countries of Asia have all had relatively high investment rates and high productivity growth rates. Investment here includes spending on education and skills and on infrastructure such as transport and telecommunications as well as on new factories. However, some countries have also enjoyed rapid increases in the number of hours worked due to population growth, greater female participation and, sometimes, longer hours.

What determines investment and productivity rates? Rates of investment are closely related to the level of savings. If current spending on goods and services is high, perhaps because wages are high or consumer borrowings are high or the government is running a large budget deficit, then there are less resources available for investment. If the economy is generating higher savings then it is more likely to have high investment. However, high savings by consumers and businesses are by no means certain to go into domestic investment. They might go into financing a government deficit or into investments overseas.

If high savings are to be used for productive investments, three domestic conditions must be satisfied.

First, investment is likely to be higher, the better the general business environment, which includes a whole host of factors, most of which are influenced if not determined by government policy. Hence, an economy which is moving in the direction of privatisation, reduced regulation and increased educational attainment is likely to see an expansion in investment over time. As we shall see in Chapter 10, policies of this kind in emerging markets have usually been correlated with advancing stock markets. Similarly, the buoyant stock markets of the USA and Europe during the 1990s were linked to progress in these areas.

Secondly, returns on capital should be high. If business can see high returns, then it is much more likely to invest. Return on capital, however, has not been the only motivator in many countries. In Asia investment seems to have been aimed at sales growth and market share rather than simply returns. Nevertheless the difficult experience of Japan throughout the 1990s and

---

[1] J.M. Keynes' most influential work was 'The general theory of employment, interest and money', 1936, London: Macmillan. 'Keynesian' economics was developed by other economists using a simplified framework and the debate continues to this day on the extent to which this framework is true to Keynes.

smaller Asian countries since 1997, especially in contrast to the USA, suggests that return on capital will be of more widespread importance in future. In practice, high returns on capital are usually associated with a particular phase of the economic cycle, but they can also be created by a wave of new technology or by a major government liberalisation programme.

Thirdly, investment is likely to be higher, the lower the overall risks in the economy. In practice, risks are likely to decline the more stable is macro-economic policy – the lower the inflation rate, the more business-friendly the government and the greater the political consensus for a continuation of these policies.

How can countries generate higher savings? One way is for governments to reduce budget deficits or even generate surpluses. Studies of the East Asian countries show that budget surpluses were an important factor in their success during the 1980s and early 1990s. The performance of the US economy in the late 1990s is also often attributed to the reduction, and then the elimination, of budget deficits. Sometimes it is argued that a budget deficit is justifiable if it is being used to finance major infrastructure investment; but experience suggests that government investment is less productive in general than private investment. Moreover, if particular government investments will indeed generate higher returns, it would nearly always be preferable for that investment to be financed privately. If the government does have a large budget deficit, interest rates will tend to be higher than otherwise, reducing private investment.

Another way for a country to have a higher savings rate is to encourage private savings. In the East Asian countries private savings are high partly because there is very little in the way of a government safety net for unemployment or old age. For the developed countries most studies focus on the desirability of reducing taxation on savings, e.g. reducing taxes on interest from deposits and on capital gains from investments.

High productivity growth is linked to a whole host of factors including good education and training, flexible trades unions, competition, dynamic entrepreneurship, moderate taxes, work ethics and of course high investment itself. It can also be linked to new technologies.

Table 1.1 shows average GDP growth rates for a selection of major countries during 1990–1999 compared with the share of investment in GDP at the beginning of that period in 1990.

Table 1.1   GDP growth and investment rates

Selected countries	Annual GDP growth 1990–99 (%)	Investment rate as % of 1990 GDP
China	10.7	35
Singapore	8.0	37
Ireland	7.9	21
Chile	7.2	25
Malaysia	6.3	34
India	6.1	25
Korea	5.7	38
Argentina	4.9	14
Poland	4.7	25
Indonesia	4.7	31
USA	3.4	17
Brazil	2.9	20
UK	2.2	19
Germany	1.5	23
Japan	1.4	32

While it broadly confirms the relationship between high rates of investment and high rates of growth, there are a number of fascinating exceptions. Ireland is perhaps the most interesting, having achieved very high growth rates despite only a modest investment rate. The reason for this is probably a combination of a much-increased workforce due to immigration and longer hours worked, together with particularly good improvements in productivity. Also, the available data may underestimate the size of investment in education.

Argentina is another country that performed well during the 1990s despite a very low rate of investment. The reason here is catch-up after the government eliminated high inflation and partially liberalised the economy, which resulted in a sharp improvement in growth. Unfortunately the benefits petered out at the end of the decade and Argentina faced a new crisis.

At the other end of the scale, Japan's lamentable GDP performance despite high investment is a measure of the very low rate of productivity achieved. A large part of this investment was government investment in infrastructure to try to keep the economy moving. Unfortunately much of it was probably unnecessary. Although business investment remains high it does not seem to be translated into growth.

DEFINING GROSS DOMESTIC PRODUCT

Why is it called GDP?

GDP is called *gross* domestic product because it includes the investment made to replace the machines that wear out in the process of producing that output. Since we do not know how quickly things really do wear out or become obsolete the calculation of net domestic product (i.e. after subtracting replacement investment) is dubious (though that does not deter the statisticians). It is called *domestic* product to distinguish it from *national* product (as in GNP) which is sometimes used. Domestic product is all production within a country, while national product is all production by the nationals of a country, including those working abroad.

The manner in which GDP is defined makes it equal to gross income as well as to gross spending. Clearly the total value of goods and services bought must be equal to the total value sold. In turn, these must also be equal to total incomes, including wages, profits, interest and rents. Remember that GDP is calculated on an 'added value' basis. In other words, the statisticians have to avoid any double counting such as including both the overall value of a new car and the value of its steel and tyres.

Calculating GDP in Practice

The precision in the statistics makes GDP look like a very accurate number. The reality of course is that it is no more than the best guess that can be made. In practice, figures are based on very sketchy data. Obviously the government statisticians cannot add up all the value of the output of the economy or indeed all the incomes or all the spending every quarter. They simply do not have the information, so they make a major computation every few years using all the available data, including income tax returns, sales tax returns and business and retail sales figures. In between they rely on the use of data that are available monthly to build up a picture which, it is hoped, will approximate the real GDP. One drawback of this approach is that, periodically, past GDP data are revised substantially when the big survey comes up with a new set of numbers.

FOUR WAYS TO ANALYSE GDP

Nominal versus Real GDP

The distinction between nominal and real GDP is basic but crucial. The difference between the two is inflation (or deflation if it is negative), in this case a measure called the GDP price deflator. It is called a 'deflator' because it pricks the balloon of rising prices and deflates the nominal figures on output, bringing them back to the real increase in goods and services output. Calculations are made as to how much of the nominal rise is due to price changes and how much is due to volume changes. However, since it is difficult to judge the effects of inflation, the calculation is subject to some doubt.

For example, suppose we know that the price of a Porsche 911 has risen 35% in the last ten years. We could conclude that this is all inflation, but Porsche would undoubtedly argue otherwise, citing improved features and options that are now fitted as standard. How much of the rise in price is due to quality improvements providing extra real value and how much is due to inflation? The statisticians have to make these decisions and they would be the first to admit that there are lots of questions over the calculations. This is particularly true the longer the period. For example, the Porsche 911 usually does not change much from quarter to quarter, but over ten years it will be a significantly different car. Fortunately, for the investor the long term is not all that important. The main question is whether the economy is growing at a fast pace or a slow pace and, fortunately, the data are generally good enough to answer that.

The Demand Components Approach

The demand components approach looks at GDP by analysing the various components of demand – economists' jargon for spending (see Table 1.2). This is the way the statisticians calculate GDP numbers and it is also the way that most economists try to forecast GDP. Note that each component has to be measured in real terms, i.e. after stripping out inflation.

Table 1.2   GDP by component: USA 2000

US$ billion	Value	% of total
A. Private consumption	6728	68
Durable goods	820	8
Non-durable goods	1989	20
Services	3919	40
B. Gross private investment	1767	18
Fixed investment	1718	17
Non-residential	1293	13
Residential	425	4
C. Change in inventories	50	1
D. Net exports	−364	−4
Exports	1103	11
Imports	1467	15
E. Government spending	1741	17
Gross Domestic Product	9873	100

Source: US Survey of Current Business. Note Gross private investment equals fixed investment plus change in inventories.

Table 1.3 Consumer spending indicators

Measures	Influences
Consumer expenditure	Income growth
Retail sales	Consumer confidence
Car sales	Unemployment
Department store sales	House prices
	Stock prices
	Interest rates

Each of these components responds in different ways to changes in variables such as interest rates, government spending and exchange rates, and so economists use this breakdown as a way of analysing the likely changes in the economy. For example, consumer spending, which depends primarily on income, also depends on such factors as consumer confidence, interest rates, the stock market, house prices, etc. The following sections look at this breakdown in detail.

Consumer Spending

Data are published on retail sales broken down into durable and non-durable goods, car sales and, after a delay, consumer spending. Retail sales (which in the USA includes car sales but not in the UK data) is the best overall indicator (Table 1.3). Durable goods and car sales are good indicators of consumer confidence since, in recession, it is the big-ticket items, and especially cars, on which consumers usually cut back. There are, in addition, the indicators that feed into consumers' spending decisions such as real wages (i.e. wage growth after inflation), employment trends (rising employment both increases consumer income and improves confidence), the rate of interest and consumer confidence. In the background are so-called wealth effects coming from stock market gains or house price increases (see Chapter 7).

The effects of the rate of interest vary from country to country. In the UK, short-term interest rates have been very important because of the prevalence of floating rate mortgages. Lower interest rates immediately impact on consumers because they have lower mortgage payments. In other countries the effect of falling short-term interest rates is less certain because lower rates reduce consumers' spending due to the fall in interest income. Bond yields are more important in the USA where mortgages are usually at fixed rates and are linked to 10-year US Treasury yields. A significant fall in bond yields leads to a wave of mortgage refinancings. These allow consumers to increase their spending on goods and services because they have lower interest payments to make, and many use the opportunity to increase their outstanding loan.

Investment

The key measures are capital goods orders (monthly for many countries) and business investment as reported in the GDP breakdown (see Table 1.4). Monthly or even quarterly data are not given too much attention because they are extremely volatile. But even though business investment is only around 15–20% of GDP in most industrial countries it tends to move up and down more strongly than consumer spending and is therefore very important for the cycle.

Table 1.4   Business investment indicators

Measures	Influences
Fixed investment	Sales
Capital goods orders	Interest rates
Purchasing Managers reports (ISM)	Capacity utilisation
Inventories	Business confidence
	GDP growth
	Stock prices

The key inputs to forecasting business spending are expectations of GDP growth, the level of capacity utilisation, the rate of growth of sales, the rate of interest and the performance of the stock market. Again countries vary as to the relative importance of short-term rates and bond yields. In Germany and Japan long rates are more important while in the UK short rates are more significant. The USA and France fall in between. Related to all these are the state of corporate balance sheets. When companies are overextended with debt they will naturally respond more quickly to higher interest rates or a downturn in demand.

Business Spending on Inventories

This is important primarily because its volatility gives inventories a key role in the business cycle (see Chapter 2). Expectations of rising demand will prompt companies to order more goods or produce more, and this extra production creates jobs and incomes which, for the economy as a whole, makes sure that the extra demand does indeed come through. However, interpreting the behaviour of inventories is always awkward. For example, let us assume that the government reports a rise in inventories. Is this due to business anticipating a rise in demand or, in fact, due to levels of sales lower than hoped, giving an involuntary rise in inventories? Also there has been a pronounced tendency for the ratio of inventories to sales, a key indicator, to trend down over the last 10 years. This is due to improvements in inventory management such as 'just in time' approaches in factories, made possible by improvements in computer technology.

Note that the way inventories are accounted in calculating GDP growth is very important for the swings in and out of recession, though it can initially be confusing. In 2000 the creation of inventories in the US economy amounted to $51 bn. In 1999 the figure was $62 bn. Therefore the contribution to US GDP growth from inventories in 2000 was −$11 bn (i.e. the change in the change) or −0.1%. In 2001 US business slashed inventories due to worries about the slowdown in sales so that inventories fell by $62 bn, compared with the increase of $51 bn in 2000. The change in the change, $113 bn, amounted to approximately 1.1% of GDP, so about one-third of the GDP growth slowdown from 2000 (4.2%) to 2001 (1.1%) was caused by inventories. At the time of writing, economic recovery in 2002 is widely expected to be led by a recovery in inventories.

Changes in inventories can have a dramatic impact on quarterly GDP figures, which are usually reported on a quarterly annualised basis. For example, in Q4 2000 inventories rose by $43 bn (at an annualised rate), but in the next quarter, Q1 2001, inventories fell by $27 bn. The *change* in inventories was therefore $70 bn for the quarter, or $280 bn at an annual rate, which translates to just over 3% of GDP. So the inventory correction cut the Q1 annualised GDP growth rate by three percentage points from what it would otherwise have been.

Exports and Imports

The key factors behind exports and imports are the exchange rate and the relative speed of GDP growth in the home and foreign countries. Fast growth at home tends to crimp exports because manufacturers are less inclined to bid keenly for foreign contracts when they are busy with the home market. Faster growth abroad obviously makes it easier to export.

To calculate GDP the statisticians use a concept called 'net exports', which is exports less imports. Note that if exports rise rapidly but imports rise equally rapidly, there is no net contribution to GDP. Monthly trade data are important for what they reveal about the contribution to economic growth from external trade. Ideally the breakdown is provided according to volume and price, since otherwise it is very difficult to reach much of a conclusion.

Investment and Productivity

The third method of breaking down GDP growth is to separate it into new output due to new investment and new output due to productivity growth (after subtracting extra hours worked). In other words, how much of the increase in output is due to new machines that can create more output and how much is due to the better use of existing machines?

In reality this can never be measured reliably because output often rises because old machines are replaced. The new machines are not adding to capacity but in fact allow more productivity growth. Nevertheless the distinction is very important conceptually. As with an individual company, countries must invest a certain amount each year just to repair and replace old machinery. It is only when investment goes above that level that new capacity is created enabling the economy to produce more goods. Hence, economists often look at the ratio of investment to GDP. If that ratio is only in the area of 10% then it is more than probable that most of the investment is simply repairing worn out machinery. If, however, the ratio is 15% or more, then a substantial amount of new capacity is being created.

However, as we saw above, high investment does not necessarily mean faster GDP growth as this depends on the new plant or equipment being used effectively. Hence, there is a need to look at the productivity of that investment, and here we are referring to labour productivity, i.e. the output per hour.

Supply of Growth

This final method of analysing GDP looks at the components of growth on the supply side. The simplest way is to divide growth into changes in employment and changes in labour productivity. Sometimes, for longer term analysis, employment trends are broken down further into changes in the size of the potential labour force and changes in actual labour force participation (e.g. more or less women or older people working).

For example, in the past, US GDP growth was assumed to average 2.5% p.a. over the long term, based on just under a 1% p.a. growth of the labour force, a small rise in labour force participation and a rise in labour productivity annually of about 1%. But during the late 1990s there were signs that productivity had risen perhaps to around 2.5% annually, so estimates of trend GDP were raised to 3.5–4% p.a. In contrast the figures for many developing countries would be more like 2% p.a. labour force growth, 1% p.a. from increased participation and 3–4% p.a. from productivity, suggesting that growth could average 6–7% p.a. over the long term.

KEY CONTROVERSY: ECONOMIC GROWTH AND THE 'NEW ECONOMY'

In the late 1990s the spectacular performance of the US economy in generating faster economic growth without an acceleration in inflation led to claims that the trend growth rate had accelerated. Many analysts concluded that the long-term trend growth rate of the economy, which used to be around 2.5% p.a., had now moved up to 3.5–4% p.a. In practice, the evaluation of this claim proved difficult and controversial with some analysts arguing that the increase was at best temporary and at worst a statistical illusion. This issue is taken up in more detail in Chapter 4 but here we can shed light on the debate by using the four analytical approaches described above.

Nominal versus Real GDP

Some of the recorded increase in growth seems to have been due to a change in the way the government statisticians divided nominal GDP between real growth and inflation. The changes were based on studies that suggested that inflation had previously been overestimated, and the very rapid technical progress in computers meant that very large differences in real productivity growth could be made by changing the way that computers were accounted. Some studies suggested that this change raised GDP growth by as much as 0.5%. Provided that computers continue to improve at the pace of the 1990s this means that, as published, the trend growth rate of the economy can indeed be higher. Nevertheless the changes are controversial not least because other countries account for computers on a different basis, which means that they could be understating GDP growth.

The Demand Components Approach

During the second half of the 1990s total domestic demand grew at close to 5% p.a., somewhat above GDP growth. The difference was made up by the rising current account deficit, effectively foreigners supplying the excess demand. Critics of the 'new economy' argued that GDP was simply responding to this rapid rate of demand growth and that productivity growth was high simply because the economy was running flat out. Strong demand was driven by fast-growing consumer spending buoyed by gains in the stock market and a fall in unemployment.

Investment and Productivity

Despite the scepticism over the new economy the acceleration in the rate of investment suggests that we should expect a genuine acceleration in growth. Private fixed investment rose from 10% in 1994 to 15% of GDP in 1999. The result was that capacity grew rapidly, helping to avoid inflation pressures. The rise in productivity was, to some extent at least, a result of this increase in investment. However, this does not guarantee that faster productivity growth will continue since that would require high investment to continue. But investment fell sharply during the slowdown in 2001 and there has been increasing evidence that companies were over-investing, particularly in the technology area. In 2001 productivity growth held up well, surprising most observers, but this may have been a lagged reaction to past investment. If the rate of investment runs at a lower level in the next few years productivity growth could slow.

Supply of Growth

A key factor in the 1990s upswing was the increased labour force participation as low rates of unemployment and high wages brought an increasing percentage of the population into the workforce. Many analysts also believed that high levels of illegal immigration played a role. Higher productivity growth has already been discussed in relation to investment. There have also been claims that changes in technology, particularly the more effective use of computers, e-mail and the internet, contributed to higher productivity.

In Europe and Japan there was no sign of a 'new economy' effect and many Europeans (as well as a few Americans) have questioned whether it really exists or is just a temporary phenomenon, reflecting cyclical factors or even a statistical artefact. However, if it is the latter, this still means that the trend growth rate of the US economy, as reported, has increased from previous levels. Unfortunately this may not translate into higher profits, since intense competition points to the benefits passing through to consumers in the form of lower prices, but it is important for assessing inflation and Federal Reserve policy as we shall see in later chapters.

CONCLUSION: GROWTH FUNDAMENTALS AND THE INVESTOR

Short-term changes in the rate of economic growth are crucial for investors because they influence interest rate policy and company performance, which in turn feed through to the markets. This is the subject of Chapter 2, which looks at the business cycle.

Long-term trends in GDP growth are important to investors for three reasons. First, countries with a higher trend growth rate usually show strong returns on stocks because profits rise at least in line with nominal GDP. Of course the markets anticipate this growth and therefore usually value high growth countries at high price/earnings ratios. They may even anticipate this growth before it occurs when they see new government policies that are likely to have positive effects. Still, returns to investors will be good provided that the high growth continues. Secondly, high growth countries often have higher inflation as the strong growth puts demand pressures on sectors of the economy such as infrastructure and skilled labour. Thirdly, high growth countries will usually have higher interest rates, both at the short and the long end, partly due to the high inflation and partly because high growth requires high investment which puts upward pressure on interest rates. However, a rise in trend economic growth due to faster productivity growth helps to ease immediate inflation pressures and makes the central bank's task easier.

For investors the key is to anticipate, or at least to spot at an early stage, that productivity growth has accelerated. As we shall see, successive waves of strong emerging stock market performance in the 1980s and early 1990s followed from improved economic growth performance in Asia and later in Latin America. More recently, the apparent improvement in US economic performance in the late 1990s fuelled a major stock market rally.

2

Business Cycle Fundamentals

Business cycles have been documented at least since the eighteenth century and seem to be an inescapable feature of the market economy. Periodically, usually near the height of an economic boom, people begin to argue that business cycles have been abolished but, so far, every upswing has ended in recession (or at least a severe drop in the growth rate) and every recession has given way to recovery. Business cycles are crucial for investors, most of whom spend a great deal of time trying to guess when the next turning point is coming. In practice the length of the cycle, the strength of the upswing and the depth of the recession vary considerably and are impossible to predict accurately. Nevertheless, it is crucial that investors are aware of the pattern.

In the simplest terms the business cycle (sometimes called trade cycle) is an alternation of periods of faster growth with periods of slower growth or decline. However, many analysts believe that there is more than one cycle. In a famous, and famously long, book Joseph Schumpeter writing in 1939 argued that there are three cycles.[1] There is a three-year cycle, which he called the Kitchin cycle (after another economist Joseph Kitchin); there is a nine-year cycle, called the Juglar cycle (another economist); and finally there is a very long cycle, the Kondratieff cycle (a Russian economist, see below).

However, since the Second World War cycles appear to have lasted anywhere between three and nine years. The existence of the nine-year cycle was in doubt during the 1950s and 1960s but seemed to return in the 1980s and 1990s, but few believe that the cycle can be predicted with any degree of regularity. Despite exhaustive attempts it remains elusive: a great deal is known about patterns of cycles but it has proved difficult to use this information in a predictive way because every cycle is different.

A TYPICAL BUSINESS CYCLE DESCRIBED

The following is a description of the usual course of a typical nine-year business cycle. The very long-term Kondratieff cycle is discussed in more detail separately below. The comments on what the markets are doing at each phase need to be treated carefully. In a sense the markets are always adjusting to new views on how long the current phase is going to last or how strong it will be, when the next phase will begin and how long that will last. Remember that cycles since the early 1970s have been more pronounced than in the first decades after the Second World War. The five phases of the business cycle are shown in Table 2.1.

Phase 1: Recovery

This is usually a short phase of a few months in which the economy picks up from its slowdown or recession. Note that recoveries are seldom seen as such until several months after they

---

[1] J.A. Schumpeter (1939) *Business Cycles*. New York: McGraw-Hill.

Table 2.1   Five phases of the business cycle

1. Recovery
Stimulatory economic policies
Confidence picks up
Inflation still falling

MARKETS . . . short rates low or falling, bond yields bottoming, stocks rising, commodities rising, property prices bottoming.

2. Early Upswing
Increasing confidence
Healthy economic growth
Inflation remains low

MARKETS . . . short rates at neutral, bonds stable, stocks and commodities strong. Property picking up.

3. Late Upswing
Boom mentality
Inflation gradually picks up
Policy becomes restrictive

MARKETS . . . short rates rising, bond yields rise, stocks topping out, property and commodity prices rising strongly

4. Economy slow or enters Recession
Short term interest rates peak
Confidence drops suddenly
Inventory correction begins
Inflation continues to accelerate

MARKETS . . . short rates peak, bond yields top out and start to fall, stock and commodity prices fall, property prices top out.

5. Recession
Production falling
Inflation peaks
Confidence weak

MARKETS . . . short rates drop, Bond yields drop, stocks bottoming, property and commodities weak

really happen. The same applies to the onset of recession and is a reflection of the delays in publishing economic data. In the recovery phase there are often stimulatory economic policies from the government in the form of lower interest rates or a fiscal stimulus. Note that these policy measures normally influence the economy with a lag of a few months and continue to provide stimulus for at least a year in the case of interest rates and around two years in the case of fiscal policy. Generally confidence is picking up among businesses and usually among consumers.

A crucial factor supporting the recovery is usually the inventory cycle whereby, after a period of retrenchment during the recession, a better balance between inventories and sales, together with renewed confidence, prompts businesses to increase inventories in anticipation of higher sales. This inventory rebuilding generates income and jobs in the economy. As we saw in the previous chapter, the way inventories are accounted can generate large swings in GDP. There may be an expansion of investment with new products and new processes. Sometimes

Table 2.2   USA: Recoveries and the stock market

Cycle		Return from the S&P Index*	
Peak	Trough	Through year	Following year
Aug. 1929	Mar. 1933	53.0	−1.5
May 1937	June 1938	30.0	−0.8
Feb. 1945	Oct. 1945	35.7	−7.8
Nov. 1948	Oct. 1949	17.8	30.5
July 1953	May 1954	51.2	31.0
Aug. 1957	Apr. 1958	42.4	11.8
Apr. 1960	Feb. 1961	26.6	−8.8
Dec. 1969	Nov. 1970	3.5	14.1
Nov. 1973	Mar. 1975	36.9	23.6
Jan. 1980	July 1980	31.5	−4.8
July 1981	Nov. 1982	20.5	22.3
July 1990	Mar. 1991	30.0	7.4
Mar. 2001	na	-	-

* Price appreciation plus dividends
Source: National Bureau of Economic Research and Standard & Poor's
Security Price Index Record

the stimulus can come from abroad with fast growth elsewhere giving good export growth as occurred, for example, in Germany in 1982–3 when the rapid pace of the US expansion provided a convenient locomotive. In this phase unemployment may still be rising, or at least not falling yet, but overtime work will be increasing. Inflation, which tends to lag the economic cycle by a year or so behind, will still be falling.

In the markets, short-term interest rates will be already low or may still be falling as the government tries to ensure that the recovery continues. Inflation will be down and unemployment up so the government may well be concentrating mainly on making sure that recovery takes hold. Government bond yields may continue to come down through this phase but are likely to be bottoming. The crucial factor here is the strength of the recovery. Stock markets usually rise strongly at this point because fears of a longer recession or depression dissipate (see Table 2.2). Cyclical stocks should do particularly well. Commodity prices rise too, especially for industrial commodities. As confidence in the economic outlook improves, riskier assets such as small stocks, higher yielding corporate bonds and emerging equities and bonds attract investors and perform well. Property prices are typically the laggard in the market. It takes time for the (typical) commercial sector overbuilding in the previous boom to be worked through, while consumers are still cautious about buying at this point when unemployment is still rising and the memories of price declines during the recession persist.

Phase 2: Early Upswing

The recovery period is past, confidence is up and the economy is gaining some momentum. This is the healthiest period of the cycle in a sense, because economic growth can be robust without any signs of *overheating* or sharply higher inflation. Typically there is a virtuous circle of increasing confidence with consumers prepared to borrow and spend more and business, facing increased capacity use, keen to invest. Unemployment falls, usually rapidly in such countries as the USA where the recession prompts temporary lay-offs, but more slowly in

Europe. Higher operating levels allow many businesses to enjoy a fall in unit costs so that profits rise rapidly. Inflation may pick up off the bottom because cut-throat price competition eases as sales improve, but only rises slowly.

In the markets short rates move back towards neutral at this time, while, further up the yield curve, bond yields are likely to be stable or rising slightly. Stocks are strong with recovery stocks in particular doing well at this stage, while commodity prices are probably moving up gently. Property starts to show some life. This phase usually lasts at least a year and often several years.

Phase 3: Late Upswing

This is where the boom mentality has taken hold, as for example in the US economy during 1997–2000. The economy grows rapidly, capacity utilisation nears a peak prompting an investment boom and unemployment falls. Property prices and rents often move up strongly at this stage prompting a construction boom. Inflation picks up, usually slowly at first, with wages accelerating too as shortages of labour develop.

In the markets, typically interest rates are rising as the monetary authorities become restrictive to try to slow down the boom and heavy borrowing puts pressure on the credit markets. Bond markets anxiously watch this behaviour and bond yields will usually be rising. Stock markets will often rise but may be nervous too, depending on the strength of the boom, and this is not usually the best time for stocks. Commodity prices are liable to soar as capacity limits are reached and, at the same time, investors looking for a hedge against inflation, take speculative positions. This is the best time for property prices. Commercial property does well as vacancy rates are low and new buildings have yet to be erected. Residential property prices typically rise strongly too as rising incomes, falling unemployment, easily available mortgages and dwindling memories of the previous slump all bring a rise in purchases and a willingness to take on larger loans.

Phase 4: Economy Slows or Goes into Recession

At this point the economy is declining but usually, because of the lags in reporting, recession is not confirmed until at least three months after it began. For example, the 1990 US recession is now dated as beginning in July 1990 (just before Saddam Hussein invaded Kuwait), but was not widely seen as occurring until October/November of that year and was blamed on the invasion. The sharp US slowdown in 2000–1 started in the third quarter of 2000 but was not really appreciated until December of that year.

In this phase, short-term interest rates move up sharply, then peak when confidence drops rather suddenly for some reason. The slowdown is exacerbated by the inventory correction as companies, seeing a drop in sales and consequent rise in inventories and suddenly fearing recession, try to reduce their inventory levels. At this point, capacity utilisation begins to drop off, but wages move on ahead since labour markets are still tight, with the result that inflation continues to rise. Inflation usually peaks around a year into recession.

In the markets short-term rates peak and then begin to fall. How quickly they fall depends on the length of time the monetary authorities want to continue the squeeze to reduce inflation. In 2001 the Federal Reserve (Fed) cut interest rates at an unusually rapid rate because it perceived inflation to be under control. Bonds top out at the first sign of a slowing economy and then rally sharply (yields fall). In 2000 bond yields were falling for much of the year well ahead of the confirmation of a slowdown. The stock market may fall, perhaps significantly, with interest-sensitive stocks, including utilities, doing best. Commodity prices top out and may fall. Property prices waver but may hold up initially, buoyed by declining interest rates. Only when vacancy rates and unemployment rise significantly do prices come under major pressure.

Phase 5: Recession

Once the recession is confirmed monetary policy is usually eased but only cautiously at first if there are still fears of inflation. Moreover, there is always a lag between cuts in interest rates and recovery. Recessions typically last six months to a year during which both consumer and business confidence decline. Profits drop sharply, particularly reported profits which include restructuring charges, but operating earnings fall too, due to weaker sales and lower capacity use. The mistakes of the boom have come home to roost, with individuals and companies likely to find themselves with assets worth less than they thought and debts that are difficult to service. In a severe recession the financial system may have a serious problem with bad debts, which makes lenders extremely cautious. Often there is a major bankruptcy or financial crisis. The inventory correction is in full flow and, as long as it continues, will tend to keep the economy in recession. Unemployment rises quickly, which starts to put downward pressure on inflation though most of the benefits are seen later.

In the markets short-term interest rates drop during this phase, as do bond yields. Depending on how badly confidence is affected stock markets may fall precipitously at first in response to reports of company losses and bankruptcies, but then recover on the back of lower interest rates and hopes for economic recovery. The stock market usually starts to rise in the later stages of the recession, well before recovery emerges. Commodity prices are weak as surplus capacity opens up. Property prices may begin to fall.

INVESTMENT AND THE CYCLE

The above description of a typical cycle makes investment sound easy. Just buy stocks once the recession is underway and buy bonds at the peak of the boom! In practice market timing is much more difficult because each cycle varies in length and amplitude (height of the boom and depth of the recession). Investors are often afraid of buying too soon or selling too late. When the market is falling fear tends to be prevalent, with investors believing that the market could go much lower; and when the market is rising 'greed' tends to be the dominant sentiment with investors frequently believing that 'it is different this time'. Moreover, since the overall pattern is well known everyone else is trying to move just ahead of the market. This is one reason why the stock market is seen as a leading indicator of the economy: investors try to jump in and out before the economy turns.

THE INVENTORY CYCLE

In addition to the long cycle described above there is also evidence of a short-term inventory cycle – the Kitchin cycle mentioned earlier. As already explained, inventories can have a powerful effect on GDP growth as companies try to keep them under control. In the up-phase of the inventory cycle businesses are confident about future sales and are increasing production in anticipation. Quite often they are right, which means that inventories do not increase significantly because the products are quickly sold. Businesses continue to

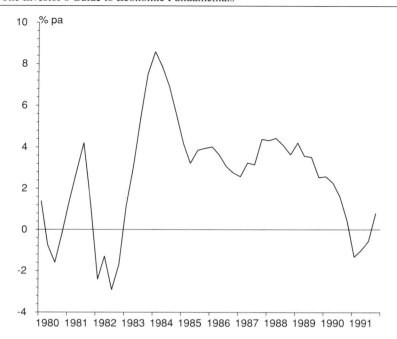

Figure 2.1   US GDP growth 1980–91
Source: Thomson Datastream

increase production, generating more overtime and more employment and therefore further sales.

At some point, however, there is a disappointment or a change in expectations of future sales so that businesses start to view inventories as being too high. In the recent past this has often been caused by a tightening of monetary policy, because the up-phase of the inventory cycle begins to generate economic growth above trend. It could also be caused by a 'shock' such as higher oil prices. At this point business cuts back production to try to reduce inventory. It does this by cutting back on overtime initially and perhaps slowing hiring or announcing redundancies. But of course then, for the economy as a whole, sales grow even more slowly than anticipated and inventories fail to come down. The result is a slowdown in growth.

The following description treats the last 20 years as two long cycles, 9–10 year Juglar cycles. It can also be broken up into five subcycles reflecting the growth pauses in 1986, 1995 and 1998. These 3–4 year subcycles look like the Kitchin cycle and are linked to inventories as well as to Fed action. The timing of the phases is the author's (see Figure 2.1).

THE US 1980s CYCLE: 1982–90

Phase 1: Recovery 1982–3

A recovery phase began in the fourth quarter of 1982 though, as usual, it was not evident until a few months later. It came as a result of a massive fiscal stimulus put into place by President Reagan in the form of lower taxes and higher defence spending. Also interest rates came down sharply during 1982, especially after August (partly in response to the Mexican debt default).

Initially inventories played a big role in leading demand. In the markets, interest rates fell until early in 1983, bond yields fell with them and then stabilised, while stock prices rose strongly. Property prices continued to fall.

Phase 2: Early Upswing 1983–6

This was a strong recovery with GDP growth averaging 5% p.a. in 1983–4, quickly taking the economy back to the unemployment rate of 7% that prevailed immediately before the recession. In the markets, the strength of the recovery encouraged the Fed to raise interest rates, and bond yields rose too. The stock market paused before moving up again from 1985 onwards. Inflation remained very modest in the early 1980s, partly helped by the rise in the dollar.

This phase lasted much longer than normal, probably for two reasons. One was that the 1980–2 recession had been a double downturn, which left scope for a longer upswing. Secondly, and most importantly, oil prices fell by around half in 1986, sharply reducing inflationary pressures world wide and allowing interest rates to fall.

Phase 3: Late Upswing 1987–8

This phase can be dated from early 1987. After the pause in growth in 1986 the economy started to accelerate again. Confidence rose sharply, helped by low interest rates and the massive devaluation of the dollar in 1985–7. The low rate of inflation (following the oil price decline) encouraged the view that the upswing still had a long way to go: in fact it was at this time that a few articles appeared pronouncing the business cycle dead! Unemployment began to drop steadily, passing through 6%, which started to ring warning bells at the Fed and then on to 5%. Inflation began to edge up again.

In the markets stocks boomed in the first half of 1987, crashed in October and gradually made their way to new peaks by 1989. Bond yields rose sharply in early 1987 but then took comfort from the stock market crash, which seemed to point to recession, and the tightening stance of the Federal Reserve. Commodity and property prices rose strongly.

Phase 4: 1989–90 — Slowdown into Recession

The avowed aim of the Federal Reserve was a 'soft landing' and the economy slowed down nicely in 1989 and into 1990. The Federal Reserve began to cut Fed Funds rate in the second quarter of 1989 and the economy bounced along at a slow rate. With the benefit of hindsight, the Fed did not cut rates sufficiently during 1990 to avoid recession. This was partly because the economy appeared to be stabilising in early 1990, a false dawn as it turned out. As 1990 continued, employment and consumer confidence weakened, as did investment. Construction spending dropped off sharply, both for houses and commercial use. This combination was already taking the economy into a mild recession in the third quarter of 1990, but then came an external shock: the invasion of Kuwait, which brought a sharp rise in oil prices and uncertainty over the outcome of the US military build-up.

Stock prices fell sharply, as did bond yields, and the Federal Reserve cut rates rapidly. But confidence had already fallen, so spending and hiring decisions were delayed. Property prices and commodity prices fell and banks looked weak.

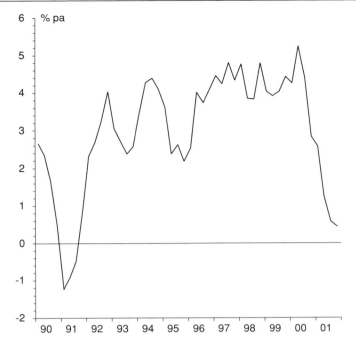

Figure 2.2   US GDP growth 1990–2001
Source: Thomson Datastream

Phase 5: Recession 1990–1

The recession lasted about nine months. Uncertainty over the Gulf crisis and oil prices combined with a classic inventory cycle to make the economy weaker. At the same time property prices were falling and consumers were worried about rising unemployment in the face of high debts. The Fed cut interest rates by 2% between November 1990 and March 1991. The recession itself was a comparatively mild recession, as measured. However this is slightly misleading because the early recovery phase was a rather extended period of sub-par growth (in stark contrast to the early 1980s upswing) so that the overall slowdown period, from 1989–92 was a painful experience for many individuals, companies and banks (Figure 2.2).

In the markets stocks fell on the invasion of Kuwait and bottomed in October before starting to pick up. The beginning of the war gave stocks a sharp boost and signs of the ending of the recession in the spring of 1991 took the market higher. Bond yields peaked in September 1990, reflecting worries about the impact of higher oil prices. Once it became clear that the economy was in recession, from about October 1990, bonds rallied, with yields dropping almost 100 basis points. Property prices fell.

THE US 1990s CYCLE: 1991–2001

Phase 1: Recovery 1991–2

The economy initially rebounded strongly in spring 1991 with the war successfully over. However after the first bounce it became locked into a sluggish and hesitant growth trend until the second half of 1992, with industrial production trending up only very slightly. Excessive lending during the 1980s brought a spate of bad loans, which hit many US banks hard during the recession and immediate aftermath. The result was that the US suffered a 'credit crunch' in the early 1990s with banks unwilling to lend. At the same time severe falls in both residential and commercial property prices in many areas hit balance sheets and confidence. The Fed responded by continuing to cut interest rates during the recovery phase to only 3% p.a., more or less the same as the inflation rate and hence very stimulatory. But economic growth averaged only1.4% p.a. during 1991–3 and unemployment failed to decline. It was described at the time as a 'jobless recovery'. However one positive result was that high unemployment brought slower wages growth and inflation was reduced to below 3% p.a. by 1993, compared with 5.4% p.a. in 1990.

Phase 2: Early Upswing 1993–8

Starting in February 1994, with the economy strengthening, the Fed abruptly began to raise interest rates to move away from the excessive stimulus of the recovery years. Between 1993 and 1998 the US economy achieved a period of strong growth with low inflation. The period was extended by three factors. First, the Fed followed an activist policy and achieved a 'soft landing' in 1995 which helped to check inflation pressures. The sharp tightening in 1994 brought a brief slowdown in 1995 associated with an inventory correction and allowed the upswing to resume. Secondly, the Asian crisis in 1997–8 led to a dis-inflationary shock, which helped to keep US inflation under control. Lower oil prices (largely due to weaker Asian demand), cheap imports from Asia and elsewhere and the strength of the dollar helped to keep inflation down. Thirdly, the US economy itself achieved a better productivity performance due, among other things, to a surge in investment. From the end of 1995 the stock market rose strongly, reflecting the improved performance of profits and strong investor confidence. Technology stocks led the way. Bond yields rose sharply in 1994 as the Fed raised interest rates and the economy accelerated. Indeed at the time this was seen as a bond market crash. From 1995 yields stabilised and fell slightly, helped by the good inflation performance and declining budget deficit. Property began to recover from the steep downturn of the early 1990s.

Phase 3: Late Upswing 1999–2000

The financial crisis of October 1998 was triggered by the Russian default (August 1998) which led to a sharp rise in spreads (over Treasury bonds) on risk assets such as emerging market bonds and 'junk bonds'. When a highly leveraged hedge fund, Long Term Capital Management (LTCM), ran into trouble the Fed responded by cutting interest rates by 75 basis points. Although it put rates up again during 1999 there was great concern that the Y2K problem (the new calendar affecting computers) would cause great economic disruption, so the Fed moved only slowly and liquidity was deliberately kept very loose in the second half of 1999. This lax monetary policy combined with a period of economic euphoria to generate very fast growth.

Since recorded inflation remained comparatively low the Fed was content to tighten only gradually, but signs of overheating increased. Consumer confidence reached record levels as did car sales, house prices boomed in hot spots like Manhattan and San Francisco and business investment grew at rates close to 10% p.a. Much of this investment was linked to computer and internet technology as the whole country (indeed the whole world) was caught up in a frenzy of investment in the new 'dot.com' companies. Many commentators made comparisons between the internet and railways or electricity, although the real enthusiasts argued that it was a much more important innovation even than those and should be regarded as akin to the industrial revolution. Only time will tell the full significance of the internet but there is no doubt of the key role it played in the euphoria of this late upswing phase. This was the period when, once again, many analysts proclaimed that recessions were now abolished, due to the changed workings of the 'new economy'.

Ten-year bond yields rose from lows of 4.3% p.a. at the time of the Russian crisis to a peak in early 2000 of 6.7%. Meanwhile the stock market boomed, led by the NASDAQ. The latter moved up from below 2,000 in early 1998 to over 5,000 by March 2001. The S&P 500 index rose about 50% during the same three years. Property price inflation accelerated during this period. Commodity prices overall showed some gains but the big mover was oil. Having fallen sharply in 1998 due to the Asian crisis, oil rebounded strongly in 1999–2000, buoyed by the US boom as well as OPEC production cuts.

Phase 4: Economy Slows, Second Half of 2000

The Fed raised interest rates further during 2000 to 6.5% p.a., but probably more important for the slowdown was two other factors. First, the rise in oil prices combined with higher natural gas prices to sharply hit consumer incomes. Secondly, enthusiasm for the new technology went into reverse. The bubble in technology stocks began to deflate, bringing major losses to many investors and paper losses to many employees with stock options. The result was that, starting in the second half of 2000, business and consumer confidence began to decline. The initial effect was a slowdown in car sales and new technology orders (both consumer and business), exacerbated by some exceptionally cold weather in the early winter months. GDP growth slowed from 4% annualised in the first half of 2000 to only 1.5% in the second half. Only in November–December did the slowdown become evident in the numbers. In 2001 business started to make drastic cuts in production to reduce inventories and also cut back on investment which had been running at high levels.

Wrong-footed by the sudden downturn, the Fed maintained a tightening bias until December 2000, then very abruptly in early January 2001 and, in an unscheduled meeting, started to cut rates. Further rate cuts followed in swift succession. From the peak of the S&P 500 index of 1,508 in March 2000 the index moved sideways until September then trended down for the rest of 2000 and into 2001. The NASDAQ showed much sharper falls as faith in the internet and technology unravelled. Bond yields trended down from the start of 2000, anticipating the slowdown and seeing an overall fall in yield of over 150 basis points by early 2001. Oil prices peaked late in 2000 then started to fall back.

Phase 5: Recession 2001

In early 2001, business confidence fell sharply and a sharp inventory correction began, subtracting 3% from annualised Q1 growth. Starting in Q2 investment dropped off too, particularly in technology products. This partly reflected the over-investment in the previous years during the boom. Meanwhile, consumer spending continued to slow but remained positive, keeping GDP growth just in positive territory, buoyed by rising house prices and still-low unemployment. The National Bureau of Economic Research dated the start of the recession from March, and recent revised GDP data (July 2002) confirm three quarters of recession. The recession ended during the fourth quarter.

In the markets the Fed cut interest rates by 3% during the first eight months of 2001, helping to maintain confidence to some extent and also probably avoiding a worse fall in the stock market. But markets still suffered badly. By August 2001 the S&P 500 composite index had fallen over 20% to below 1200, then following the terrorist attacks on 11 September it fell to a low of under 1000 in late September, a peak-to-trough decline of more than one-third. NASDAQ stocks fared much worse, falling to a low of 1,500 in September 2001, compared with the peak of over 5,000 in early 2000. Bonds yields were volatile during the recession, but yields essentially stayed in touch with the 5% level reached during the slowdown phase. They fell sharply after 11 September to 4.3% but soon bounced back to 5%. However, residential property prices continued to rise reflecting the unusually early and sharp decline in interest rates during this recession and continuing relatively high consumer confidence. Although the Conference Board and Michigan surveys of consumer confidence showed sharp declines in 2001 they remained well above previous recession levels. Non-residential property prices stalled.

THE CURRENT CYCLE: 2002–

Phase 1: Recovery 2002

At the time of writing (spring 2002) a new recovery seems to have just begun. The reader will know whether or not this turns out to be true. Most economists expect an upturn helped by the particularly low level of inventories as well as low interest rates and the fiscal stimulus. But business remains very cautious and some people fear a double dip. If recovery does continue in 2002, the 2001 recession will have been unusually mild, which would account for the unusually good performance of property prices. The stock market should trend up, though there are worries about the already high valuations. Bonds will be nervous because of the unusually small 'output gap' opened up in such a mild recession and the rapid growth of money supply which could point to higher inflation.

TWO APPROACHES FOR INVESTORS

For investors there are two ways to approach the business cycle. One is to attempt to spot the turning points and shift asset allocation between bonds, stocks and cash accordingly. Equity managers will also try to shift the balance between cyclical stocks and growth stocks and defensive stocks. But in practice the timing is very difficult. The reader will probably detect the author's difficulty in identifying the precise position of the business cycle at the time of writing. A cautious approach, in face of this uncertainty, runs the risk that stock weightings may be too light when they rise. Most professional investors only change their asset weighting within certain limits and always keep a core of bonds and stocks in their portfolios.

The second approach is to ignore the business cycle completely and concentrate on picking good companies or identifying investment themes. This is a longer-term approach, looking through the business cycle rather than trying to forecast it. Many professionals use a combination of both approaches.

Table 2.3 US leading indicators

Average workweek (hours)	Building permits
Initial jobless claims	Stock prices
Consumer goods orders	Money supply
Slower deliveries	Treasury yield curve
Capital goods orders	Consumer expectations

Source: Commerce Department

THE ROLE OF LEADING INDICATORS

To identify where we are in the business cycle economists rely heavily on leading indicators and business survey results. The leading indicators index in most countries is an average of 9–12 indicators which, historically, have been found to lead the business cycle by a few months. However the lead time varies considerably—for example, in the USA, from as low as one or two months up to 18 months or more. Several of the components of the index are watched particularly closely, for example, weekly unemployment claims, new orders and consumer confidence (Table 2.3).

Note that employment is not a leading indicator but a coincident indicator, i.e. it is in line with the cycle. Its popularity as an indicator, particularly in the USA, is twofold. First, the employment report does in fact contain a wealth of other information including hours worked and wages. Secondly, it is reported only 3–4 weeks after the survey is taken. Hence, for example, the February employment report (based on a survey near the beginning of the month) will be released at the beginning of March.

HOW DO DEPRESSIONS FIT IN?

The word depression is usually understood to mean a slump in output of 10% or more, with a massive rise in unemployment. This was the experience in the 1930s, especially in the USA. Since the Second World War downturns have usually been described as recessions, which is partly euphemistic but also reflects that, at least until the 1970s, downturns in most countries were very mild. The typical post-war recession has resulted in drops in output of between 1 and 4% and rises in the unemployment rate of a similar order. There are probably two reasons for this.

First, governments now play a very active role in re-stimulating an economy that is in recession. They safeguard the banking system to avoid the kind of collapse seen in the USA in the 1930s. They often use one or both of fiscal and monetary policy to kick-start the economy. Not only does this directly end the recession but knowledge of the willingness to use fiscal policy influences expectations so that the blind fear that was seen in the early 1930s is ruled out. Japan's efforts to avoid a depression in the 1990s provide a good example. Fiscal policy was used actively, interest rates were reduced to zero and the banking system was supported. At the time of writing, Japan's economy is still very weak and going through its third recession in ten years but a full depression has been avoided.

The second factor is that modern economies are now more resilient to major recessions or depressions because the public sector itself is so much larger. In most countries government spending amounts to around 40% of GDP and changes only slowly in the event of a recession. The serious downward spiral seen in the early 1930s is therefore more muted. These so-called 'automatic stabilisers' ensure that the government's budget deficit opens up automatically in a recession, providing a source of demand that partially counteracts the private sector's lack of spending.

WHY DOES THE CYCLE EXIST?

Explanations vary from theories related to sunspots (which were thought to influence agriculture) to sophisticated mathematical models based on expectations and investment behaviour. Some economists argue that the cycle does not exist as a natural cycle; it is simply a pattern that we think we observe but is really a random phenomenon. However, probably the best way to look at the question is to ask why booms end and why (some time later) recoveries begin.

There are broadly three types of factors that seem to bring the boom to an end. First, there are the inherent or natural economic factors in the cyclical situation. For example, during the late upswing phase investment is usually strong. This in turn makes economic growth itself strong and investment is undertaken on the expectation that growth will continue very strong. After a while demand slows for some reason and companies suddenly find themselves with excess capacity. When they cut back on new investment the result slows the economy. Another factor can be that prices rise too far and people hold back on spending. However, while these issues are often present they are not usually the triggering factor that ends a boom and takes the economy into recession.

The second type of factor is some sort of shock to the system from a political event such as a war or perhaps a rise in oil prices. The recessions in 1974–5, 1980–2, 1990–1 and 2001 all involved a dramatic rise in oil prices although, as mentioned above, the 1990 US recession did in fact begin just before Saddam Hussein's invasion of Kuwait and the 2001 slowdown was also linked to the slowdown in investment in technology.

The third factor is higher interest rates. The monetary authorities often deliberately bring booms to an end because they want to rein in inflation. They may intend or at least announce that they intend to engineer a slow down or a *soft landing* but it is very difficult to fine-tune the economy. In some countries the timing of monetary policy is linked to elections though, in most major countries now, central banks have been made independent. The idea was to slow the economy just after an election so that the boom phase would coincide with the next election. Unfortunately this often meant delaying a necessary rise in interest rates until after the election, which tended to make the subsequent slowdown worse.

WHERE DOES THE RECOVERY COME FROM?

During a recession it is often very hard to see where the recovery is going to come from. Who is going to start spending again when all around everything is depressed? Typically there are four important factors. First, the authorities are likely to be actively stimulating the economy. Lower interest rates boost the stock market, encourage spending and borrowing and also lower the burden of existing debt. Fiscal policy directly puts more money into the economy. Secondly, during the recession consumers and business are actively reducing debts. This is often what keeps the recession going. At some point, with the help of lower interest rates, they may become more relaxed about borrowing. Also as spending on big-ticket consumer or investment items is delayed, a backlog of potential demand builds up which finally comes through, once confidence improves a bit. Thirdly, asset prices fall during the slowdown and recession, eventually to the point where people are prepared to buy again. Finally the inventory cycle plays a key role.

KONDRATIEFF CYCLES

In 1925 a Russian economist called Nikolai Kondratieff published a book called *The Long Waves in Economic Life*, which claimed to identify a 50–60 year long cycle.[2] In its strict form the Kondratieff cycle is supposed to consist of a 20–25 year upswing, followed by a 20–30 year downwave. The downwave does not mean that the economy is in decline for the whole time, only that prices (or inflation) are on a downward trend while average growth is slower and recessions tend to be long and deep while upswings are short or mild. The theory behind the cycle is that it is due to the long life of capital goods and the tendency for periodic investment booms.

Many studies have attempted to find long cycles but few have found the regular cycle that Kondratieff claimed (based on detailed statistical studies). There is also a problem in that, given the length of the cycle, there can only be four cycles since the industrial revolution began in the 1780s which, for statisticians, does not amount to many observations! Also, given the huge changes in the structure of economies over such long periods it seems doubtful whether the cycle would continue to remain the same length. Another criticism that is sometimes levelled is that many of the key turning points in the world economy seem to be linked to wars. But Kondratieff was writing in a Marxist tradition so that he saw wars not as random events but as part of the system. In fact he argued that wars normally occur in the upswing.

Nevertheless, the world economic slowdown of the 1970s encouraged renewed interest in the Kondratieff cycle. In 1925 Kondratieff dated the beginning of a downswing as around 1914–20. That points to the beginning of the next downswing due 50–60 years later, in the 1970s. This would fit with the sharp economic slowdown from the mid-1970s onwards (triggered by the oil crisis) and would also fit with the peak in inflation that occurred in 1974 or 1980 in most countries. Later analysts dated the beginning of the upswing in that cycle as around 1940, of course associated with the Second World War. Hence the good news is that the downswing phase should be nearing an end somewhere between 1995 and 2005!

If a Kondratieff upswing is starting at present then future slowdowns or recessions should be relatively mild and contained, and the performance of the economy should be relatively good, until around 2020. During recent years this has struck a chord with many people who see the new technologies such as computers, the internet and biotechnology as particularly potent. A new upswing would also mean that the disinflation process since the 1970s is nearing an end and that inflation could be on an upward trend again over the next couple of decades.

CONCLUSION: BUSINESS CYCLE FUNDAMENTALS

For many fundamentals-based investors, at least half of their time is spent trying to anticipate the next move in the business cycle. However, forecasting is very difficult. When the economy is in recession, how long it will last and how strong the recovery will be become overriding questions. Moreover, cycles differ in their impact on the major asset classes so there is always new history being written. The most common mistake is to forget or to deny that the cycle exists. Investors frequently start to believe that the upswing must go on for ever or that the recession will never end. This usually proves costly. However, trying to time the cycle precisely can also prove costly if the investor gets it wrong. Hence the approach taken by most investors is to alter asset class weightings, or time purchases and sales with one eye on the cycle, but not to place excessive bets upon timing the cycle correctly.

---

[2]N.D. Kondratieff (1935) An English translation appeared in *Review of Economics and Statistics*, 17 (6), 105–15.

3

Is Inflation Dead?

In recent years inflation has fallen to low levels while some countries have even seen deflation in the form of falling prices. However, the old fundamental relationships between inflation, unemployment and growth still exist, just at lower inflation rates. In some ways the analysis of inflation and unemployment is another way of looking at the business cycle. During recessions, unemployment rises and inflation tends to fall, while during the boom unemployment falls and inflation rises. But it is worth analysing these two aspects in more detail both to understand the timing of the cycle and to look at the long-term trends in inflation that have played such a crucial role in determining investment returns since the early 1970s.

THE PHILLIPS CURVE

The idea that there is a fixed relationship between inflation and unemployment was suggested by an economist called A.W.H. Phillips in 1957.[1] He plotted the unemployment rate against the inflation rate for 100 years of UK data and showed that high inflation was associated with low unemployment and vice versa. This plot became known as the Phillips curve. During the 1960s the Phillips curve became the subject of an enormous amount of economic analysis and discussion. The question, which was debated endlessly, was whether governments could choose where they wanted the economy to be on this curve. For example, could governments choose to accept a slightly higher level of inflation and thereby achieve lower unemployment? Many economists thought so in the early 1960s and argued that this would be worth doing.

However, in the late 1960s and 1970s both inflation and unemployment rose to higher levels and it became clear that such a choice does not exist over the long run. Governments can stimulate the economy to achieve a lower rate of unemployment, and inflation will naturally rise, but the economy eventually slows and unemployment rises. It is now generally believed that, over time, the level of inflation is independent of the rate of unemployment. This does not alter the short-term observation that a rise in unemployment will lower inflation, but it does mean that ultimately it is no use accepting a higher rate of inflation and hoping that this will give a permanently lower rate of unemployment. It was this realisation that led to a revolt against Keynesian economics in the 1970s and also lay behind the strong drive in the 1980s to reduce inflation. Nevertheless, the short-term relationship between inflation and unemployment remains crucial and is at the heart of central bank policy and the business cycle.

WHAT CAUSES INFLATION?

In looking at the causes of inflation, economists have traditionally divided into two camps. One, the monetarist camp, sees a growth in the money supply as the cause of inflation by pushing up demand for goods and labour. The other looks for the causes of inflation in the supply

---

[1] A.W. Phillips (1958) The relation between unemployment and the rate of change in money wage rates in the United Kingdom 1861–1957. *Economica*, 25 (November), 283–99.

and demand for goods and labour which is then accommodated by rising money supply. The monetarist approach is generally out of favour with policy-makers now. The problem is that the relationship between money and inflation has proved to be unstable and unpredictable in recent years, particularly in the short term. With monetarism very much in the background, attention now focuses more on the supply and demand for goods in the economy, though monetary growth remains an important indicator (see Chapter 5 for a full discussion of monetary policy).

Inflation is like a heavy moving vehicle with a great deal of momentum. It takes a lot to slow it down or speed it up. For example, suppose inflation is at 3% p.a. and workers are used to obtaining 5% p.a. in annual wage negotiations. It will usually require a sharp rise in unemployment to reduce that wage growth to, say, 3% p.a. but this will only gradually produce a drop in inflation. The rise in unemployment required, especially if labour markets are not very flexible or if unions are strong, may be substantial. Very often price inflation is slow to respond to lower wage growth because the context is one of economic slowdown, when business costs per unit of output are rising and companies may at first try to raise margins.

At any one time a particular level of inflation, whether 2% or 4% p.a., tends to be built into the system. The key question for the markets is whether the balance of forces in the economy is making inflation slow or accelerating it.

INFLATION TARGETING

Inflation targeting was first introduced in the 1980s in New Zealand and spread rapidly in the 1990s to include the UK, Euroland and numerous developing countries though not, so far, the USA. The idea is for the government to set an inflation target, usually a range in the region of 0–3% p.a., and task an independent central bank to use interest rate policy to achieve it. For investors the importance is twofold. First it institutionalises low inflation and therefore makes it much less likely that a new period of high inflation will emerge. Secondly, it provides a useful framework for forecasting central bank policy since the tools available to private forecasters are the same as those used by the monetary policy committees.

However, as always there are many complications. First, the system varies somewhat from country to country. For example, the European Central Bank (ECB) was given the task of price stability in the Maastricht Treaty and itself defined the target as 0–2% p.a. price inflation. The Bank of England has a 'symmetrical target' of 2.5% p.a. (set by the government) and undershooting is treated as just as much a failure as overshooting. Secondly, the system is relatively new and has not withstood many cycles. Thirdly, it is likely that central banks will tolerate periods of temporarily higher inflation due, for example, to oil prices, as in 2000–1. They would probably do the same in war-time. Finally, there are those who say that this is fighting the battles of the 1980s and the new threat will be deflation, i.e. falling prices. Taking the very long period, i.e. hundreds of years, inflation has been unusual outside war-time.

WHY DID INFLATION PICK UP IN THE 1960s?

For most people alive today inflation is a fact of life and has been for as long as they can remember. In investments and markets it has been a crucial factor for more than 40 years. However, except during war-time, price inflation during the nineteenth century and through the twentieth century prior to the 1960s was negligible. Indeed the price level in the UK fell for a large part of the nineteenth century. In the USA the main period of inflation was during the Civil War. Prices dropped for long periods otherwise. The period of relatively high inflation between the late 1960s and 1990 is therefore an unusual period historically. Why did it happen?

An obvious point is that in fact there was a war, the Vietnam War. The cost of financing that war and the stimulus it provided to the US economy (since it was not offset by tight monetary or fiscal policy) took unemployment to low levels for some time and inflation accelerated. This inflation was then transmitted to other countries, initially via the fixed exchange rate system of the time. Although that war ended many years ago it has taken a couple of decades to slow the momentum.

A second factor was the run-up in world commodity prices, particularly during the 1970s. For a time in the early 1970s it was widely believed that this rise reflected a dwindling in world natural resources. It is clear now, however, with the prices of most commodities back to the level of the early 1970s in real terms, that this was not a long-term trend but a cyclical move. In 1970, after over 20 years of strong growth in the USA and Europe, commodity-producing capacity had temporarily fallen behind. Once prices moved up in the 1970s more capacity was created and prices were eventually driven down again. This has helped in the disinflation process since 1980.

A third general factor was the bias towards faster economic growth in most countries. Faster growth means a more rapid rise in living standards, which is politically popular. Because inflation was slow to establish itself, and because people became accustomed to low inflation with the help of floating interest rates and indexation, it took many years for policy to turn decisively against inflation. The significant year was 1979, when Paul Volcker, the new Chairman of the US Federal Reserve, switched policy and raised interest rates sharply, Mrs. Thatcher was elected to power in the UK, and the Exchange Rate Mechanism was introduced in Europe.

Finally, inflation really took off when countries moved to floating exchange rates. Of course some countries, such as the UK and Italy, had relatively high inflation rates even before the system of fixed exchange rates broke down in 1971 and therefore needed periodic devaluations. But once the discipline of the system was taken away completely, many countries went through a period of much higher inflation, freed from its constraints.

INDICATORS OF INFLATION

The most commonly quoted measure of inflation is the consumer price index (CPI) but there are a host of others. The CPI (or retail price index, RPI, in the UK) is a basket of commodities weighted roughly according to an average family's budget. It is often distorted by sharp movements in food prices and energy prices and by movements in indirect taxation, e.g. value added taxes or other taxes, and also by movements in interest rates. Hence, for example, the UK publishes its RPI both in full and excluding food and energy, and also excluding the effects of changes in mortgage rates (RPIX). Rising food and energy prices can of course add to inflation over the long term but, very often, sharp monthly rises are subsequently reversed.

A second keenly watched indicator is the index of wholesale or producer prices, which measures the price of a basket of goods at the wholesale level. Another indicator is the GDP deflator. This is the index used to translate the calculation of nominal GDP into real GDP and therefore represents the price of all goods produced domestically. Finally, in the USA, Federal Reserve chairman Greenspan has indicated his preference for the consumer expenditure deflator, which covers a more comprehensive range of consumer spending than the consumer price index.

Another way to think of inflation is to treat it as the sum of three components, *wage growth* minus *productivity growth* plus *margin growth*. If wages are increasing at, for example, 5% p.a. and productivity growth is increasing at 2% p.a., then if producers and retailers are not altering their margins prices are likely to be increasing at 3% p.a. If they are trying to raise margins then price inflation is likely to be higher than 3% and vice versa.

Margins tend to rise during the economic upswing and contract during a slowdown or recession so that price inflation fluctuates more than wage inflation. Nevertheless, while margins do impact on recorded price inflation it is the trend of wages that has more long-run importance. Notice that, using this approach, if productivity rises, a higher level of wage growth is possible for the same rate of inflation. The best measure of wages is hourly earnings, or, after taking productivity growth into account, unit labour costs. In the USA the employment cost index is watched very closely because it includes the price of benefits such as health insurance.

MEASURING THE FORCES DETERMINING INFLATION

Economists look at two basic ideas in trying to measure whether the economy is positioned in such a way as to raise inflation or reduce inflation. These are called the output gap and the natural or non-accelerating inflation rate of unemployment (NAIRU).

The Output Gap

The output gap is a measure of the extent to which the economy is running above or below its comfortable maximum level of output, i.e. whether there is a gap between the current output of the economy and what it could be. If output has risen well above its trend line then the economy is likely to be overheating and vice versa. Inflation tends to fall about a year after an output gap emerges during the recession phase of the cycle. Similarly, inflation rises about one year after output goes above trend. Sometimes it is obvious whether the economy is well short of capacity or if it is showing signs of severe overheating. At other times it is a more questionable measurement. For the USA and the UK in the late 1990s it became a very difficult assessment when it was thought that the trend rate of growth of the economy might have increased. The output gap opens up when the actual output of the economy drops below estimates of the trend or underlying growth rate of the economy.

Figure 3.1 shows the relationship between US inflation and capacity use, as a proxy for the output gap. When capacity use rises above about 82%, reflecting an economy moving beyond its potential output, there has been a clear tendency for inflation to rise. The relationship worked less well in the 1990s, a point to which we shall return below.

The Natural Rate of Unemployment (NAIRU)

The other way of measuring the forces on inflation is to look at the so-called 'non-accelerating inflation rate of unemployment', or NAIRU for short, (also called the 'natural rate' of unemployment). This is the level of unemployment which is neither so low that wages are likely to move up nor so high that wage settlements are likely to be trending down. As its name suggests, the non-accelerating inflation rate of unemployment is a rate that is neutral for inflation, neither boosting it nor restraining it. The NAIRU used to be called the natural rate because some economists argued that the economy would naturally return to this level if left to itself, although this is a matter of debate.

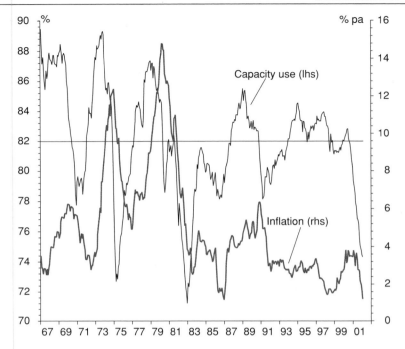

Figure 3.1   US inflation and capacity use
Source: Thomson Datastream

Inevitably there are substantial disagreements on the level of the NAIRU in each economy. It was generally thought to have risen in the 1970s and 1980s for a number of reasons discussed below, but then to have fallen in the 1990s. Note that for the markets a key factor is what level of unemployment the monetary authorities regard as the NAIRU rate, or at least a range at which they start to become concerned. For example, the Federal Reserve traditionally regarded 6% as a level below which wage pressures were likely to increase and therefore usually began tightening once unemployment approached that level (Figure 3.2). However, this level has come into doubt in recent years with the good performance of inflation despite low unemployment, and some observers would now put it below 5%.

These concepts are important because they explain why, just because economies pick up and start to grow, inflationary pressures will not necessarily re-emerge straight away. After a long recession like the early 1990s, the output gap and unemployment rate were well above what would be regarded as natural rates. Hence countries could grow at a relatively rapid pace, above trend growth rates, for at least a few years before inflation re-emerged. At the same time, a combination of recovery with low or declining inflation does not mean that inflation has gone away permanently, only that it is at bay.

Why is the NAIRU not Zero?

In the USA the NAIRU is believed to be in the 4–6% range, while in Euroland it is thought to be nearer 8%. Why is the NAIRU not zero and why does it vary from country to country? First, there are people who have lost their job and take some time to find another. For various

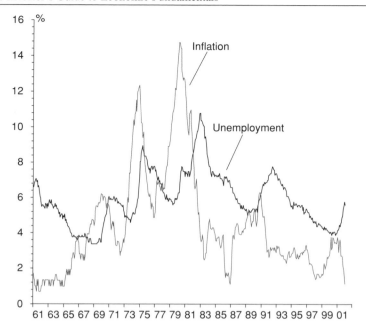

Figure 3.2   US inflation and unemployment
Source: Thomson Datastream

reasons people spend time finding a new job (even when the economy is buoyant). This may be because they have a financial cushion and therefore can afford to look around rather than accept the first job that comes their way. Or perhaps as jobs become more and more specialised it takes a little longer to find the right one.

Secondly, there is so-called structural unemployment — although this word 'structural' covers a multitude of factors. Generally, it means that people have the wrong skills or are in the wrong place to find jobs. For various reasons, including lack of adequate incentives or problems with relocating because of inefficiencies in housing markets (e.g. people cannot find cheap rented accommodation near their place of work), people either do not learn new skills or remain in areas of high unemployment. As the pace of structural change in the world economy accelerates, this problem has become more intense.

The third reason for unemployment is inadequate incentives to take work. If, by taking work, people lose too many benefits and face too much taxation, then the incentives to work are not great. In many countries, particularly in Europe, it would appear that there has been an increase in the number of people who register as unemployed and receive benefits but also do casual work in the 'black economy'. Such people may be disinclined to return to normal taxed work because they would be worse off. High rates of tax and generous benefits make this a particular problem in Europe.

The first three causes of unemployment determine the NAIRU or natural rate. The final cause of unemployment is lack of 'demand' owing to the state of the business cycle. At times weak demand can persist for a prolonged period, taking unemployment well above the natural rate and depressing inflation. If this situation persists for long enough (as, for example, in Japan), the economy may even see deflation.

IMPLICATIONS OF A LOW INFLATION ENVIRONMENT

After 20 years of relatively high inflation, the 1990s saw much lower inflation and even, in some countries, falling prices. In most of the industrial countries, inflation has converged to levels of 3% or below. Lower inflation is generally associated with higher economic growth, and this reflects four factors.

First, lower inflation means that there is a more stable environment for company planning. High inflation tends to bring uncertainty over future prices for both inputs and outputs, including foreign exchange, wages, interest rates, etc. While management can hedge against some of these uncertainties, it can usually do so only for the short term and at a cost, but there are others over which it has no control. Investment, therefore, becomes a less risky business in a period of low inflation.

Secondly, with low inflation, the financial environment is more stable, allowing for a reduction in real interest rates (the difference between nominal rates and inflation). The danger of a sudden sharp acceleration in inflation is reduced and investors therefore require less of a risk premium. Lower rates of interest encourage more investment, boosting economic growth.

Thirdly, low inflation can improve business cash flow. In periods of high inflation and high interest rates the cost of borrowing effectively becomes front-loaded because the initial interest payments are high while the repayment at the end of the term of the loan is in devalued money. Any investment financed by borrowing will therefore generate a less positive cash flow in the first few years in an environment of high inflation.

Fourthly, low inflation promotes growth by making changes in relative prices much more transparent both to consumers and businesses. When the general price level is moving upwards and price lists are frequently revised, it is harder for people to ensure they are paying or asking the right price. Since the market system relies for its efficiency on price signals, it is important that inflation does not obscure them.

Overall, a low inflation environment is good news for economic growth and therefore good news also for investment returns measured in real terms. The problem, however, is that the transition from high inflation inevitably includes a period of slow growth, high unemployment and reduced profits. It also changes the relative attractions of different asset classes.

INFLATION AND INVESTMENT RETURNS

The general level of inflation has had a crucial influence on investment returns over the last three decades. The rise in inflation between the mid-1960s and 1980 was devastating for long-term bonds, and a poor environment too for equities. It did, however, generate excellent returns in property and commodities because real interest rates were often negative. After 1982 both stocks and bonds enjoyed a long-term bull market as stock valuations rose substantially and bond yields fell substantially.

Property has continued to do fairly well in many countries, though with much longer cyclical bear markets. In the low inflation environment of the early 1990s, property prices fell in the USA, Japan and Europe. Prices moved up during the second half of the 1990s (except in Japan) in response to strong growth but the effect was smaller and more localised than in the 1980s. Price strength reflected excess demand in areas of strong economic growth such as Silicon Valley, or financial centres like New York and London. Industrial commodities, especially metals, picked up sharply in 1994 in response to strong US growth, but for much of the 1990s low general inflation held them back in comparison to the 1970s.

At the time of writing inflation is relatively low in most countries and an output gap has opened up. Does that mean that inflation is likely to go down another gear, taking inflation to 0% in Euroland and perhaps 1% in the USA and the UK? Such a level would push bond yields into the 2.5–4% range and provide new capital gains to holders of long maturities. It would also help justify price/earnings multiples in the mid-20s. Or is disinflation over now?

It would seem that there is no intention among governments or central banks to push inflation below the 1–3% range. Not only is this level comfortable but a lower rate would risk a period of deflation, which carries some problems of its own (see below). However, central banks may not be able to prevent a further fall in inflation, particularly in an increasingly globalised world with substantial overcapacity and fierce competition.

One of the problems facing investors in the 2000s is that low inflation means that nominal returns are comparatively lower, even though real returns are as high or higher than before. In the 1970s or 1980s it was common for investments to return over 10% p.a. in successive years. But US inflation averaged 5.8% p.a. between 1967 and 90, and if inflation averages only 2% p.a. in the 2000s, returns in single figures should be expected. This may lead investors to seek higher risk investments even though the reality is that they do not necessarily need to do so. In the end it is the real return, after inflation, that matters for investors.

THE THREAT OF DEFLATION

Deflation simply means falling prices, the opposite of inflation. However, there is fear associated with deflation because it has often been followed by recession or even depression in the past. Moreover, for investors, deflation in asset prices means losses on stock or property investments (compared with cash) which are magnified if the investment has been partly bought with borrowed money. Here we focus on deflation of the general price level.

For much of the nineteenth and the first half of the twentieth century deflation was common outside war-time. Generally speaking, although the price level rose during wars and strong economic upswings, it fell back again during peace-time and economic weakness. The reason was the gold standard system, which essentially limited the supply of money to what could be mined. Since the real economy was growing and therefore the demand for money rising, the amount of goods being produced tended to outgrow the supply of gold. The result was deflation.

Starting in the 1960s the world went through a major period of inflation with the overall price level rising several times in the main industrial countries and hundreds of times in some high-inflation countries in Latin America. Much of the story of economic policy in the 1980s and 1990s was about how to defeat inflation and by 1995 the authorities had largely succeeded. In the industrial countries inflation was generally down to 3% p.a. or below, and most developing countries had brought it down to single digits.

Starting with Japan in 1995, and then China and Hong Kong in 1998, deflation reappeared. Suddenly the price level was falling and policy-makers began to focus on how to fight deflation. Deflation is a real possibility in other countries too. For example, the US recession and then subsequent weak recovery from 1990 to 1994 reduced inflation from 5.4% to 2.6%, a reduction of nearly three percentage points. With inflation at 2.5% in 2001 a similar weak period could easily see deflation emerge.

Deflation is a threat to the economy for several reasons. First, it tends to undermine debt-financed investments. If the price of an asset, whether a new machine or a consumer's house, falls in value the 'equity' amount (i.e. the cash advanced) falls at a leveraged rate. For example, if the value of a property financed with a 67% loan-to-value mortgage then falls by 2% the value of the equity declines by 6%. This naturally makes both banks and investors nervous and some-times leads to panic sales to save what is left. This can lead to asset deflations of the kind seen in the USA in the 1930s, the UK in the early 1990s and many Asian countries in the late 1990s.

Secondly, deflation undermines the power of central banks (see also Chapter 5). Once interest rates reach zero they can go no lower since people would keep cash under the bed rather than pay interest to the bank for keeping it. As we shall see, monetary policy may still have some power but it has to work through flooding the markets with liquidity and/or depressing the exchange rate rather than through interest rates.

Thirdly, deflation can make people delay purchases. Why buy something now when it will be cheaper in future? A slow rate of deflation, say up to 2% p.a., may not have much impact but anything greater could be negative for the economy.

A combination of all these factors means that central banks prefer to keep inflation slightly positive rather than slightly negative. If they succeed in keeping inflation around 1–3% p.a. over the long term then there are clear implications for investors. Bond yields are unlikely to average below 4–5% p.a. Stock and property prices will trend up gradually over time. For example, the Bank of England's current 2.5% p.a. target implies that the price level will double every 28 years or so. This is a far greater degree of financial stability than in recent decades but does nevertheless leave property prices on a rising path for the long term.

What if deflation becomes the norm? Remember that if an investor owns a property which falls 10% in value over a period of several years, but the general price level falls by the same amount, then he is no worse off—provided the property was owned outright. If the property is mortgaged then he will have lost out substantially. The same applies to stock market investments. Any investment with a fixed pay-out such as a bond or annuity, or a final salary pension, will gain. Clearly bonds are the best hedge against deflation while any kind of borrowing is risky.

But is prolonged deflation really likely? In the past it was caused by the limited money supply provided by the gold standard system. Now, with governments controlling the money supply with paper money there is really no reason for deflation to persist. The period of deflation in China and Hong Kong in recent years was lengthened by the fixed exchange rate systems, particularly in Hong Kong; and in Japan the problem seems to have been caused by a dysfunctional banking system and a central bank too frightened of re-igniting inflation and the asset price bubble to push enough money into the system.

However, in future the weak period of the economic cycle could easily be a period of deflation, even if the upswing phases see positive inflation. The overall effect could be that the price level over a number of years is relatively stable. This is probably good news for the economy but again, for investors, the main point is that it is a totally different environment to the last 40 years — in general good for stocks and bonds but bad for property and commodities.

CONCLUSION: INFLATION REMAINS FUNDAMENTAL

Although inflation has fallen to low levels over the last 40 years it could still re-emerge if central banks become less vigilant. We shall return to this theme in Chapter 5. However, as long as inflation remains low, overall investment returns in nominal terms will be lower than before. The two asset classes which outperformed during the period of high inflation will continue to do less well. Stocks will continue to thrive, while bonds will only make capital gains if inflation declines further. However, the threat of deflation makes it likely that central banks will worry more about growth than inflation in coming years.

4

The New Economy: Myth or Reality

Talk of a 'new economy' first surfaced in the middle of the 1990s and by the end of the decade some aspects of it had become widely accepted, not least because of its embrace by Alan Greenspan, Chairman of the Federal Reserve Board. His willingness to let the economy grow much faster than had previously been thought prudent was based on his belief that the trend rate of growth was now higher than before and that low unemployment was less of an inflation threat. Also, the performance of the US economy between 1995 and 2000 seemed to bear out that optimism. Economic growth averaged over 4% p.a. while core inflation remained under 2.5% p.a.

At the risk of some oversimplication, it is possible to identify three broad views of the new economy, what I shall call the 'conventional view', the 'strong version' and the 'sceptical view'. In the 'conventional view', for various understandable reasons, the new economy is performing better than before. For example, using the concepts discussed in the preceding chapters, it means that the trend rate of GDP growth has accelerated from the generally accepted long-term rate of 2.5% p.a. to a 3.5–4% p.a. rate, due to higher productivity growth. It also means that the natural rate of unemployment may fall from its earlier 6% level to perhaps 5% due to structural changes in the labour market.

However in the late 1990s some enthusiasts took the argument further: the 'strong version' view suggested that the economy was behaving in completely different ways from before and now needed a different method of analysis. Proponents questioned the inevitability of the business cycle, arguing that changes in inventory management made possible by new technology could eliminate the typical overshooting patterns seen in the past. They also rejected the conventional relationship between inflation and unemployment, arguing that heightened competition due to deregulation and globalisation left firms with no pricing power. This should keep inflation low, almost whatever the level of unemployment. Clearly this would be good news in itself, but would also help to keep the upswing going since the Federal Reserve would not need to raise interest rates too much to constrain the economy. This 'strong version' of the new economy clearly contradicts much of the analysis in Chapters 2 and 3 above.

The sceptics denied the existence of a new economy altogether, arguing that the apparent improvement in productivity was due to a combination of statistical illusions and an economic boom unleashed by an incautious Federal Reserve. They argued that inflation was held down by the strength of the US dollar and weak economic growth in other countries, particularly after the Asian crisis in 1997. These sceptics doubted the importance of the new technology and questioned the way that statisticians were calculating productivity gains within the computer sector.

For many investors belief in the new economy, particularly in the strong version, provided justification for what were by then historically high valuations for stocks because it promised continuing strong economic growth, a reduced risk of recession and low inflation. Some analysts argued that the new economy would generate continued strong profits growth, though this argument was probably flawed since history suggests that, at least in the long run, faster productivity growth will flow through to consumers via reduced prices or higher wages. The new economy argument was inextricably linked with the technology boom, which was seen as a key driver of the new economy and lay behind the bubble in the NASDAQ stock index. However, since the collapse in technology stocks and economic recession in 2001 the new economy has lost some credibility and is generally viewed much more cautiously.

Essentially the new economy has three elements: higher productivity growth, changed inventory and cycle behaviour and improved inflation performance. They are analysed in turn below.

FASTER PRODUCTIVITY GROWTH

The rate of growth of productivity in the US economy did accelerate markedly in the late 1990s and, at least through early 2002, productivity growth has held up relatively well. The latest data show that during 1996–2000 labour productivity per hour rose at 2.7% p.a., significantly higher than the average of the previous 20 years of only 1.5% p.a. (Figure 4.1). The late 1990s data are slightly lower than was originally reported due to data revisions but are still very impressive. Nevertheless they relate to only five years. If the whole economic cycle is taken, from 1991 to 2001, productivity growth was 2.1% p.a., almost the same as the last cycle 1983–90, when the average was 1.9% p.a.. This highlights the problem of choosing data periods for comparison. Hence the question of whether productivity growth will remain strong in the next few years is still open, though the 1.8% increase in 2001, despite the recession, is very encouraging.

All analysts are agreed that the acceleration in productivity growth in recent years is, in some way, linked to the growth of computer and telecommunications technologies. 'Strong version'

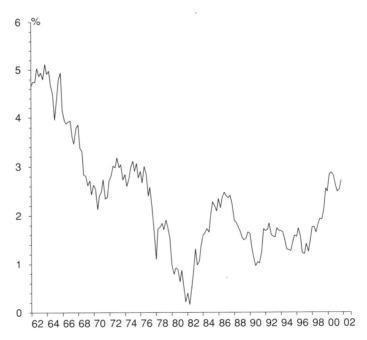

Figure 4.1   US output per hour (5-year moving average).
Source: Thomson Datastream

enthusiasts put the emphasis on the gains from the networking of personal computers and the benefits obtainable from developments such as e-mail and the internet. These technologies make it possible to improve management information systems, flatten corporate hierarchies and improve procurement processes (particularly through just-in-time inventory systems and outsourcing supplier contracts). Anecdotal evidence suggests that gains in the retailing sector may have played a particularly important part here.

However, another part of the productivity gain (noted particularly by the sceptics) is the strong productivity gains *within* the technology sector, as processing speed and memory capacity improved at a rapid rate. For example, if the US computer sector comprises 2.5% of GDP and productivity in this sector rises at 30% p.a., then 0.75% p.a. is added to overall US productivity growth. The measurement of the productivity increase within the computing sector is contentious. If a computer manufacturer turns out a computer with twice the processor speed and twice the memory of the model sold last year and is able to sell it for the same price (the ubiquitous £999), should this be regarded as a doubling of productivity in that factory? On paper the answer is yes, but sceptics argue that most users will not take full advantage of the doubling of computing power so that the product is not really twice as good.

The conventional view of the productivity improvement focuses more on the macro numbers and the link with higher investment spending. Many analysts were impressed by the fact that productivity growth accelerated in the second half of the upswing since periods of unusually high productivity growth have usually occurred at the beginning of an economic cycle when capacity use is being increased, rather than four years into an economic expansion. But the conventional view would link the acceleration in productivity to the investment boom. Private fixed investment rose as a percentage of GDP from a fairly stable 9–10% between 1983 and 1994 to an average of 13% from 1995 to 2001, with a peak of 15% in 1999.

Overall then, the recorded increase in productivity growth was partly due to measurement changes, partly due to specific productivity gains *within* the technology sector, partly due to the cyclical strength in the economy and partly due to higher investment. The difference between the three views of the new economy is shown by the way the gains are apportioned between them.

In general, both the sceptical view and the 'strong version' view have lost ground in the past few years. The sceptics' view, which attributed all the gains in productivity growth to measurement changes and the strength of the boom, was too pessimistic. Productivity growth held up well during the recession in 2001 and anecdotal evidence of productivity gains from greater use of computer technology continue to abound. However, the 'strong version' view has not held up well in the face of the bust in the technology sector and questions over the accounting of technology. The conventional view — i.e. the higher rate of productivity growth will continue — will depend partly on whether investment remains high. During 2001 investment started to fall back but still remained relatively high as a percent of GDP.

In Europe there has been very little sign of a rise in productivity. In fact productivity growth slowed in the second half of the 1990s, though the plus side was that employment grew quickly. There could be several reasons for this slowdown, some of which support the new economy view and some of which create doubt. First, there is anecdotal evidence that European companies have been slower to adopt new technologies and, in particular, slower to restructure businesses to take full advantage of new investments. This may be due to the more difficult labour environment as well as more conservative practices generally. Secondly, Europe has a smaller computer sector and therefore benefits less from the productivity growth within the sector. Most of the major companies at the heart of the sector, e.g. Microsoft, Cisco, Intel, Oracle etc., are US companies. Thirdly, there is some evidence that different government accounting approaches have measured the technology sector differently, contributing to different GDP growth rates. The Bundesbank calculated, for example, that if Germany used the US system for measuring productivity, GDP and productivity would have grown by about 0.5% p.a. more than reported. Finally, Europe did not enjoy the same economic boom as the USA in the late 1980s so did not gain from the productivity gains that (temporarily) go with a boom. Nor did it experience an investment boom, which would have raised productivity growth.

BETTER INVENTORY CONTROL ELIMINATING RECESSIONS

The 'strong version' of the new economy placed considerable emphasis on the view that the introduction of computer-based technology and networks would reduce, or even eliminate, inventory cycles because companies would be able to react much more quickly than before to a drop in sales. It was expected that inventories would adjust by smaller amounts over shorter periods and not necessarily set off the traditional downward sequence for the economy of lower sales, reduced production to cut inventories, leading to less overtime and less employment and resulting in still lower sales.

The evidence from the 2001 US recession is mixed. The inventory recession was *deeper* than ever before, with inventories cut by a remarkable 1.2% of GDP in the fourth quarter of 2001 (annualised rate). Overall the 2001 recession was due to this inventory cut-back combined with a sharp fall in business fixed investment. But there is some evidence that the inventory correction was *faster* than on previous occasions, which may have been helpful for the stability of the economy. Some analysts argued that the inventory correction was over before the full effects of the downturn could feed through to consumer spending.

The 'strong version' argument was dealt a blow by the fact that a key area of inventory correction was in the technology sector itself. At the end of 2000 producers suddenly found that the production of computers, servers and their components was well ahead of sales. This was caused by the end of the Y2K investment boom combined with the end of the 'dot.com' boom. The latter also resulted in substantial volumes of nearly new equipment coming back onto the market. But inventory in the technology sector can depreciate extremely quickly so companies moved very rapidly to cut production. Since many of the component parts are manufactured in Asian countries, and many of these countries are relatively concentrated in one area, one consequence was a very rapid and steep recession in countries such as Singapore and Taiwan.

In summary, in the 2001 recession inventories remained a key component of the cycle and hopes that the new economy would help to eliminate the business cycle proved unfounded. Paradoxically inventories of technology products played a particularly important role. However, there is some evidence that the unusually fast inventory correction played a role in limiting the severity of the recession.

PERMANENTLY LOWER INFLATION

The 'conventional view' here is that various elements of the new economy may have lowered the natural rate of unemployment or NAIRU. Sceptics argued that this was an illusion and that the relatively good performance of inflation was due to special factors. The 'strong view' of the new economy argued that neither firms nor employees could any longer push up prices or wages because of the new, much more competitive environment. Firms will simply not pay higher wages because they cannot raise prices. Instead they will either improve productivity,

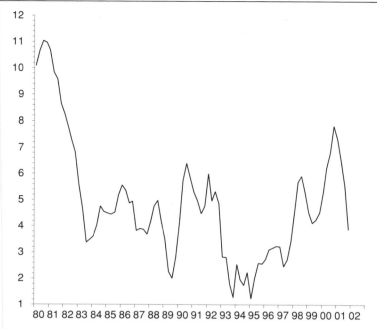

Figure 4.2   US wage growth (compensation per hour)
Source: Thomson Datastream

outsource at home or abroad, or go out of business. On this view companies have no 'pricing power' because any attempt to raise prices in response to higher costs leads to lost sales to other producers, whether domestic or foreign.

There are several elements involved in this story, which we can dissect using the 'old economy' theory of the preceding chapters. First, as discussed above, the natural rate of unemployment may indeed have fallen. In the case of the UK there is strong evidence that this has happened, at least looking at the long-term picture. Wage inflation in the UK appeared to edge up only slightly in 1999–2000 and at a much lower level of unemployment than before. This is probably a result of labour market liberalisation undertaken by the Conservative governments during the 1980s and early 1990s, and not much, if any, due to new technology. In the USA, the market was relatively liberalised already but there were new measures such as 'welfare to work' and the tolerance of greater immigration, which may have made some additional impact. Nevertheless, wages did appear to accelerate from about 1996 onwards, when unemployment went down to the 5–6% level, though only slowly (Figure 4.2).

Secondly, globalisation has undoubtedly increased and has gone hand-in-hand with the technology revolution. The fax machine in the 1980s made it easier to use suppliers in another country but the advent of sophisticated computers with e-mail makes it far easier to look overseas for suppliers than ever before. Lower wages elsewhere undoubtedly put pressure on developed country wages and reduce union power. The pattern in all developed countries shows that highly skilled people have seen an increase in real incomes relative to lower skilled or unskilled people. In the good times, unskilled people have still enjoyed some wage growth but the differentials have widened.

Figure 4.3 Trade-weighted US dollar index
Source: Thomson Datastream

Thirdly, the second half of the 1990s saw relatively slow economic growth outside the USA. Europe performed relatively poorly, initially because of the fiscal tightening in many countries ahead of the introduction of the Euro, and later under the impact of the Asian and Russian crises. Japan continued to struggle with the aftermath of the 1980s bubble while the smaller countries in Asia suffered a major financial crisis and recession. As a result there was plenty of excess capacity in the world, which encouraged increased exports to the USA.

Fourthly, and closely linked, was the strong dollar (see Figure 4.3). Even a relatively closed economy like the USA, with 'only' about 15% of GDP traded, receives a major disinflationary benefit from a strong currency; and during 1998–9 this was exaggerated by weak oil prices. The result was that import prices fell sharply during 1998–9, and helped to pull down general inflation.

Again, the evidence seems to favour the 'conventional view'. The natural rate of unemployment or NAIRU probably has fallen in the USA and the UK over recent years. In the USA part of this may be attributed to the increased impact of international competition linked to new technology. But the NAIRU still exists, at a slightly lower level and the conventional analysis of the risks from inflation if unemployment goes below that level remains valid.

CONCLUSION: OUTLOOK FOR THE NEW ECONOMY

Productivity in the US economy accelerated sharply in the second half of the 1990s. The increase was partly due to measurement changes, partly due to specific productivity gains *within* the technology sector, partly due to the cyclical strength in the economy and partly due to higher investment. The difference between the three views of the new economy — the 'strong version', the conventional view and the sceptics' view — is shown by the way in which the gains are apportioned between them.

The 'strong version' of the new economy also argued that the new technology allowed better control of inventories, which could eliminate the business cycle. The 2001 recession put paid to that theory although there is some evidence that the recession was relatively mild because of the speed of the inventory adjustment.

Nor did the 'strong version' claim, that the theory of the natural rate of unemployment is outdated, stand up during the last cycle. Wage growth did start to rise from about 1996 onwards once unemployment moved down into the 5–6% range. However, it can be argued that the effective NAIRU is a little lower than before and that the increase in wages was relatively muted this time.

If productivity is still growing healthily by the time you read this book, it will be very good news for investors. It will mean that the economy is still able to manage relatively high GDP growth, between 3 and 4% p.a. compared with the previous trend growth rate of 2.5% p.a. It will also mean that it is much easier for the Fed to keep inflation under control. That in turn will mean that the Fed has less need to raise interest rates sharply at certain periods to deal with inflation, which thereby makes a recession less likely. In turn price/earnings multiples on the stock market of 20 and higher (well above long-term averages) can be justified. However, if the new economy story becomes discredited and the late 1990s becomes viewed as a disreputable economic boom, markets will likely have a much more difficult time.

5
Understanding Central Banks

The main instrument of monetary policy is the short-term rate of interest. The exact interest rate instrument varies from country to country but is usually an overnight rate or another very short-term interest rate which the central bank can control directly. This rate influences the rest of the yield curve, with a declining impact as it goes out in time. At the far end of the yield spectrum, 30-year bond yields are only indirectly affected by overnight rates and indeed, in response to a move in money rates, can move in the same direction or the opposite direction or not at all.

A cut in short-term interest rates will stimulate the economy and vice versa though the size of the impact also depends on the level of interest rates relative to inflation, i.e. the 'real' interest rate and a host of other factors. A cut in interest rates will also usually lower the exchange rate, though this relationship has become less certain in recent years.

One group of economists — monetarists — believes that changes in the money supply are a better indicator of the stance of monetary policy than either interest rates or trends in the economy itself. But most economists and governments now distrust pure monetarism and only look at money growth alongside all the other indicators.

WHAT ARE CENTRAL BANKS TRYING TO DO?

In day-to-day markets changes in monetary policy or expectations of change dominate market activity. For the longer term investor, monetary policy is important as being one of the key determinants of the business cycle. The monetary authorities cannot make recessions and recoveries to order, but they certainly try, and monetary policy is their main instrument. Several countries experimented with direct control of the money *supply* during the 1970s and 1980s but the results were widely seen as unsatisfactory (see below on monetarism). Hence monetary policy now is geared to setting the short-term rate of interest at a level that will generate the appropriate level of *demand* for money (or perhaps more accurately for credit) in the economy.

When the economy is weak the question becomes: What rate of interest will get the economy growing fast enough to bring unemployment down? When it is strong interest rates are raised to slow growth. The ideal is to keep the economy growing at something close to its natural or trend rate of growth. If unemployment is relatively high and there is spare capacity generally, then a rate of growth higher than the trend rate will be tolerated for a while. If the economy is threatening to overheat, then the authorities will aim for a 'soft landing', a period where growth is slower than the trend rate. If they get it wrong and a recession emerges then they will cut rates sharply to restore growth. Finally, if there is a major crisis which threatens the financial system, they will cut rates sharply and 'flood' the economy with liquidity, as was seen in 1987, 1998 and 2001. The key variables that the monetary authorities watch are the pace of economic growth, the amount of excess capacity still available if any (the 'output gap', see Chapter 3), the level of unemployment and the rate of inflation.

However central banking is not easy. A useful analogy is to think of being in a pilot's seat trying to control an aircraft (i.e. the economy) into land. The anxious passengers, the markets, try to guess what the next move will be. A touch more on the airbrakes is used to slow the plane (e.g. a rise in interest rates), or keep things steady (no change) because the plane is nicely on the glide-path. Pursuing the analogy, the key instruments to watch are the altimeter, i.e. where the economy is in relation to full capacity (the ground!), and the rate of descent indicator which shows how quickly the economy is moving towards full capacity.

Imagine further that neither the central bank nor the markets can look out of the front window of the plane, but only behind them, as data on the past movement of the economy become available. Also, that there is a delay between any action by the Fed on the controls and the plane responding.

There is another element we can introduce into the analogy. As well as the pilot and the markets there is also the 'owner' of the plane, the government, which in most countries plays a role. Governments are interested in making sure that the plane is flying high when elections loom and they certainly do not want a crash landing. Fiscal policy can have a major effect on the plane and central banks have to take into account fiscal measures. Generally speaking, if governments loosen fiscal policy, e.g. more government spending or tax cuts, the monetary authorities will keep interest rates higher than otherwise, and vice versa. Interest rates could still fall, but only if the economy was weakening for other reasons.

INDEPENDENT CENTRAL BANKS AND INFLATION TARGETING

Over the last decade most countries have shifted to a system with an 'independent' central bank and many have introduced inflation targeting. This was a response to the disastrous inflation of the 1970s and the belief that monetary policy had become too politicised. The real extent of independence is somewhat debatable. Central Bank chairmen are usually political appointees and their objectives are defined by politicians, but the process is generally fairly transparent and the possibility of a return to the days when politicians cut interest rates shortly before elections or did not respond to the economy overheating because of the political consequences, is probably at an end. Nevertheless, if economies see a prolonged period of economic weakness and/or deflation, central banks may lose some of their credibility and, in time possibly, their independence.

The second major change, inflation targeting, was a response to the failure of monetarism to deliver a usable policy approach. While in theory the quantity of money can be directly controlled by the government, in practice attempts to implement this approach led to wild gyrations in interest rates and considerable economic instability. Moreover, once the money supply was targeted in this way it seemed to behave differently. An alternative for small, open economies is to follow an exchange rate target. But this approach has had limited success with, for example, the break-up of the European Exchange Rate Mechanism in the early 1990s and the Asian currency crisis in 1997.

Nevertheless, the USA does not have an explicit inflation target. Most analysts believe that the Federal Reserve has an implicit target range of the order of 1–3% p.a. and beyond 3% p.a. the Federal Reserve will be trying urgently to slow the economy. Japan introduced an inflation target in 2001 aiming at 'price stability', although it does not appear to be fully operational. Many commentators recommended that Japan should establish a target of 1–2% p.a. but, with the price level currently falling, there is concern that an explicit positive inflation target might, if it was credible, lead to a sharp fall in bond prices. Japanese bonds in recent years have yielded only around 1–2% p.a., but yields would be expected to rise to the 3-4% p.a. range if inflation averaged 1% p.a.

Whether inflation targeting will remain the norm in future is hard to tell. Experience suggests that monetary regimes change periodically, as conditions alter and fashions shift. On the other hand, arguably the most successful central bank of all, the German Bundesbank, navigated through all these shifting currents without major changes in its approach which has always been to aim for low inflation and not to tolerate any significant acceleration. The approach taken by the European Central Bank is dominated by this tradition. So perhaps the experience gained in the last 30 years, without the fixed exchange rate system, really will make central bank behaviour more predictable and more stable than before.

One major caveat, however, is the problem of deflation. As discussed in Chapter 3, a falling price level means that the traditional monetary policy of using interest rates to change the demand for money, and therefore the economy, becomes more difficult and perhaps impossible. Ironically therefore, just as central banks have settled down to a regime of inflation targeting, they could find that inflation disappears altogether. This has already occurred in Japan and has the effect of eliminating the effectiveness of interest rates and returning attention to direct control of the monetary base (see below).

OFFICIAL INTEREST RATES

The primary instrument of monetary policy is the short-term interest rate. The monetary authorities alternately squeeze or flood banks' balance sheets with money in order to raise or lower short-term interest rates to their target level. In the USA the key rate is the Fed Funds rate, while in some other countries it is an overnight money rate or a repurchase rate. In the UK the banks' base rate is the key rate. These overnight or very short-term rates in turn influence the whole of the yield curve. Many countries, including the USA, Japan and Germany, have a discount rate, i.e. the rate at which banks can borrow from the central bank. This is usually below prevailing money rates and is available to banks only in exceptional cases.

Key Official Interest Rates to Watch

USA	*Federal Funds rate* — the Federal Reserve's key rate. It is an overnight deposit rate for banks.
Japan	*Official discount rate* — the floor for rates.
Euroland	*Repurchase rate* — the key operating interest rate.
UK	Bank of Englands's *dealing rates*. Used to control bank's *base rates*.

THE YIELD CURVE

The yield curve (Figure 5.1) is a chart of interest rates from overnight rates to 30-year bond yields, or even beyond, at any particular moment in time. To use a different flying analogy from the one above, the yield curve can be seen as a kite string with the monetary authorities hanging on to one end and the 30-year bond yield being the kite at the other end. The lower part of the string is not going to be far up or down from where the central bank is holding it, but at the other end of the string, at longer maturities, the kite could be very steeply up in the air or sloping downwards to the ground. If the markets think that the government might lower its short-term rate soon, then 3-month interest rates will often be below overnight rates. If the government tugs down on the string and reduces short-term interest rates the effect, as kite-flying enthusiasts know, might take the kite higher with a steeper angle on the string (yield curve).

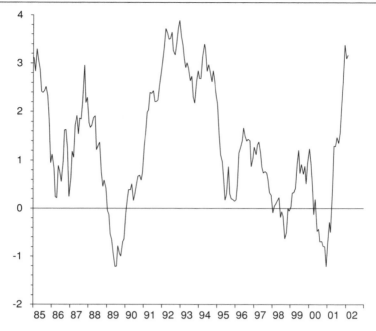

Figure 5.1   US yield differentials: 10-year yield — Fed Funds rate
Source: Thomson Datastream

A 'normal' yield curve has an upward slope, i.e. bond yields above money-rates. If investors are to be induced to lend for a longer period, they must be offered a higher return to justify the risk. The risk here is that short-term interest rates move up at some point. Suppose an investor has just bought a 3-month security with a coupon (i.e. interest payment) of 3% p.a. If interest rates suddenly rise to 4% p.a. he can hold the security for the rest of the three months then buy another one yielding 4% p.a. Assuming that interest rates stay at 4% p.a. for the next nine months he will have earned 3.75% p.a. over the whole period. But if he had just bought a 1-year security yielding 3.3%, he will earn only 3.3% over the period. At the time he buys the 1-year security it offers a higher yield than the 3-month security to try to guard against the risk of a rise in interest rates. But in this example, of course, it is not enough.

One of the implications of this analysis is that the yield curve is likely to be more steeply upward sloping the greater the risk of a sudden rise in interest rates. Hence when, during the late 1970s and 1980s, markets became very concerned about the risk of higher inflation, yield curves were relatively steep. From the early 1990s onwards the perception grew that the days of high inflation were over and that deflation was an increasing risk. The result has been a tendency for the slope of the yield curve to be less steep.

Another way of thinking about the risk is in terms of the volatility of the price of the security. For investors holding to maturity this is irrelevant but they are losing out on better interest rates now available in the market. For those focusing on the price, the longer the maturity, the greater the fall will be when interest rates rise (on a mark-to-market basis).

If investors think that government controlled interest rates are headed up then the yield curve will be especially steep. If, however, investors think that the government may be going to cut interest rates, then long-term rates may be below short-term rates, i.e. the yield curve is 'inverted'. Usually, at the height of an economic upswing the yield curve is inverted while, at the end of a recession and beginning of a recovery and during the early upswing phase, the curve will be steeply upward-sloping. The yield curve is a good leading indicator of the economy.

INTEREST RATES AND THE ECONOMY

A cut in interest rates will normally stimulate the economy and vice versa, though the precise impact is always uncertain. The change in short-term interest rates affects the economy through a number of different mechanisms which vary in their effects at different times. The best way to look at this is in terms of the components of GDP (consumer spending, business spending, government spending and foreigners' spending).

Consumers tend to spend more when interest rates are lower for various reasons. First, lower rates encourage more borrowing particularly for the big-ticket items such as cars and kitchens. In the UK, where most housing finance is at floating interest rates, consumers benefit very quickly from lower mortgage payments. In other countries where fixed rate mortgage finance is more common, lower interest rates may have some negative impact on consumers by reducing interest income. However, in the USA lower interest rates are very important in stimulating refinancing of mortgages. Consumers enjoy the benefit of lower fixed interest rates but also, commonly, take out a larger loan when they remortgage, reducing their equity and thereby freeing up money to spend.

Secondly, lower interest rates usually bring a fall in yields across the spectrum, which means higher bond and stock prices. This in turn should encourage consumers to go out and spend through a wealth effect; business will be more inclined to spend too for similar reasons; investment projects are more attractive if they can be financed at lower interest rates; and the cost of working capital and of holding inventories goes down. Also, lower interest rates often mean higher share prices, which encourage businesses to invest. Small businesses in particular are often very much influenced by interest rates.

In the short run, however, interest rates probably influence business spending more through being signals about the direction of the economy (e.g. lower interest rates point to faster growth ahead) which encourages retailers to order more goods and companies to produce more in anticipation. Lower interest rates also help by improving business balance sheets, to the extent that they use floating rate debt. Interest rates work on foreigners' spending by influencing the exchange rate. Usually a cut in rates will lower the exchange rate and therefore stimulate exports. Figure 5.2 shows US interest rates from 1980 to 2002.

ASSESSING THE POLICY STANCE

The extent to which a particular move in short-term interest rates will stimulate the economy is always difficult to judge in advance. We do know that the full effect is not complete for a year or more. Although confidence may receive an immediate boost from lower interest rates, the impact on spending takes longer.

The effect of a cut in rates also depends on the absolute level of interest rates not just the direction of change. For example, if interest rates have been raised from 3 to 6% to deal with inflation and then, in response to a recession, are lowered to 4%, the lowering of interest rates might stimulate the economy, but interest rates are still at higher levels than before. Some economists believe that this is the key to understanding monetary policy. In other words, what

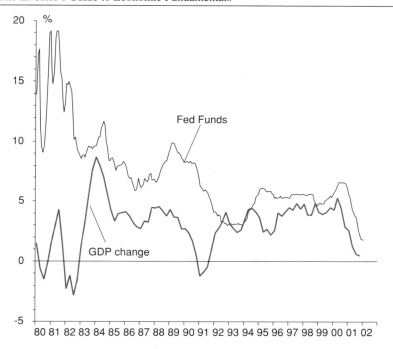

Figure 5.2   US interest rates and the economy
Source: Thomson Datastream

matters is not whether interest rates have most recently been moved up or down but where they stand in relation to their average or neutral level.

Economists often look at *real* interest rates, i.e. the difference between interest rates and inflation, to judge how easy or tight policy is at that moment. In the above example, if inflation is running at 1% p.a. and interest rates are at 4% p.a. the real interest rate would still be 3% p.a., which would normally be judged comparatively high to stimulate spending. Ideally the calculation of the real interest rate should use *expectations* for inflation rather than just the latest figure. If the economy is weak then inflation is probably headed downwards, i.e. inflation expectations are lower than actual inflation and the implied real interest rate is correspondingly higher.

The trouble with using real interest rates, as a guide is that they have varied at different points in history (Figure 5.3). The whole of the 1980s' economic upswing took place with comparatively high real interest rates, whereas in the 1970s real interest rates were mostly negative. In the 1990s real interest rates were generally much lower again. One reason was that fiscal policy in the USA and Europe was generally contractionary in the 1990s, in contrast to the early 1980s. In other words, budgets were being tightened, which acted as a drag on GDP growth. Another reason (see above) was that expectations of inflation were lower so that there was a smaller risk premium against the chance of an acceleration to a higher rate. Indeed, investors frequently saw a greater risk on the downside, i.e. towards lower inflation or deflation. Nevertheless, if inflation stays at moderate levels real interest rates are likely to show more stable trends in future and may be more useful in assessing monetary policy.

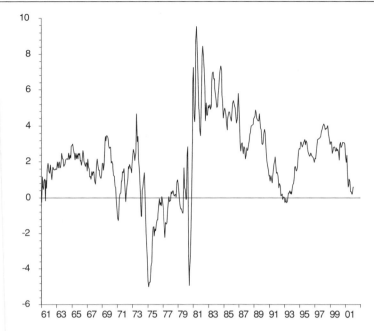

Figure 5.3 US real interest rates
Source: Thomson Datastream

THE TAYLOR RULE

One way to assess the central bank's stance and to predict changes is through the so-called Taylor Rule, named after the academic economist John Taylor, who was appointed US Treasury Under-Secretary in 2001. In essence this rule is a formal way of linking the short-term interest rate to the rate of growth of the economy and inflation. There are a number of forms in use but a simple approach is as follows. Decide on a figure for the trend rate of growth of the economy and the target inflation rate. Almost all central banks now have either an explicit inflation target or a range. Some also indicate what they think the trend rate of growth of the economy is likely to be. Although the USA does not have a formal inflation target most economists take 2% as the mid-range of a comfortable level.

As a result, if growth and inflation are both exactly rising at trend, the short-term interest rate should be equal to their sum. For example, if the USA is forecast to achieve 3% growth (assumed to be trend) and 2% inflation, then the Fed would be happy with a Fed Funds rate of 5%. However, if the forecast inflation rate and/or the forecast growth rate of the economy is above the trend or target level, interest rates need to be raised by *half* the difference between the forecast and the trend. And, of course, vice versa if inflation and/or growth are forecast to be below target and trend. (See the Glossary for the formula in detail.) For example, if inflation is forecast to be 3% and the target is only 2% then, if growth is forecast to be exactly on trend, interest rates need to be 0.5% higher, i.e. 5.5% in the example above. But if, at the same time, forecast growth is 1% *under* trend then there is no need to raise interest rates above the neutral level because the slow economy will bring down inflation in any case.

Historically central banks have followed an interest rate path quite close to this formula, and although no central bank has adopted it explicitly, it is a useful 'rule of thumb' both for central bankers and the markets. In practice, several difficulties arise. First, while an inflation target can be agreed easily or may be mandated by the government, what is the trend rate of growth of the economy? In the late 1990s most analysts and the Fed concluded that trend growth in the US economy had risen from the old 2.5% p.a. rate to at least 3.5% p.a. But this remains highly contentious. Remember also that, if growth is on a higher trend, that implies a higher neutral rate of interest in itself, 5.5% in the above example. Another problem arises if the economy has a substantial amount of excess capacity or is clearly overheating, when a more extreme and less gradualist stance might be justified. Finally, central banks also need to take account of significant upward or downward movements in asset prices which could upset the economy.

MONETARY CONDITIONS INDICES

Another tool for both central banks and investors is a Monetary Conditions Index. This is based on the idea that the impact of a particular monetary stance can best be assessed by looking at a combination of indicators including changes in interest rates, changes in exchange rates and sometimes changes in asset prices. Thus, even if the nominal and real interest rates do not change one year, a fall in the exchange rate will be a stimulus to the economy, as would a rise in stock prices. These indices therefore attempt to capture the combined effect. Some countries, for example Canada, publish such indices; for others there are indices that are published by banks or brokers.

The weighting between interest rates, the exchange rate and asset prices should vary between countries. For small countries the exchange rate is often of crucial importance since foreign trade can represent 30% or more of GDP, so the exchange rate is likely to have a large weight in the index. For the USA or Euroland the exchange rate is less important since foreign trade is only 10–15% of GDP. The weight for asset prices has probably been increasing over the years, and is likely to be more important for the USA and the UK — with the substantial role played by stock markets and housing prices in the economy — than for continental Europe.

THE MONETARIST VIEW

The difficulty with using real interest rates as an indicator of policy stance is one reason why many monetarist economists believe that changes in money supply are a better indicator of the position of monetary policy. Another reason is that monetarists believe that changes in money supply occur *before* changes in the real economy and therefore can be used as a leading indicator of the economy. (See the appendix to this chapter for an explanation of how money is created.)

Most monetarists would disagree little with the paragraphs above describing the relationship between changes in interest rates and the economy. However they would regard the interest rate story as being only a 'transmission mechanism' between the money supply and the real economy. For example, a rise in the money supply causes a fall in interest rates which causes the economy to strengthen.

However, monetarists split into two groups on this point, with some believing that changes in the money supply *cause* changes in the real economy and in prices, while others believe that money supply is just a particularly good indicator. It is thought to indicate movements in the economy with a lead time of between three months and two years.

Monetarist Experiments 1976–85

Monetarism goes back to the early twentieth century and before, but it was largely forgotten about between 1940 and 1970. It has long been known that, over the long term, a relationship exists between the money supply and the economy. Even Keynes himself, frequently accused of ignoring money, in fact wrote most of his major works on the subject of money. However, after the Second World War his followers, known as the Keynesians, accorded money very little importance. They argued that fiscal policy should be the main instrument of control over the economy. It was only in the 1970s, when these policies seemed to fail and inflation accelerated, that monetarism was rediscovered by mainstream economists and policy-makers.

During the 1970s inflation reached crisis levels and governments seemed unable to control it. There was a widespread rejection of Keynesian economics and macro-economic policy began to follow a monetarist approach. The monetarist experiments in the USA and the UK around the end of the 1970s and in the early 1980s were founded on the belief that controlling the money supply was the key to controlling inflation. Some even argued that it would be relatively painless, a claim now usually forgotten. The German Bundesbank used a partial monetarist approach until 1999 when its role was taken over by the European Central Bank. The ECB continues to pay more attention to money growth than the Federal Reserve although in the early years of monetary union there are worries over whether old relationships between money and the economy, which worked in Germany, will work for the region as a whole.

Governments tried directly to control money supply, under Mrs Thatcher in 1979-81 and under Paul Volcker at the Federal Reserve during 1979–82, and the result in both cases was a sharp rise in interest rates. This was not very surprising, but what did surprise everybody was a sharp rise in money supply, at least at first. This was partly due to the rise in interest rates itself which encouraged people to hold wealth in interest-bearing securities, included in broad money measures, rather than stocks or bonds which are not.

Eventually inflation did come down substantially but only through the usual mechanism of a severe recession and high unemployment. Meanwhile money growth was high and volatile and the historical link between money and inflation seemed to have broken down. By the mid-1980s both the US and UK authorities had rejected the idea that money could be relied upon as the sole or even the main guide to policy.

Some people now regard that as a mistake. For example, in the UK, rapid money growth from about 1985 onwards did signal the excessive boom of the late 1980s, the rise in asset prices and the acceleration in inflation. Other indicators showed that, not only asset prices themselves but also the dramatic fall in unemployment and the pace of growth of the economy, but unfortunately none of the indicators was heeded until it was too late. Forecasts repeatedly suggested that growth was just about to slow. The 1980s experience did see the authorities swinging back to giving money a greater role, but only in the context of other indicators.

In the late 1990s rapid money growth was very evident in the US economy. Broad money grew an average 9.2% p.a. between 1996 and 2000, well ahead of nominal GDP growth of 6% p.a. Undoubtedly this was a contributory factor in the stellar performance of the stock market and to some extent the housing market. The rise was tolerated by the Fed, partly because the trend rate of growth of the economy was believed to have accelerated and this therefore meant an upward adjustment in money supply as well as the stock market. It also developed partly because the Fed was anxious to avoid a problem with the Millennium Bug, which might have disrupted markets.

The ECB still sets monetary targets, but if money now goes outside these targets they will not necessarily respond, nor will the markets immediately draw conclusions. The reason is that money supply can be distorted by changes in behaviour or by changes in government policy towards financial institutions. A series of such changes in the last 20 years have left many central bankers sceptical of the usefulness of money, even as a reliable indicator.

Which Money Measure?

A key problem for monetarism and a major topic of debate among monetarist economists is which measure of money supply should be used. Ideally the measure would include only money that people hold ready for spending, e.g. cash and current accounts. But experience has suggested that other forms of money, including short-term deposits, may also be held for spending soon, so most monetarists prefer to look at wider measures. However, the wider the measure the more likely that some of the accounts may not be intended for short-term spending.

Money measures are listed from M0 to M3 or M4 with slight differences in definition between countries, though the concepts are similar. The narrowest measure of money M0 is also called the monetary base and consists of just banks' reserves at the central bank and cash in circulation. This is a closely watched indicator of the short-term strength of the economy. Past evidence suggests that M0 is closely correlated with spending in the economy, though without more than a few weeks' lead time. Money supply M1 is M0 plus sight or demand deposits. M2 includes large time deposits, while M3 includes large time deposits and money market funds.

In times of higher interest rates, people tend to hold more assets in higher interest accounts than in current accounts. They may also hold fewer bonds or stocks. Economists have spent an enormous amount of time analysing the relationship between the level of interest rates and the form in which people hold their money. One of the biggest issues in the literature on monetarism is whether or not this relationship is stable. If it is stable, then when we see a rise in the quantity of money we will know whether it is simply due to changed interest rates or whether it indicates faster economic growth.

The Velocity of Money

Velocity is the measure of the speed with which money goes round the economy. Each individual or company spends money or writes cheques and passes them to others who may keep that money in their account for a few weeks and then themselves write cheques or draw out cash to spend. The stock of money is, of course, less than the value of GDP because money is flowing around from person to person. If the amount of money in existence is equal to one-tenth of the value of one year's GDP then the velocity is measured as 10 times. Of course each measure of money has a different velocity.

The key question for monetarism is whether the velocity of money is stable. It does not necessarily have to be constant. We know that it might be affected by changes in interest rates. We also know that long-term trends may be involved — for example, as people increasingly use credit cards or use money for transactions not included in GDP. But neither point matters if the authorities can make allowances for higher or lower interest rates or long-term trends. We would still know that a rise in money supply after allowing for short-term cyclical factors or long-run trends implied an increase in transactions.

However, we would not automatically know whether an increase in the value of transactions represented an increase in prices or an increase in the number of transactions. Nor could we know whether it represented an increase in demand for current output (i.e. GDP) or an increase in transactions of assets, for example more house sales.

Velocity has been Unstable

In practice velocity has changed over time and sometimes in an unpredictable way, which makes the relationship difficult to sustain. The stable relationship that appeared to exist in the 1960s and 1970s became less stable in the late 1970s and 1980s. It is believed that this could be due either to the financial innovations of the later period or it might have to do with the effects of targeting money supply. One of the key Bank of England officials involved in managing the UK's monetarist experiment, Charles Goodhart, coined 'Goodhart's law' which stated that whichever monetary aggregate is chosen as a target variable becomes distorted by the very act of choosing it as a target!

The rapid growth of money supply in a number of countries in the mid-1980s and again in the late 1990s was, initially at least, linked to the rapid turnover in assets such as property and shares. Only some time later did the economies become sufficiently heated for a general rise in prices. Whether the build-up of general inflation could have been avoided if governments had managed to slow the economy early enough is an unanswerable question. In the 1980s governments were tightening policy sharply in 1987 but then reversed for six months or more after the October stock market crash.

In the 1990s money growth again accelerated in the USA during the late phase of the cycle from 1998 to 2000 (Figure 5.4), but the Fed was comfortable with ignoring it because general

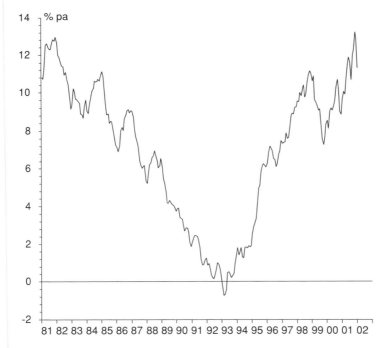

Figure 5.4   US money growth M3
Source: Thomson Datastream

inflation was low, partly due to the Asia crisis. Also the Fed believed that the natural rate of growth of the economy had accelerated so that a faster rate of economic growth could be tolerated. Finally, the strength of the dollar suggested to some that monetary policy was relatively tight. However, this was probably to ignore the impact of the private sector boom in boosting the currency.

Money as an Indicator

Monetarist economists still believe that careful analysis of money data is revealing. Indeed, if we accept Goodhart's law, this may be more likely if governments are not using monetary targets. Non-monetarists have given up, or use money supply only alongside all the other data, partly because they doubt the usefulness of monetary developments as an indicator of economic developments and partly because they know that central banks are looking at everything else too. Money supply is included in indices of leading indicators but only as one among several indicators.

Most governments still find that money developments are not very helpful in making short-run policy and prefer to look out of the window, even the back window to see where they are, rather than rely on money numbers. For this reason the markets now pay far more attention to data releases on employment and production than they do to money supply. The longer term investor, however, should definitely not exclude monetary trends from his calculations.

MONETARY POLICY AND THE EXCHANGE RATE

The basic rule is that a government cannot have an interest rate (or monetary) policy independently from an exchange rate policy. The reason is simple: if the government tries to maintain a particular exchange rate then interest rates may have to rise at times if people do not believe that the exchange rate is sustainable, or fall at other times to prevent the exchange rate rising.

Another rule, however, which became very clear in Europe in 1992-3 and in Asia in 1997, is that a pure exchange rate policy will not necessary work. In effect, although governments can raise short-term rates to astronomically high levels (for example 1,000% at an annualised rate overnight), if markets do not anticipate that this level can continue, the government is liable to be forced to devalue.

However, if the government is pursuing an exchange rate policy then interest rates are the easiest and quickest way to do it. A cut in interest rates will usually bring the exchange rate down, encouraging the economy. Similarly, a rise in interest rates often slows the economy and reduces inflation, particularly through maintaining or raising the exchange rate. The mechanism here is that a high exchange rate puts pressure on domestic producers to control prices, and that feeds through the whole economy.

CONCLUSION: MONETARY POLICY FUNDAMENTALS

Central banks try to maintain inflation in their target range by using interest rates to stimulate or stifle economic growth, to keep it close to trend. If inflation goes significantly above trend, the central bank will need to push GDP significantly below trend for a period, to pull inflation back. To judge the current stance of monetary policy it is best to look at all the indicators, including real interest rates, monetary growth, Monetary Conditions Indices and the Taylor Rule.

A cut in official interest rates is good news for stocks, usually good news for bonds (but not always) and usually bad news for a currency (but not always). It is good news for bonds and bad news for currencies if the markets regard the cut as likely to be maintained because of the weakness of the economy. However, a cut will be bad news for bonds and good news for the currency if it seems to point to a rapid strengthening of the economy.

APPENDIX: HOW IS MONEY CREATED?

Money can be created both by the government and the private sector. These two types of money are sometimes called 'printing press money' and 'fountain pen money'.[1]

Printing Press Money

Historically, printing press money goes back a long way. Centuries ago governments minted new coin to pay for wars (if they controlled the gold or silver mines). Or clipped existing coins and melted down the silver and gold to create new coins. Nowadays printing press money is created when the government borrows from the banking system to finance its spending (instead of selling debt to the *non-bank* private sector).

For example, suppose the government writes a cheque to pay for some services and issues a Treasury Bill to cover the spending. The government banks with the central bank (let's say the Bank of England) so that the cheque is drawn on the Bank of England. The recipient pays it into his bank (lets call it Anybank), increasing his bank deposit and therefore the money supply. Anybank will present the cheque to the Bank of England, which then credits Anybank's account at the Bank of England. Anybank will then probably have more on deposit with the Bank of England than it needs so will buy Treasury Bills issued by the government.

Notice that in reality the government has not simply printed money. It has issued a new Treasury Bill and written a cheque. So the government will have to repay the Bill at some point by raising taxes. But there is more money in the system. The recipient of the money is likely to spend it on something else and the next recipient on something else. So it courses through the economy creating new economic activity.

If the government wants to avoid increasing the money supply in this way it needs to sell securities to the *non-bank* private sector, usually longer term securities. Then money is withdrawn from the system to pay for the government's spending. This is sometimes known as 'full-funding' to distinguish it from 'underfunding' (the latter means creating printing press money as described above). Governments sometimes also use 'overfunding', which is a way for the government to withdraw money from the banking system by selling more long-term bonds to the non-bank private system than it needs to fund its deficit. The extra funds are used to buy short-term instruments — usually Treasury Bills but also sometimes privately issued short-term securities.

Fountain-pen Money

Fountain-pen money is money created by the private sector. Suppose a businessman, Mr Gates, comes up with a wonderful new project and goes to his bank, Anybank, for a loan of £1 million. The bank manager agrees it is a great idea and provides a loan, which he does by simply

---

[1] G.T. Pepper and M.J. Oliver (2001) *Monetarism under Thatcher: Lessons for the future.* IEA

crediting Gates' account. In accounting terms Anybank's assets and liabilities must increase by the same amount of course. This transaction adds a new asset, equal to the loan, on the asset side of the balance sheet and a new liability, equal to the deposit, to the liability side. In the not-so-distant past this transaction would require two simple fountain-pen entries in the books. Now, of course, just a few keystrokes.

This description is somewhat simplified because Anybank might not be comfortable expanding its balance sheet in this way, for two possible reasons — capital requirements or reserve requirements. Capital requirements are often referred to as the Basle Agreement or BIS capital requirements because they are an international agreement negotiated under the auspices of the Bank for International Settlements based in Basle. At the time of writing a new agreement is under discussion, called Basle II, but this would not change the discussion here.

Banks are required to keep certain minimum ratios of capital against their assets, so Anybank might turn down the transaction because it had already reached its target ratio of capital to assets and did not want to reduce its capital ratio. In practice capital requirements are unlikely to restrict the growth of balance sheets for the system as a whole. In the short term most banks operate well above the minimum capital requirements and if loan demand is strong will likely accommodate a new loan. Over the medium term the banking system can simply increase its capital base and, of course, is likely to do so if loan demand is strong. This can be done by retaining profits to add to capital, and profits are likely to be strong if loan demand is strong. Banks can also raise new capital in the markets, and again this is likely to be easier if the demand for credit is booming.

Reserve requirements have the potential to bite, though only if the central bank is using a reserve requirement system to directly control banks' balance sheets. While this has been done at times in the past, it is not current practice in the major central banks. Reserve requirements were abolished in the UK in 1981, and although they are retained in the US, they are not the crux of monetary policy. Reserve requirements work in the US by requiring banks to maintain non-interest-bearing deposits, called Federal Funds (Fed Funds), at the Federal Reserve, equal to a certain percentage of their deposits, for example 3%. If banks have more than the minimum on deposit with the Federal Reserve, they are allowed to trade them overnight with other banks at a rate called the Fed Funds rate. Yes — that is where the famous Fed Funds rate, the key operating rate for monetary policy, and the real crux of monetary policy, comes in.

Now, if the Federal Reserve was following a policy of directly trying to control the money supply, it would have a strict target for the quantity of reserves in the system. In effect it would be saying 'No, we are not going to allow any more loans because all the money we are going to allow is already out there'. Anybank would know that if it wanted to expand its balance sheet to make the loan to Mr Gates it would have to bid for the reserves at the Federal Reserve, and probably pay a higher price (i.e. a higher Fed Funds rate).

Something similar to this approach was used during the monetarist period of 1979–81, as we have seen. But, as usual, if you target a quantity, then the price has to adjust and price movements can be substantial, creating considerable volatility. Hence, although the USA still has the reserve requirement system it is not the central mechanism for controlling monetary policy. As in other countries, the Federal Reserve uses the price of money, i.e. the interest rate, working through affecting the demand for money (or more accurately credit) as its method of monetary control. So Anybank would not need to pay a higher rate for the extra reserves.

6
Fiscal Policy

Fiscal policy is the second main policy area that the authorities can use to manipulate and control the economy. Generally speaking, fiscal policy is a slower and more ponderous instrument than monetary policy, both more difficult to change and slower to act on the economy. Whereas the impact of changes in monetary policy usually takes around three months to start to come through and is likely to be exhausted after 12 months, fiscal policy generally acts over a period of between nine months and two years. However, it should be noted that fiscal policy's primary use is in so-called pump-priming. It is doubtful if fiscal policy can have any long-term impact and indeed some economists argue that it may not even work in the short term.

In analysing fiscal policy, or the so-called 'fiscal stance', it is crucial to remember two points. First, it is *changes* in the fiscal deficit that matter, not its level. For example, although the Japanese budget deficit has been running at 8% of GDP or more for many years this is not imparting a continuous stimulus to the economy. But if, in a given year, the deficit rises to 10%, that could represent a stimulus. Conversely, a reduction in the deficit could represent a contraction in the fiscal stance, that is tighter policy.

Secondly, only those changes in the deficit that are due to *deliberate changes* in government policy matter. The budget deficit will constantly be changing in response to the economy. During recessions the deficit tends to rise because tax revenues fall and government spending on unemployment benefits increases. In contrast, when the economy grows strongly, the budget deficit naturally falls. However if, in a given year, the deficit rises because of a reduction in tax rates or a rise in government spending, then there is a stimulus.

The tendency for the deficit to rise in recessions and fall in booms is an important source of stability for the economy, helping to avoid major downturns or depressions. The power of so-called 'automatic stabilisers' has only really emerged since the Second World War as government spending has risen to 30–50% of GDP and therefore the amounts in relation to the economy mattered. Before the Second World War, government spending in most countries amounted to only around 10–15% of GDP.

MEASURING THE STANCE OF FISCAL POLICY

Some governments prefer to obscure the extent to which changes in the budget deficit are due to government action and the extent to which they are in response to the economy. But the OECD regularly publishes measures of the 'structural balance' of the government finances, expressed as a percent of GDP. The structural balance calculates what the deficit would be if the economy was at its trend output level, i.e. neither in recession nor overheating.

Changes in the structural balance (the last column in Table 6.1) represent actual fiscal policy. A fall in the structural deficit or rise in the surplus (i.e. a positive change) is a tightening of policy and vice versa. In the early 1990s many countries used fiscal stimulus to offset the recession — for example, the USA in 1991–2 and the UK and France in 1992–3. However, after about 1994 only Japan was using fiscal stimulus; the other major countries were all

Table 6.1   Fiscal stance 2001

% of GDP	Financial balance	Structural balance	Change in structural balance* 2000–1
USA	0.6	0.7	−0.6
Japan	−6.4	−5.8	+0.8
Germany	−2.5	−2.0	−0.7
France	−1.5	−1.7	−0.1
UK	1.1	1.2	−0.7
Italy	−1.4	−0.6	+0.2

Source: OECD Outlook, December.
* A positive sign indicates tightening

tightening to some degree and continued to tighten in the second half of the 1990s. In Euroland this was driven by the need to meet budget deficit targets in order to qualify for EMU. In many of the Anglo-Saxon countries it was driven by a strong aversion to deficits, both among governments and at the popular level. In 2001, however, the US government put in place a massive fiscal stimulus in response to the recession while Germany and the UK also provided a fiscal stimulus.

THE UK EXPERIENCE 1980–2002

The UK provides a fascinating example of how ordinary financial deficits and structural deficits are influenced by the economic cycle and fiscal policy. Remember the basic rule that structural deficits are influenced only by policy while the financial deficit moves with both policy and the economy.

In 1978/9 the UK had a high deficit on both measures (see Figure 6.1). At that time the economy was growing rapidly and had moved above trend level, with unemployment down

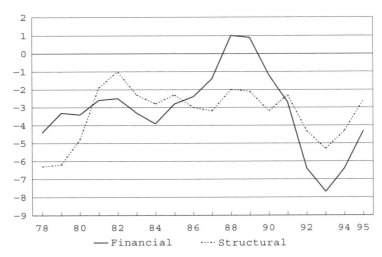

Figure 6.1   UK: General government balance, financial and structural, as percentage of GDP

to 4.5% in 1979. Hence the financial deficit was less than the structural deficit. Between 1980 and 1982 both deficits were sharply reduced despite a severe recession. This was partly due to the fiscal austerity introduced by the incoming Conservative government led by Mrs. Thatcher, and substantially due to the sharp rise in government revenues from North Sea oil. Of course, because of the recession, the structural deficit moved lower than the financial deficit.

The tightening of fiscal policy was extremely controversial at the time since most economists thought that it was a mistake to tighten during a recession. However, the tightening did not prevent an economic recovery because it was more than offset by falls in interest rates. Japan faces a more difficult problem now. Although it needs to tighten fiscal policy because of the high and rising level of government debt, tighter fiscal policy cannot be offset by lower interest rates.

Through most of the 1980s the UK structural deficit remained at around 2–3% of GDP but, as the economic boom took hold from the middle of the decade, the financial balance improved relative to the structural balance and in 1988 moved into surplus. The government was reluctant to tighten, partly because of forecasts, wrong as they turned out, that the economy was about to slow down on its own, as well as signals such as the 1987 stock market crash.

During the 1990–2 recession the UK financial deficit naturally soared. But the structural deficit also rose in 1992–3, indicating an expansionary fiscal policy. This may be seen either as a rational response to the impotence of monetary policy (until September 1992 when Sterling left the Exchange Rate Mechanism) or a calculated (and successful) bid for re-election by the Conservative government.

The figure also shows trends in 1994–5. The combination of large tax increases and tight spending curbs brought the structural deficit back to the 2–3% range by 1995. The financial deficit was still higher, reflecting the expectation of continuing slack in the economy. Both the structural and financial deficit continued to drop in the late 1990s, moving into surplus in 1998. Many people were surprised by the tough stance by the incoming Labour government in keeping to very tight spending plans put forward by the outgoing government, especially since few analysts would have expected the Conservatives to keep to those plans, but Labour performed a U-turn starting in 2000, with much higher plans for government spending on health and transport. As a result the surpluses are starting to give way to modest structural and financial deficits. Provided economic growth remains healthy, these present no threat to the economy, especially since the UK has relatively low debt/GDP ratios. However an unexpected large recession would find the UK swinging into a larger deficit than would have seemed likely a few years ago.

WHY FISCAL POLICY DOES NOT ALWAYS WORK

Many economists question the effectiveness of fiscal policy. A few believe it is totally ineffective while most believe that, although it can have an effect in the short term, the impact may be uncertain and can be partially offset by other factors. There are three broad arguments why fiscal policy may not work.

A Theoretical Argument

First, there is an argument that tax-payers are not easily fooled. They recognise that the government deficit will have to be paid for in the end through higher taxes, even though it is temporarily financed by bond issues. According to this theory people will view a reduction in taxation or increase in government spending as an increase in their future tax liability and therefore will increase their savings in response to it, ready to pay higher taxes at a later date. While this is a neat theoretical argument it seems to presuppose that tax-payers look 10 or 20 years into the future and regard events then as holding a high degree of certainty. In an uncertain world, both for individuals and for the economy, this theory (technically known as the Ricardian equivalence theory) seems rather implausible.

Crowding Out

The second and much more realistic objection to fiscal policy is the 'crowding out' thesis. According to this idea, if the government increases its spending and finances it by issuing bonds then the effect will be a rise in bond yields which crowds out spending by businesses and households unwilling to pay higher interest rates. The stimulatory effect of the government deficit is therefore cancelled out.

Most economists and governments believe that crowding out is less likely under two conditions. First, if the economy is in recession, then private spending is likely to be weak and spare resources in the form of labour and equipment are easily available. Secondly, if this easier fiscal policy is accompanied by an easy monetary policy then any tendency for interest rates to rise will be offset.

Much depends on timing. If the fiscal expansion is late to take effect, when the economy is already picking up, then it can raise interest rates. This is always a risk given the long lead-time in fiscal policy. Or, if the monetary authority is independent, it may see it as its duty to raise interest rates to offset the fiscal stimulus. As the economy strengthens, household savings typically come down as people start to believe that the worst of the recession is over and unemployment is becoming a dwindling threat. Similarly business is likely to be accumulating inventories, which means increased borrowing, and perhaps looking to new investment. Hence crowding out is a possibility if fiscal policy is implemented at any time other than during a recession.

On the other hand, there will be times when a relaxation in both fiscal and monetary policy will be of great concern to the bond markets because they will anticipate higher inflation at a later stage. If governments appear to be too keen to stimulate the economy when perhaps it is not very weak, or inflation is seen as too high, then the bond markets may sell off substantially.

'Temporary' Policy

The third problem with the use of fiscal policy is when governments try to use it as a temporary device. For example, a special income tax surcharge for one year, or perhaps an income tax cut to be financed by a rise in other taxes after a two-year delay, will impart a temporary budget deficit to the economy and therefore should stimulate spending. The problem is that if households or businesses know this is strictly temporary they may not react very much. Nevertheless it is hard to believe that even these approaches will not have some impact, particularly if supported by monetary policy. The question is: How much impact?

LINKAGES WITH MONETARY POLICY

When looking at policy it is useful to consider the overall mix of fiscal and monetary policy. If fiscal and monetary policies are both tight, then the situation is unambiguous and the economy

Table 6.2   Policy mix and the yield curve

Monetary policy	Fiscal policy	
	Loose	Tight
Loose	Steep	Moderate
Tight	Flat	Inverted

is certain to slow after the necessary lags. Similarly if both monetary and fiscal policy are expansionary, then the economy can be expected to expand. However very often the policy settings are at odds with one another — for example, with tight fiscal policy and loose monetary policy, or vice versa. These situations create both opportunities and risks for investors.

Policy Mix and the Yield Curve

The fiscal/monetary mix often shows up in the shape of the yield curve, i.e. the relative position of short-term interest rates and long-term bond yields. Table 6.2 illustrates the four possibilities. When both fiscal and monetary policy are loose the yield curve tends to be steeply upward sloping, i.e. bond yields are substantially above short-term rates. When fiscal policy is tightened while monetary policy remains loose, bond yields tend to fall and the yield curve comes back to a more moderate upward slope.

If monetary and fiscal policy are both tight then the yield curve is typically inverted, i.e. short rates move above long bond yields. Finally, when monetary policy is tight but fiscal policy is loose the yield curve tends to be flat, i.e. not much difference between short-term rates and long bond yields. These four possibilities are well illustrated in the following examples from the US experience.

THE US EXPERIENCE 1980–2002

In the early and mid-1980s President Reagan simultaneously cut tax rates, particularly at the top end, and increased defence spending. Cutting tax rates was, and is, a policy favoured by so-called supply-side economists and associated with an economist called Arthur Laffer. Whether or not lower tax rates had a structural impact on the economy remains a matter of dispute, but President Reagan's actions certainly involved a major loosening of fiscal policy. The US structural budget deficit increased by 1.8% of GDP between 1981 and 1983 and the effect strongly stimulated the economy. In response the Federal Reserve kept interest rates high with the Fed Funds rate remaining above 9% p.a., even though inflation came down to 3–4% p.a.

In the markets bond yields also remained high, averaging 11% p.a. in 1983 despite low inflation. This was because of the combination of high bond issuance, strong private demand for capital, a rapidly growing economy and high short-term interest rates. As a result the yield curve was comparatively flat in this period. The dollar soared in the early 1980s reaching a peak in February 1985, attracted by the high nominal and real interest rates available. The stock market also liked this policy despite the high interest rates since the growth in the economy generated a strong recovery in profits.

In the late 1980s, when inflation began to rise, monetary policy was tightened again while fiscal policy became neutral, taking short rates above long rates (an inverted yield curve). In

1991–2, as the economy slowly recovered from recession, both fiscal and monetary policy were loosened, leading to a steeply upward sloping yield curve. Then in 1993 President Clinton's new budget package tightened fiscal policy leading to a strong rally in bonds and a flattening of the curve. In early 1994 interest rates were raised but monetary policy was initially still seen as too loose. Bond yields rose by a similar amount keeping the yield curve still moderately steep. In early 1995 the yield curve flattened as the markets began to anticipate a slowdown in the economy, and believed the Federal Reserve had tightened enough.

In the second half of the 1990s the structural deficit continued to fall and then became a rising structural surplus. This helped to keep Treasury bond yields relatively low, since the government began to buy back bonds. The prevailing political mood at this time was very much in favour of cutting the deficit, partly as a reaction to the deficit years of the 1980s and also because of worries over the rising social security burden in future when the social security budget goes into deficit.

In 2001 the sudden slowdown in the economy prompted a change of heart and a large tax cut was introduced to try to reverse the slowdown. The original motivation of the tax cut was a return to the supply-side approach, on which incoming President Bush had campaigned. But when the economy slowed, President Bush switched the emphasis to its stimulatory role in the sense of increasing demand, and Congress supported this approach. Nevertheless the size of this tax cut was smaller than the Reagan tax cuts. If the economy performs well in 2002–3 surpluses will probably re-emerge. If it is weak, the surplus is likely to disappear and be replaced by a deficit.

There are two lessons of this experience, similar to the UK experience. First, running a surplus during a strong upswing makes it easier to accept a swing into deficit during a recession. Secondly, long-term forecasting of budget positions should be treated very cautiously. A few years of slower than expected growth or a switch to a stimulatory policy can have radical effects.

FISCAL POLICY AND REAL INTEREST RATES

If fiscal policy is stimulatory it will tend to raise *real* interest rates (i.e. interest rates minus inflation) and if fiscal policy is contractionary it will tend to lower real interest rates. The reason is the effect of 'crowding out' as described above. When the government is borrowing in the markets it is competing with the private sector for funds. This drives up interest rates, particularly at the medium and long-term end of the yield curve. The effect is to take bond yields higher than they might otherwise be and strengthen the currency. Similarly if fiscal policy is contractionary then real bond yields, and therefore often nominal, bond yields will be falling. At the same time the exchange rate will tend to be weak.

Of course if monetary policy is expansionary at the same time as fiscal policy, then there is no reason for any particular pressure on interest rates at the short end of the curve. Banks will be awash with liquidity and there is no real 'crowding out'. However, further up the curve, bond markets may be concerned about the inflation implications which is why this combination tends to generate a steep upward sloped yield curve with an unusually large spread between short rates and long rates.

FISCAL POLICY IN HIGH-INFLATION COUNTRIES

For countries with low inflation there is little direct link between fiscal policy and the level of inflation. For example, in 1999–2000, when the US ran a budget surplus, inflation was accelerating because the private sector was booming and oil prices were rising. However in countries with high inflation, 10% or more, there is usually a direct link between fiscal policy and inflation. Inflation is often being generated by 'printing press money' (i.e. central bank financing) to pay for the budget deficit.

Using money growth to finance a fiscal deficit is sometimes referred to as the 'inflation tax'. Instead of collecting a normal tax like income tax or sales tax the government allows (or forces) the central bank to buy its bonds, which means that the central bank is pushing money into the economy. This money creates inflation, which, in effect, imposes a tax on anybody who holds bank deposits or cash. Even during high inflation most people unavoidably have some deposits and cash. When those deposits are worth, for example, 5% less at the end of the month than at the beginning of the month, this represents a tax, collected by the government issuing the currency.

Fiscal policy in high-inflation countries becomes almost entirely a question of whether and when the government can control its basic fiscal position. Typically the problem is that it is difficult to raise ordinary taxes further because of resistance to paying taxes, through evasion and avoidance. In periods of high inflation it is often very difficult to collect taxes at all because tax-payers know that if they can delay paying, even for a month or two, the effective burden is reduced. Also typically these governments are unable, due to social and political pressures, to cut spending or subsidies. Success in reducing inflation depends on solving the fiscal problem. Any number of new currencies, price freezes or currency pegs, will not work without it. The story of countries such as Turkey and Argentina in recent years revolves around these issues. Fortunately fewer countries than before are suffering from high inflation, i.e. using the inflation tax. There is, however, an increasing tendency for emerging countries to rely heavily on internal debt, which has been creating new problems.

FISCAL POLICY AND DEBT

Countries that borrow substantially eventually acquire a large government debt (Table 6.3). There is no particular level beyond which debt can be said to be excessive although it is sometimes argued that a ratio of debt/GDP below 60% (the level specified in the Maastricht Treaty for entry into EMU) is satisfactory and can be managed. When debt moves up to near the 100% level or above, as for example in Italy, Canada and Belgium in the early 1990s and

Table 6.3   Public debt/GDP 2001

%	Gross	Net
USA	55.0	39.2
Japan	130.5	57.1
Germany	58.0	40.1
France	64.1	41.4
Italy	107.3	95.1
UK	52.6	30.7
Canada	99.8	60.6

Source: OECD.
Note: Net debt includes government financial assets including social security surpluses (notably large for Japan)

Japan more recently, then the effect is to severely constrain government policy. For emerging countries the debt limit is usually somewhat lower.

The scope for fiscal stimulus in a recession is reduced if debt is high because of the effect on confidence and the dangers to the debt position. This becomes of critical importance if interest rates are already low so that there is little room for monetary stimulus by reducing interest rates.

In practice it becomes difficult to reduce the budget deficit because of the large volume of interest payments. For example, a government with a debt/GDP ratio of 100% facing interest rates of 7% p.a. will pay an interest payments bill of 7% of GDP. With government spending in most industrial countries in the range of 40–45% of GDP, this means that 15–17% of total government spending is on interest payments. Reductions in spending therefore have to focus on the other 85% of the budget or on raising taxes unless interest rates can be brought down. For these countries, then, there will be a tendency for bond yields to be high owing to the risk of default and the volume of issuance in the markets. The markets may also demand high bond yields in case the government tries to inflate its way out of the problem.

Reducing government debt/GDP ratios takes many years. It is unlikely that even a very stringent policy will reduce the ratio by more than about 5% of GDP per year. For example, Belgium succeeded in cutting its net debt/GDP ratio from 125% in 1995 to a projected 92% in 2002. If a country starts with a ratio of 100% it will usually take at least a decade to reduce the ratio to an acceptable 50% level. Many people expect government debt to emerge as the dominant problem in Japan in the long run.

CONCLUSION: FISCAL POLICIES AND MARKETS

From the discussion above we can generalise as follows. A deliberately stimulatory fiscal policy (i.e. a rise in the structural deficit) will usually be bad for the country's bond market. The reason is partly that it implies more bond issuance (though that in itself does not always matter) but more importantly that it points to a stronger economy in one or two years and therefore higher inflation than would occur without the stimulus.

Quite often a stimulatory fiscal policy will also be good for the currency because of the effect of higher interest rates and bond yields. It will also often be good news for stocks because of the prospect of faster growth and higher profits. However, both stocks and the currency could go the other way if the stimulatory fiscal policy is seen as mistimed or reckless. It would be mistimed if it occurred at any time other than in a recession, either because the economy recovered earlier than expected or it was put in place to win an election by a spendthrift government. A stimulatory policy would be reckless if it occurred when the government's debt ratio was already worryingly high.

A tightening of fiscal policy is generally good for the bond markets. If it is offset by looser monetary policy it is almost always good for bonds. The currency is likely to fall in both cases because of lower interest rates. The stock market will usually respond well to tighter fiscal policy, particularly if it is accompanied by looser monetary policy, provided only that it does not appear over-severe, risking a recession. Stock markets will react particularly favourably if the tightening is part of a long-term programme to reduce government debts.

7
Asset Prices and the Economy

For investors, foreseeing the future performance of asset prices is the key to high returns; but asset prices also feed back into economic performance in various ways. Moreover, the increase in wealth holdings in recent decades, and especially in the last decade, has made these interactions more important than ever before. The most important assets are housing and stocks though the relative importance of each varies between countries. Rising asset prices provide a positive wealth effect to consumers which can be substantial — for example, during the UK housing boom of the 1980s or the US stock market boom of the 1990s. Similarly, a collapse in asset values impacts on consumer confidence and encourages more savings, as seen in Asia in the 1990s. The effects of gearing, i.e. borrowing, can exaggerate these effects.

More subtly, asset prices often provide a signal to central banks and investors as to what is happening in the economy and what might happen next. For example, a strong rise in house prices indicates that consumer spending is likely to be buoyant in coming quarters. As well as feeling wealthier many consumers will re-mortgage or 'over-mortgage' as they move house, gaining money to spend. Rising house prices associated with high turnover (as is usually the case) is also likely to mean more spending on furnishings, etc., boosting retail spending. A rise in stock prices can have a similar effect on consumers' spending, and will also generally affect company behaviour since it implies a greater potential gain from new investment.

The size of wealth effects is generally estimated at between 3 and 6 cents on every dollar in the USA, but somewhat less in other countries. In other words, for every dollar in increased wealth consumers will spend 3–6 cents more, though the full effect may take up to four years to come through according to some studies. There is some evidence that the impact of increases in housing wealth is greater than the impact of stock market wealth, probably because consumers use higher house prices to increase borrowings. The effect of falling asset prices is less well established though it might be expected to be similar.

WHY ASSET PRICES MATTER

It is helpful to distinguish between real assets and financial assets. Real assets are those which provide some direct benefit to the user, for example, houses, cars or machines for making things. We could also include education and skills. Financial assets are claims for future payments of interest or dividends. This category includes securities such as bonds and stocks, also bank assets such as loans and mortgages and also assets such as pensions and life insurance. Obviously anybody who holds a financial asset believes that the obligor to the claim has some real assets with which to make payments — for example, a job that pays a salary, or a business or perhaps an ability to tax, if we think of government bonds.

Asset prices matter increasingly not only because they are being valued higher, as we shall see below, but also because the modern economy is becoming increasingly rich in assets. One of the definitions of an emerging market is that it has few assets. Not only few factories or machines, and often a small housing stock with people living in crowded conditions, but also limited education and skills. Financial assets are usually limited too. Measures such as the ratio of bank credit to GDP tend to be low while stock and bond markets are small. Mortgage and consumer credit markets are undeveloped, and the main borrower is very often the government.

Advanced economies have more real assets as individuals become increasingly wealthy and economic activity relies more on real assets to make things, rather than just labour inputs. People live in bigger and better houses and have more cars. Workers have valuable machines as well as substantial education and training to make them more productive. Advanced economies also naturally have more financial assets. It makes sense to use borrowings and equity participations to finance a company, while, for individuals, the desire to borrow reflects the expected pattern of life-time earnings. In the early years of a career people borrow to buy houses and cars, knowing that their future labour as well as education will enable them to meet payments. Meanwhile they pay into a pension in anticipation of retirement.

A major trend for at least 20 years is the reduced role of bank lending in the economy and the increased role of securities of one form or another. To some extent this has been made possible by computers which, for example, can bundle together hundreds of mortgages, with different amounts and pay dates into one security. But it also reflects a desire on the part of investors to hold securities rather than simply bank deposits. This process is known as dis-intermediation, i.e. a reversal of the traditional role of banks as intermediators between lenders and borrowers.

Dis-intermediation is driven by the fact that borrowers can often borrow at a lower rate by borrowing directly from lenders rather than through the banks. Banks must hold capital (i.e. shareholders' money plus certain types of long-term bond issues — money lent to the bank on a long-term basis). They also have operating costs. So banks tend to work by lending to individuals or companies where intimate knowledge of circumstances is crucial or where the loan is secured on a particular (real) asset. Sometimes these can be repackaged as asset-backed securities. Other times they are held on the balance sheet.

THE INCREASED VALUE OF ASSETS

In the USA the value of net household assets relative to income rose from 479% in 1990 to 637% in 1999. The ratio fell back during the bear market in stocks in 2000–2 but remained well above earlier levels (see Figure 7.1). The stock market itself rose from being valued at 40% of GDP in 1980 to 140% in 1999. Between 1999 and July 2002 both these ratios fell, but it would require a fall in the S&P 500 index to around 700 to return the ratio to the 1994 level. Housing assets also increased in value, reflecting space and planning limitations as well as improvements in the quality of housing.

In the UK planning restrictions have driven housing values particularly high. Over the long term, house prices might reasonably be expected to increase in line with average wage growth (see Chapter 15). With the average house now valued at approximately £100,000 a 5% p.a. average increase in prices, in line with a 5% rise in average earnings, represents 3–4 times the annual increase in probable after-tax salaries for the average person. In other words, if the average person receives a pay rise of around £1,500 in a year he will probably also notice that his house is worth £5,000 more.

Asia traditionally has had high housing valuations too. As in the UK one reason is very tight planning restrictions. Japan's land prices reached stratospheric levels in the late 1980s when the parkland surrounding the Imperial Palace in central Tokyo was calculated as being worth more than all the land in California! However, since 1980 land prices have fallen by more than 70% and continue to fall. In Hong Kong the government owns all the land and has only sold it for

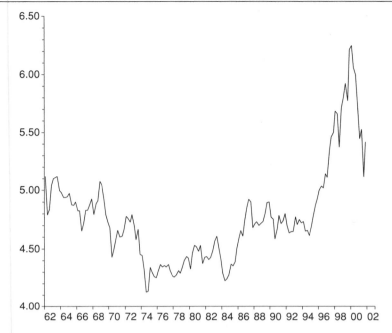

Figure 7.1   USA: Household net worth/income.
Source: Thomson Datastream

housing at a slow pace, calculated to command high prices. While this has enabled income taxes to be very low, it has also distorted the housing market and, more seriously, the whole economy.

In Hong Kong and much of the rest of Asia, housing values have been driven by the very rapid pace of growth of demand. Populations have been growing fast, but also, as living standards rise, people demand bigger and better houses. In economic jargon housing is seen as a 'superior' good, i.e. as incomes rise people are likely to spend relatively more on it, as opposed to something like bread or rice which will dwindle as a proportion of spending.

In continental Europe the picture is a little different, reflecting the more dispersed population, notably in Germany, and consequent easier planning rules. Lack of competition among mortgage lenders and real estate agents in some countries may also have raised the costs of transactions, limiting the growth of the market. There may also be cultural differences, for example in southern Europe, which discourage young people from moving away from their parents' house until they are married.

In the 1990s most stock markets also rose in value as a percentage of GDP. Most of the rise was due to higher valuations as price/earnings ratios rose in response to lower interest rates and inflation. In some countries there was an increase in the amount of stock issued, but this was not the case in the USA where companies generally bought back stock. In Asia stock markets have fallen in relation to GDP over the decade because of the huge decline in Japan and, later, in many other countries.

The size of bond markets has also grown in most countries. Government bond markets increased rapidly in size during the 1970s and 1980s as budget deficits rose in the face of clamorous social demands for spending and the slower pace of economic growth. This was also the tail-end of the period of 'Keynesian economics' which emphasised the role of budget deficits in stimulating growth. In the 1990s, with the dramatic exception of Japan, government debt has been stabilised in most countries and reduced significantly in the USA and other English-speaking countries (e.g. the UK, Canada) as part of a new drive to limit the potential damage from high debts. In Europe the Maastricht Treaty requirements for entering the EMU also forced many governments to start to reduce their debts, most notably Belgium and Italy.

The major exception is Japan. Slow economic growth and deliberate Keynesian-style fiscal stimulus have taken Japan's government debt/GDP ratio up to 130% on a gross definition and, given the continuing large deficit, the ratio is unlikely to stabilise much below 170% of GDP over the next few years on even an optimistic scenario. Moreover, these figures do not include various other government liabilities, particularly future pension liabilities. This is also a problem in continental Europe.

Private sector bonds have also been increasing rapidly in importance. For many years a major asset in the USA, they have expanded in three major waves internationally over the last 20 years. First, there was the beginnings of the 'junk' bond market in the USA as weaker companies began to borrow heavily on the markets, rather than use bank credit. Secondly, there has been a huge increase in borrowing by developing countries, both governments and private borrowers. Thirdly, and most recently, there has been a surge in issuance of euro-denominated paper as the emergence of a single currency in Europe has made possible a large liquid market.

HOW ASSET PRICES AFFECT THE ECONOMY

Rises and declines in asset prices affect the economy through a combination of wealth effects on confidence, changing the ability to borrow by increasing collateral and price signalling effects. It is helpful to divide the discussion between consumers and businesses.

The Behaviour of Consumers

There is plenty of evidence of a so-called 'wealth effect', as consumers spend more in response to an increase in the value of their wealth. Estimates vary but it is usually held that an increase in the value of stocks in the USA probably increases consumer spending by between 3 and 6 cents for every extra dollar of wealth. In other countries it is thought that the spending rate may be slightly less. Housing wealth is thought to increase spending by a somewhat larger amount. The effect is not instantaneous, however, as consumers adjust their spending only gradually to higher wealth, perhaps out of caution or perhaps because it takes a while to adjust to being better off.

Table 7.1 Household net wealth

	1989	1994	1999	2001e
USA	500	475	632	530
UK	682	584	750	720
Germany	Na	554	596	580
Japan	901	755	753	700

* As % of household income, end-year.
Source: OECD.

A word of caution needs to be injected at this point because it may be questioned why a rise in asset prices will automatically encourage the population as a whole to spend more. For example, if house prices have risen, people living in the house are not better off in any meaningful sense. And why don't younger consumers spend less (i.e. save more) since they will have to pay more for housing later? This argument can be extended to stocks too, at least at the theoretical level. Suppose the dividends of a company are expected to be $1 per share this year and rise at 10% p.a. indefinitely. If you can buy the stock at $50, implying a 2% current dividend yield ($1/$50) this is more rewarding than if the cost is $100. Hence, if stocks are rising purely because of higher valuations, the rise in values for one person represents a loss for others.

This rather theoretical argument therefore suggests that a rise in the stock market only represents a genuine rise in the country's wealth if the rate of growth of dividends is expected to rise, presumably because the economy is performing better than before. This was indeed the argument of the 'new economy' theorists in the late 1990s as we have seen.

In the case of housing this theoretical argument does not apply because what economists call 'the value of housing services in the future', or the 'use value' of housing does not change. This is why some economists argue that, if consumers are rational, there should be no wealth effect associated with housing. However, in practice consumers do seem to respond to asset price increases. Are they irrational? The reason could be that an increase in house prices leads to an expectation of further price increases. Hence the owners of housing and potential young buyers may feel better off; but this is not really a rational argument, since higher house prices now, all else unchanged, implies a slower pace of increase in future.

If asked, many householders would say that an increase in the value of their house means that they can retire later to a smaller house or a cheaper house and live well off the difference. This is true but it still leaves young people having to pay more for the house being sold. It could be argued that, if rents have not risen, then young people are no worse off because they can just carry on paying on the same rent. But if there is no one to buy the older people's house when they retire, then the price will not be so high after all.

Another argument that seems to have some validity is that rising house prices really work through increased borrowing. Although consumers have a life-time of earnings they usually can borrow only limited amounts secured on income alone. They need the security of property to borrow substantial amounts. Nevertheless, even taking into account the increase in borrowing that usually accompanies a housing price boom, there is still a wealth effect beyond that. This remains a puzzle at the theoretical level. Or perhaps we should say that economists have yet to explain in theory what obviously happens in practice!

The effect on the economy is that higher asset prices tend to depress the savings rate (see Figure 7.2). Remember that savings is simply measured as income less spending so that greater borrowing to finance spending also depresses the savings ratio. The US savings ratio rose in the 1970s as consumers struggled to boost their wealth in the face of a weak stock market and losses on bonds and deposits due to inflation. But since about 1982 rising stock prices have boosted wealth and allowed consumers to slow down on their savings (or increase their borrowings).

Asset Prices and Business

Higher asset prices also have a profound impact on business behaviour. This can work through two mechanisms: a greater ability to borrow against assets, and a greater incentive to create new assets, given their higher value.

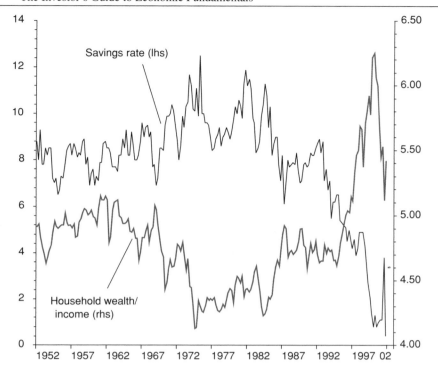

Figure 7.2   USA: Savings rate and wealth.
Source: Thomson Datastream

The main asset to borrow against is property, i.e. land and buildings. This can be a factor for large companies but is extremely important for small companies and start-ups. Most of the latter are funded out of second mortgages and family loans, but higher stock prices can also provide the capital for start-ups. The rise in asset prices is therefore a major factor in the economic cycle by encouraging a high rate of new company formation at an advanced stage of the boom, due to the easier availability of finance.

The incentive to create new assets is that if businesses see that their share price values the business at several times the cost of their investing, there is a massive incentive to invest. The ratio of the market value of a business to the replacement value is known as Tobin's Q, after the economist James Tobin, and is used in assessing the valuations in stock markets.

A simple way of looking at this is as follows. Suppose you own a chain of 100 pizza restaurants, you have $2 million in cash reserves and the market values your company at $102 million. The market is therefore valuing the average restaurant at $1 million. If you calculate that the total cost of starting a new restaurant is only $500,000 then you should spend the cash to start 4 new restaurants as soon as possible, because afterwards the company should be valued at $104 million. (You should probably borrow enough money to start even more restaurants, depending on the cost of borrowing.) Tobin's Q is 2 in this example. If, however, it would cost $2 million to get the restaurant going, it would be better to give the $2 million back to the shareholders since you will lower the value of the company to $101 million by investing (101 restaurants and the cash is spent).

Again, it is easy to see how this effect reinforces the economic cycle by exaggerating investment when the economy and stock market are booming, and depressing investment during an economic downturn. In theory, assuming that the stock market is correctly valuing new restaurants, so many new restaurants are eventually started that the return from each one starts to fall. So after a while the value of a new one falls into line with the cost of setting it up. At this point investment slows, which across the whole economy contributes to the slowdown phase of the economic cycle.

ASSET PRICES AND ECONOMIC POLICY

A large move in asset prices either upwards or downwards is a potential threat to policy-makers as they attempt to keep the economy on a steady sustainable upward track. A large move upwards threatens to spark an unsustainable boom as spending increases. If over-exuberant consumers borrow too much, or companies invest too much, the boom may end with excessive debt. If asset values then decrease rapidly a process of 'debt deflation' can occur, threatening economic growth for some time. The Japanese experience since 1990 is a good example. There, since the government guaranteed the banking system, a depression on the lines of the 1930s has been avoided, but economic growth has been minimal for over 10 years.

Hence the monetary policy authorities are increasingly watching asset prices as well as ordinary consumer prices for signs of excessive growth. Money growth is a good early warning because large asset price gains are nearly always associated with strong growth in broad money aggregates. However, the authorities are usually reluctant to directly target asset prices for several reasons.

First, in countries where politics influences monetary policy, there will naturally be resistance to monetary policy that seeks to dampen asset prices. Higher housing or stock prices are usually vote-winners both directly and because of the boost to the wider economy. On the other side, if asset prices are falling precipitately, there may be pressure to reverse the decline because of the economic pain. In several Asian countries, including Japan, Hong Kong and Taiwan, this has taken the form of direct purchases of shares, either by the government itself or by government or quasi-government agencies such as public pension funds. It may also take the form of very stimulatory monetary policy, designed to push up general inflation, even at the risk of problems at a later stage.

Secondly, there is a respectable argument which says that the authorities cannot be as knowledgeable as the markets about what the right valuation should be. Chairman Greenspan of the Fed has argued this point very cogently. The rise in the US stock market during 1996–8, he argued afterwards, probably reflected the improvement in the performance of the US economy, particularly higher productivity growth. In a sense, he was using this argument to criticise his own famous speech at the end of 1996 where he used the phrase 'irrational exuberance'. He was saying that, in 1996, he did not foresee the boost in US productivity growth, which justified higher market valuations, but the market did.

However, most commentators believe that the authorities should try to act if they see clear bubbles developing because of the potential disruption involved. Unfortunately this is not as easy as it sounds. Often bubbles are only obvious when they burst. Sometimes they may be obvious to many before that, but only when they are already substantially inflated in which case direct central bank tightening is likely to burst them. In 1990 the central bank of Japan set out to burst the housing bubble, because house prices had risen to such high levels that it was becoming socially divisive as well as threatening to the economy. But it was already much too late to burst the bubble without substantial damage. In the USA in 2000, the Federal Reserve raised interest rates mainly because it was worried about the strength of the economy and consequent inflation risks, but one of the side effects was to prick the technology stock bubble.

THE EXPERIENCE OF JAPAN

In the late 1980s both stock and property markets in Japan went to extraordinary valuations (Figure 7.3). The stock market reached price/earnings multiples of 60 times earnings and a ratio of 120% of GDP. Dividend yields fell to only 0.5% p.a. And the Japanese market accounted for 45% of the world equity market even though Japan produced only about 10% of world GDP. (By 2001 the Japanese equity market was less than 9% of the world index.) Property prices were even more extreme, with rental yields becoming negligible and values per square metre in central Tokyo reaching astonishing heights. The government's land price index for six big cities tripled between 1985 and 1990.

The drivers for this bubble were, as usual, optimism and liquidity. Optimism was driven by a positive view of the economy, with strong growth and low inflation. It is hard to believe now, but at that time Japan was seen as a major economic threat to the US economy. The techniques used for efficient production, including total quality control and just-in-time inventories, were seen as setting Japan well ahead. By the late 1980s Japan's success in manufacturing had gone well beyond efficient production of simple products and Japan was already a leading player in new products and design.

Figure 7.3   Japan's bubble.
Source: Thomson Datastream

Economic growth averaged 5.4% p.a. from 1987 to 1990, after a dip to 3.1% in 1986. Productivity growth grew at a rapid 4.6% p.a. over the same period, helping to control inflation. Profits grew at an average of 8% p.a. during the 1980s, well ahead of inflation, and there seemed to be no reason why rapid growth could not continue. Meanwhile business investment rose from 18% of GDP in 1985 to 25% in 1990.

The liquidity bubble began with the agreement by the Japanese authorities to boost economic growth after the world slowdown of 1986. The USA already faced a weak dollar and felt that it was time for Germany and Japan to become the locomotives of growth. Germany largely demurred but Japan responded positively to this request. The Official Discount Rate was cut from 5% in 1985 to 2.5% in 1987 and stayed there until 1989. Money supply (measured by M2 + CDs, Japan's main measure) accelerated to over 10% p.a. during 1987–90, well ahead of inflation of around 3% p.a.

This phenomenon was widely seen as a bubble outside Japan but not generally within the country. Many observers were shocked in 1987 when the US stock market crashed in October (following a minor bubble) but the Japanese market, almost alone in the world, hardly reacted. This immunity cheered Japanese investors and the market went up to new heights over the following two years.

Investors justified the levels of the stock and property market in terms of expectations of continued profit gains for stocks and excess demand for space for property. On the property side, Japan had very restrictive zoning (planning) laws and the earthquake risk tended to limit the introduction of tall buildings.

The turnaround in 1990–1 seems to have come from two sources. First, the central bank tightened monetary policy and, secondly, investment fell back. The discount rate was hiked to 6% in 1990 and only reduced gradually after that, despite a sharp economic slowdown. The rise in interest rates was explicitly aimed at reducing land prices, not just at combating inflation, which in fact was not much of a problem. The fall in investment reflected partly the rise in interest rates and reduced expectations for economic growth. But it probably also reflected the massive over-investment in capacity that had taken place.

From the peak at the very end of 1989 stock prices fell 46% in nine months and remained low throughout the 1990s, dipping to new lows in 2001. Land prices started a long slide which saw the six big city index give up all of its gains from 1985 to 1990 by 2001. Undoubtedly this fall in asset prices has had a negative effect on Japanese economic growth since then. Average GDP growth from 1991 to 2001 was only 1% p.a. with productivity growth averaging zero. The ratio of business investment to GDP fell from its peak of 25% in 1990 to 18% in 2001, though this remained relatively high by world standards.

The fall in asset prices was accompanied by a general deflation of prices. It also brought huge amounts of non-performing loans, rendering the financial sector close to bankruptcy. Bad loans were privately estimated to be some 20–25% of GDP in 2001. Banks also faced the problem that part of their capital base (according to a special provision for Japan in the Basle capital arrangements) is made up of gains on stock holdings. At the end of the 1980s these were substantial and gave banks a major cushion. After the stock market collapsed a large part of these gains disappeared. Bank lending grew slowly until 1997 but outstanding loans then started to fall from 1997 onwards.

In many ways the surprising fact about the Japanese economy since 1990 is that it has not performed even worse. The collapse in asset prices resembles the US experience in the 1930s but there has been no sign in Japan of the general economic slump that was seen in the USA. Presumably either the wealth effect has not been too great or it has been offset by other factors.

Nevertheless, at the time of writing, there is no sign of a generalised improvement in the economy.

One major opposing factor has been the fiscal position. The government allowed the budget to swing from a surplus of 2.9% of GDP in 1990 to a deficit of 7% by 1999. Some of this swing represented a conscious Keynesian-style stimulus concentrated on construction projects, but most was caused by leaving spending and tax levels in place in the face of slower economic growth.

A key difference with the US experience in the 1930s is that the Japanese government underwrote the banking system and did not allow depositors to lose money. The result is that, although money and credit growth has been weak, it has not collapsed as it did in the USA in the 1930s.

Turning the Japanese economy around is likely to involve four main elements. First, measures to remove the bad debts from the banking system, which is important to enable the banks to be restored to health, and to foreclose on insolvent businesses. Secondly, measures to open up new areas of the economy for investment and growth. Japan has been moving gradually to do this for many years — for example, with reforms in the financial sector and retailing — but there is plenty more to do. Thirdly, a start at reducing the budget deficit so that the growth of government debt can be slowed and eventually reversed. Finally, active measures by the Bank of Japan to boost money growth in the economy.

The first and third of these measures will tend to weaken the economy, which is why the second and fourth are so important. Boosting money growth is likely to support asset prices to some extent and should at least put a floor under the stock market. The property market may be nearing the bottom and it needs a buoyant economy with rising rents to restore it to health.

ASSET PRICES AND MONEY GROWTH

Interestingly, the problem of asset price inflation and bubbles may take us back to a monetarist view. Remember that monetarist theory postulates a relationship between money growth and the value of transactions in the economy. If money growth is too high then the number of transactions may rise for some time but eventually prices rise. Often 'transactions' is taken to refer to GDP, but of course it also includes purchases and sales of stocks, houses and second-hand cars. None of these is included in GDP (except new houses), and in practice such transactions are very large in relation to GDP.

Hence it is likely that one symptom of a bubble (monetarists would say 'cause') is a rise in money growth substantially ahead of nominal GDP growth. If GDP is rising at 3% p.a. with inflation of 2% p.a., then nominal GDP is rising at 5% p.a. If we observe money growth of (say) 10% p.a., the excess will probably go into asset price inflation. This was indeed the case in the UK and Japan in the late 1980s and in the USA in the late 1990s.

Maintaining asset prices on a stable path may become increasingly important in future years. Not only will it be important for keeping the economy itself on a reasonably stable path, but asset prices are becoming of increasing importance politically. Consumer welfare is increasingly dependent on stocks and housing, while the shift to funded pension schemes based on 'defined contribution schemes' as opposed to final salary schemes means that people will increasingly depend on a positive trend for asset prices in their old age.

CONCLUSION: ASSET PRICES AND THE ECONOMY

Asset prices are playing an increasingly important role in the economy. Booms and busts in stocks and property markets are important for the economic cycle and can, for example in the case of Japan, have long-term structural consequences. Rising asset prices stimulate consumers to spend through the wealth effect, the ability to raise borrowings and by boosting confidence. Increases in housing wealth probably have a greater impact than increases in stock market wealth. Businesses too spend more if asset prices are rising, because of the attraction of creating new assets.

The authorities will need to pay increasing attention to asset prices. In the past there has been a tendency to respond to a sudden downward move in prices with lower interest rates. But central banks have rarely moved to head off a bubble, partly because this might be unpopular and also because it is risky, as the Bank of Japan has found out. However, with interest rates in most countries now low, central banks have less scope to react to a sudden fall in asset prices. It may therefore be more important than before to avoid the risk of a bubble developing.

8

Globalisation and Capital Flows

Globalisation means that trade and capital flows are rising at a multiple of GDP growth rates. Countries are increasingly specialising in production while companies are stepping up foreign direct investment (FDI) and portfolio investors are increasing their overseas holdings. The key fundamentals to grasp are the relationships between the current account, the savings–investment balance in the economy and investment flows.

KEY CONCEPTS

The trade balance is usually defined as the difference between exports and imports of goods, although the US Commerce Department now includes data for services, which are growing rapidly. The 'current account' of the balance of payments is the most useful overall indicator of trading flows. It includes trade in services and also income and payments on capital, including interest payments, dividends, workers' remittances, etc.

Any current account deficit has to be balanced by a surplus (a net inflow) on the capital account (Table 8.1). Countries with current account surpluses, for example Japan, must see a net capital outflow. The capital account includes the balance of bank lending and borrowing, portfolio flows (e.g. purchases and sales of bonds and shares) and FDI flows (direct investment in plant and machinery and the takeover of domestic companies).

The current account balance is also equal to the difference between total domestic savings and total domestic investment, which is known as the savings–investment balance. For example, a country which is investing (in new machinery, buildings, houses, etc.) more than its total domestic savings can only do so with an inflow of foreign capital and this requires a current account deficit. Conversely, countries with a high domestic savings rate and a lower investment rate must, by definition be running a current account surplus and exporting capital. Japan is the prime example.

The 'basic balance' includes the current account and long-term capital flows such as direct investment and portfolio flows. It is useful because it gives an indication of what may be the more stable flows, before the short-term balancing items such as bank lending and changes in central bank reserves. Also, with the increasing role of long-term capital flows in the world economy, the basic balance has become a useful indicator of the direction of exchange rates. The 'overall balance' is the sum of the current and capital account before changes in reserves.

WHY DO CURRENT ACCOUNT IMBALANCES MATTER?

Often current account deficits or surpluses do not matter, especially if they are small, and sometimes even when they are large. For example, Australia has run a current account deficit for much of the last several decades, with the money invested in resources. In these cases deficits are merely a reflection of capital inflows, since for a country to receive a net capital inflow it must, by definition, have a current account deficit. But they do matter to investors, at least sometimes, for the following main reasons.

Table 8.1   Main items in the balance of payments

Listing	Definition
Current Account	Key overall trade measure
Exports of goods	Sales of goods abroad
Imports of goods	Purchase of foreign goods
Trade Balance	Goods trade balance
Services: Credit	Sales of services, e.g. insurance, software, plus spending of foreign visitors
Services: Debit	Purchase of foreign services
Income: Credit	Dividends, interest, etc. received from abroad
Income: Debit	Payment of dividends, interest, etc.
Private transfers	Net private payments, e.g. remittances from workers abroad
Official transfers	Net official payments, e.g. overseas aid
Capital Account	
Direct investment	Net direct investment in plant and machinery, etc.
Portfolio investment	Net purchases/sales of shares, bonds, etc.
Other capital	Sum of other items:
Resident official sector	Official borrowing or lending
Deposit money banks	Net change in bank lending
Net errors and omissions	Often very large
Overall balance	Sum of all above items
Change in reserves	Must equal previous line

First, they are frequently a sign of inflationary pressures and may indicate that the current economic upswing is unhealthy or unsustainable. An economy that is growing rapidly tends to have higher consumption and investment making the investment rate rise above the domestic savings rate, implying a current account deficit. If the economy could not import then domestic prices would probably rise, leading to inflation. With the deficit, inflation is hidden and only comes out later when the rising current account deficit leads to a currency depreciation.

Secondly, a current account deficit implies the risk of currency depreciation. Obviously this will impact any investment directly, unless it is hedged, but also currency depreciation could bring with it a period of instability and adjustment which impacts the investment indirectly. Domestic currency bonds are particularly risky investments at this point since the foreign investor will face a currency loss as well as, probably, a fall in the market value of the bond due to inflation fears.

Thirdly, a current account imbalance means that the country is increasing its net foreign liabilities. If the deficit is financed through debt then the country may be building up an unsustainable burden. Latin American countries have repeatedly faced this problem. With low domestic savings rates and yet strong social and political pressures for growth, governments tend to rely heavily on borrowing, testing the limits of lenders and then periodically defaulting. If the deficit is financed through foreign investment the prognosis is much better since the investments are more likely to create productive assets.

However, note that whatever the type of foreign liability, whether debt, stock ownership or direct investment, it requires servicing, i.e. interest payments or dividends. This is included in the current account as an outflow. This means the larger the net liability the greater the difference between the overall trade and services balance and the current account balance. If the liabilities become sufficiently large it is perfectly possible for the country to be running a surplus on

Figure 8.1   USA: Current account as percentage of GDP
Source: Thomson Datastream

trade (including services) but a deficit on the current account. A key implication of this is that, if the country needs to correct the current account deficit, it may need a proportionately larger move in its exchange rate to generate the necessary increase in exports or fall in imports. This is the situation in which the USA now finds itself, due to the build-up of a large net liability position in the last 10 years (Figure 8.1).

WHAT CAUSES CURRENT ACCOUNT IMBALANCES?

Key Role of the Savings–Investment Balance

The key factor in determining current account deficits or surpluses is whether, in the economy overall, individuals, businesses and the government are saving more than they are borrowing, or vice versa.

Savings are defined as the difference between incomes and *current* expenditure, as opposed to capital expenditure. Incomes include both individual and company incomes and government tax revenues. Current expenditure includes spending on any product that is used up immediately, which is taken to be all household spending on goods and services (even though many items like cars and refrigerators last some length of time). For businesses it includes spending on wages and salaries, telephone bills, etc., but not computers or other machinery. Governments nearly always spend more than they receive in tax revenues and therefore their net savings position is negative.

When, in economics, a company buys equipment or builds a house for sale or rent, it is investing. When an individual or business spends less than his/its income on current expenditure and uses the difference either to increase bank deposits or to buy stocks or bonds or to put towards investment, this is defined as saving. If total investment spending is greater than savings in the economy, then the need for finance causes pressure in the credit markets, interest rates move higher and money will flow in from abroad. The inflow of money causes the exchange rate to appreciate. After some time exports slow and imports rise, soon bringing a current account deficit and a matching capital inflow.

Twin Deficits

Countries with large current account deficits often have large government budget deficits. This is directly linked to the savings–investment balance. The balance of government savings plus private savings equals the current account balance (as a matter of definition). A government budget deficit means that the government is spending more than its income from taxation and must borrow the difference. Economists sometimes call this 'dis-saving' or negative savings. If the private sector is a net saver then the current account need not be in deficit, but if the private sector is merely in balance, or in deficit, then the current account will be in deficit.

How Excess Savings Cause Current Account Surpluses

If savings are higher than investment (as is usual in Japan) then the economy has funds to spare, interest rates will tend to be low in real terms (i.e. after inflation) and investors domestically will look to overseas markets for a higher yield. The outflow of funds will cause the exchange rate to fall, which will, in time, bring higher exports and lower imports. The country will move into a position of current account surplus with a matching capital account deficit as the excess savings flow abroad.

Critics of Japan often ignore, or conveniently forget, this theory. For example, Japan is sometimes criticised for having barriers to imports because of its relatively 'closed' distribution system. But removing these barriers would not necessarily reduce the trade surplus. For example, if Japan were suddenly to open up its markets, imports would certainly rise. But unless the savings–investment balance changed too, exports would rise as well to offset the rise in imports. The most likely way for this to happen would be for the exchange rate to fall. A paradox is therefore that the US companies who urge an opening up to more imports might be shocked to discover that the relative competitiveness of Japan actually improves as a result. Some US companies who may currently face real blocks to their exports would benefit, but others would suffer.

THE CYCLE OF CAPITAL AND TRADE FLOWS

Since capital flows can change faster than trade can adjust, countries often move through a cycle of exchange rate over- or under-valuation, gradually changing trade and eventual exchange rate correction.

The USA provided a very good example of this in the 1980s. When Ronald Reagan became President he quickly moved to cut taxation and increase defence spending, which resulted by 1982 in a large budget deficit. Since he also cut taxes on business investment and at the same time the Federal Reserve brought interest rates down, the US economy took off from the 1981–2 recession at a very smart pace. Interest rates rose because savings fell short of investment, resulting in heavy pressure on funds and encouraging an inflow of capital. This was a classic 'twin deficit' situation.

But capital can only flow into a country (on a net basis) to the extent of its current account deficit. The first effect, therefore, was to send the dollar surging to high levels as a way of creating a deficit. By 1985–6 the high dollar had hurt exports and encouraged imports so that the current account deficit had widened considerably and the matching net inflow of capital was almost identical to the budget deficit. Interest rates domestically therefore began to come down and this process was encouraged at the time by the Federal Reserve and the US government, as well as foreign governments. It took several more years, however, for the resulting fall in the exchange rate to improve the trade position. By then the economy had slowed, domestic demand for funds had decreased and the economy was finally back into equilibrium from the shock that President Reagan had imposed.

The rise in the dollar against the euro during 1999–2001 followed a similar pattern. This time the savings imbalance in the USA was caused by a fall in *private sector* savings as US business boosted investment in response to new technology and rapid economic growth, while the personal sector cut savings as unemployment fell and the value of household assets rose. The result was an inflow of capital pushing up the dollar and consequently generating a rising current account deficit. However in contrast to the 1980s interest rates did not rise dramatically, partly because the government did not have a deficit. This time the inflow was mainly long-term capital in the form of foreigners buying stocks and bonds and companies buying US companies. The attraction was high returns from those investments, analogous to the high returns foreigners looked for from government bonds in the 1980s.

At the time of writing the dollar remains fairly strong against the euro (0.85–0.90) compared with most estimates of long-run equilibrium in the 1.0–1.20 range. This reflects the continued high levels of investment in the US economy and low savings. But the current account, already at over 4% of GDP, probably does not need to go any higher to accommodate the savings–investment imbalance, so the dollar is unlikely to move higher for any sustained period. Indeed it may fall back because its strength has already done the job of opening up the current account deficit. At some point, most likely when the USA next faces a recession and a consequent rise in savings and fall in investment, the dollar will be driven down. Interest rates and investment returns will fall, capital inflows will decline and the process of improving the current account will require a weaker dollar.

This adjustment could prove quite difficult. The USA in the 2000s faces a far more difficult foreign asset–liability position than at the end of the 1980s. Then, the USA still had a net foreign asset position, albeit reduced by the current account deficits of that time. Now the USA has built up a foreign liability position of over 40% of GDP. This means that the fall in the dollar required could be proportionately greater.

Temporary versus Chronic Imbalances

A temporary rise in the trade deficit is often due simply to faster economic growth in that country than elsewhere. Faster growth sucks in imports and, with growth elsewhere being slower, exports are likely to do less well. If the country with faster growth is reaching capacity constraints, it may even be that goods destined for the foreign market are diverted to home markets where margins may be higher. When this is the primary reason for a trade deficit, policy-makers and the markets are likely to be relatively relaxed about the exchange rate and regard the correction of the deficit as likely to be achieved through either slower growth at home or faster growth elsewhere.

Some countries show a long-run tendency to investment higher than savings or vice versa. For example, the USA, the UK, Australia and Canada all tend to run current account deficits over the long term. Japan and Germany (pre-unification) tend to run surpluses. There is usually no strong market pressure for surpluses to be reduced. However, deficits may be unsustainable if they cannot be financed.

FINANCING OF CURRENT ACCOUNT DEFICITS

Often the crucial question of how long a deficit can continue depends on how easy it is to finance that deficit. If the economy is growing rapidly with strong investment, strong productivity growth and high levels of confidence, then interest rates and investment returns are likely to remain high for some time and inflows of capital will continue. If, however, the current account deficit is being financed with high interest rates that look unsustainable because the economy is weak, then the situation is likely to last only a limited time. This was clearly the situation of some of the European Exchange Rate Mechanism countries in 1992/3 and also of Thailand and many of the Asian countries just before the 1997 crisis.

SUSTAINABILITY OF DEFICITS

Sometimes the way in which the current account deficit is being financed is informative. If it is through direct and portfolio investment then that may be a signal that the deficit is part of a high investment path for the economy and that the situation will be sustainable. But if the money is coming into bank deposits, taking advantage of high interest rates, then the situation may be less sustainable.

Another key factor in financing current account deficits is whether the markets see the level and growth of foreign debt as sustainable. For example, Australia has had a trade deficit throughout its history and in itself this has not become a problem. The doubts have arisen, sometimes creating a weak currency, when the deficit has become too large and the level of foreign debt has risen too fast.

If foreign debt is rising at, say, 5% per year but the economy is growing at 5% p.a. or more (in nominal terms) then the ratio of foreign debt to GDP will grow only slowly (depending on the initial position) and the situation may be stable in the long term. If, however, foreign debt is increasing at 5% per year and the economy only expanding at 2% p.a. then the situation will not be sustainable in the long run. The latter is more likely to be true if the overspending by the population is mainly traced to higher levels of consumption.

For example, in the USA during the 1980s deficits were not associated with higher levels of investment. This did not necessarily mean that there was a problem but it did mean that the country was borrowing for present consumption rather than to increase the rate of growth of the economy. Since the mid-1990s US deficits were associated with a private sector deficit (with the government moving into surplus), and investment rose strongly. Hence, provided this turns out to reflect a sustainable rise in productivity and investment returns, the prognosis is better.

TRADE DATA AND THE MARKETS

When Trade Data are Important

The components of the trade balance — exports and imports — often tell us something about GDP growth in the economy. If both exports and imports are strong the country is doing well in overseas markets but also is growing fast and is therefore sucking in imports. If exports are doing well but imports are not, then the message is ambiguous.

Very often, and especially if an economy is reasonably close to being in balance on trade, this is all that investors are concerned with when looking at trade data. However, at certain times — and particularly when trade balances are a long way from zero — the releases may be taken by the markets as important for the direction of exchange rates. Sometimes the link is directly through policy while other times the markets believe that, with or without government backing, the exchange rate will move.

For example, during the middle–late 1980s the US trade deficit was the most important monthly data release, much more significant for the markets than the monthly employment data which has generally been the most important release in recent years. The reason was that the US trade deficit was widely regarded as unsustainable. When the government-orchestrated decline in the dollar between February 1985 and 1987 did not immediately improve the trade deficit, the markets anticipated that, either through further government action or through the natural forces of supply and demand, the dollar would need to go lower still. The USA could return to this situation in coming years if that country registers a combination of disappointing economic growth and a weak exchange rate.

Trade and Exchange Rates

In a free-floating system the exchange rate is influenced by the net savings–investment balance in the economy. For example, Japan, with its chronic tendency to save more than it invests, has a tendency towards an under-valued exchange rate normally. In contrast, the UK and the USA, with lower savings than investment, usually have an over-valued rate.

Of course these are not completely static. During the late 1980s Japan enjoyed an investment boom which took investment up to near the level of savings. In consequence the exchange rate strengthened, as less capital flowed out, bringing a reduced current account surplus. After the economy went into recession in 1991, investment dropped sharply opening a larger gap between savings and investment and the current account surplus rose in direct consequence. This pushed the yen still higher in the early 1990s, but by mid-decade, with a large current account surplus and increased investment spending by the government, the yen had overshot and savings–investment pressures took it back to much lower levels.

At times Japanese investors have shown some reluctance to place money overseas but the money still flows out in other ways, either through the banking system, through foreign direct investment or through foreign issues of yen bonds. In addition, many foreign investors have periodically borrowed yen, a very low interest rate currency, to buy other assets — the so-called 'carry trade'. They were hoping to gain, or at least not lose, on their yen position while also gaining on their other position. With the interest rates of other countries also falling to low levels in 2001, the carry trade lost some of its attractiveness.

With fixed exchange rates, the savings–investment balance still controls the current account of the balance of payments. But instead of working through the (nominal) exchange rate it works through changing costs. A devaluation or fall in the currency comes to the same thing as a decline in wages (relative to another country), except that changes in wage levels take longer. If the required changes do not look like happening fast enough then the exchange rate link may well break. This was the problem for Argentina in 2001. Although wages were under downward pressure for several years, the slow pace of fiscal adjustment and weak economic growth meant that Argentina finally could not avoid devaluation.

THE *J*-CURVE EFFECT

The effect of a devaluation will eventually be to improve the balance of trade. But the initial effect may be to worsen the trade position because prices change before volumes adjust. This is known as the *J*-curve effect and it may take one or two years before the trade deficit moves back in the right direction.

Take the UK as an example with its trade in 2001 standing at approximately £200 bn in exports and £230 bn in imports, with a trade deficit of £30 bn. If sterling is devalued by 10% against all currencies the immediate effect may be to raise the trade deficit. Exports will initially stay at the same level because volumes do not immediately change and companies do not immediately raise prices. Meanwhile, since imports are invoiced in dollars or euros, the value of imports in sterling immediately rises. Hence the trade deficit worsens, tracing the downward part of a letter 'J'. With time British producers will be able either to raise prices (in sterling) or increase volumes or both, while the volume of imports will fall because British buyers switch to domestic products. The trade balance will improve, the long side of the letter 'J', and after a period of time, usually at least a year, the trade balance will be stronger than before the devaluation.

FREE TRADE VERSUS PROTECTIONISM

The trade regime chosen by a country is often an important factor in its economic performance. Most economists are passionate believers in free trade as the ideal policy. There are two general lines of argument behind this belief. The first is a theoretical one, known as the theory of comparative advantage, first fully argued by David Ricardo in the mid-nineteenth century. This theory does not just say that a country can gain over another country by concentrating on producing whatever it is better at producing. It is a more subtle and much richer argument than this (which incidentally would be called the 'Theory of Absolute Advantage'). What comparative advantage means is that a country should concentrate on producing goods that it can produce *comparatively* well even if it is less efficient at everything else than another country. The exchange rate will take care of competitiveness.

For example, the USA can probably produce aircraft and shoes using less labour than India through the use of more machines. That does not mean that India should not produce either of those items, only that it should produce the one at which it is relatively better, compared to the USA. The exchange rate makes sure that an hour of labour in India costs much less in the USA and so India finds itself competitive at exporting shoes. If the USA raises trade barriers to try to protect its domestic shoe industry it will make the economy less efficient and lower overall living standards. Similarly, if the Indian government tries to promote a domestic aircraft industry whether through protection or subsidies, it too will be reducing overall efficiency and living standards.

In the modern world it is often argued that the relevance of this theory is limited, and there have been many attempts to discredit it. It has been shown theoretically that a government might be able to use protectionist policies to improve its country's living standards under certain conditions, but it would still be better for the government to use other policies, such as subsidies, rather than protectionism. Moreover, the backing for free trade is still firm among nearly all economists because of the second argument — i.e. it is much better to leave trade, and indeed the economy generally, to free markets. Economists believe that, although protectionism might be effective in theory, once trade policy becomes a political issue the decisions taken are much more likely to be based on practical and political factors than economic or efficiency factors.

For investors, the key point to remember here is that any moves in the direction of free trade imply faster growth for the country that is liberalising, as well as lower prices or slower inflation. Conversely, moves towards protectionism tend to mean higher inflation and slower growth.

The Politics of Trade

In practice trade is frequently a very hot political issue, with powerful lobby groups both for protectionism and for liberalisation and a strong popular involvement in the issues. Some economists have argued that there is a bias towards protectionism although fortunately there are forces in favour of liberalising as well. Let's list both sides:

First, there is a bias towards protection because individual interest groups protecting a particular industry are often able to powerfully influence politicians while the consumers who would gain from continuing free trade are dispersed and unorganised. For example, the heavy protection of the US and European car industries in the 1980s and 1990s was to the benefit of car producers, enabling jobs, incomes and profits to be held up while, to the rest of the population, prices of cars were much higher than necessary. But the 95% of the population who suffered were only partly aware of it and in any case suffered less than an individual car worker or company would have suffered. Politicians are able to draw their own conclusions from this equation.

Secondly, if a country has a trade deficit then the people perceiving themselves to be suffering from imports are likely to be a bigger lobby group than the people who perceive themselves as gaining from exports, and so there may be a bias towards protection. Trade protectionism became a minor issue in the USA in the late 1990s, despite the large trade deficit, because during the boom there were plenty of jobs and plenty of profit opportunities. If unemployment runs at a higher level in the next few years protectionism is likely to resurface as a major issue, given the large trade deficit.

Thirdly, there is a view, that one way to expand exports to countries with real or perceived barriers is to threaten to cut imports. A number of disputes at the World Trade Organisation have resulted in import 'sanctions' of this sort, punishing countries for their protectionism. Most economists are ambivalent on this. If the net result is greater trade all round then everybody is happy. If, however, the threats have to be put into play, the result is worse. The policy is therefore dangerous and, of course, is not in the interests of the country trying it, only the producers directly affected. It is important to remember that the benefits of freeing imports are felt primarily by the country doing the liberalisation, not by other countries. Lower domestic prices and more competition for domestic producers forces efficiency gains and makes everybody better off.

On the positive side, there are an increasing number of multinational companies and banks that regard free and liberal trade as important for their business. The more that companies outsource their parts — which applies to service companies as well as manufacturing companies — and the more that companies produce in a variety of countries, the more they are in favour of freeing trade. Globalisation therefore provides a stronger lobbying group for free trade.

Finally there is a very powerful ideological case for free trade, traditionally carried by the US Presidency and some other countries including the UK and Germany. This is reinforced by the historical memory of the problems in the 1930s, which were partly caused by resorting to protectionism in the face of world recession.

CAPITAL FLOWS

As we have seen, in the modern world of free capital movements it is increasingly the net flows of capital, caused by savings–investment imbalances, that drive the exchange rate. There are three broad reasons behind private capital flows.

First, relative interest rates and yields generally, e.g. on stocks, are frequently a crucial factor. Countries with high rates and yields will attract an inflow. In the 1990s the USA was an outstanding example of this as high interest rates and strong returns on stocks attracted massive inflows and drove the dollar up. Of course, if investors see high yields but worry about exchange rate depreciation then they may buy bonds or stocks but hedge the currency. The effect of the hedging is to offset the inflow of capital associated with buying the bond so that there is no net inflow. This will register in the balance of payments of the receiving country as an inflow of long-term capital and an outflow of short-term capital.

Secondly, countries with low exchange rates may attract an inflow, even with only moderate interest rates, because investors expect a currency appreciation. The euro benefited from this in the second half of 2001. What may be happening sometimes is not so much that investors flock into deposits and wait for the currency to appreciate but investors who already hold bonds or stocks remove hedges because the balance of risk has shifted with the currency being low. The effect of removing a hedge is equivalent to an inflow of capital.

Finally, some capital flows are relatively unaffected by interest rates or exchange rates and reflect long-term or structural factors. For example, the attractiveness of dollars as a currency to hold or as a means of payment throughout the world, but particularly in Latin America and eastern Europe, means that the USA can enjoy a continuous effective inflow. Some of the dollars spent by Americans on imports stay out there rather than coming back to pay for US exports. Another structural flow is direct investment. Although it is not unaffected by interest rates and exchange rates, most of it is driven by other factors. Moreover direct investors may be inclined to leave their investments unhedged because they are very long term.

All these capital flows are on the increase as capital controls are removed and international investment becomes increasingly important. In many countries there is a gradual shift from public provision of pension schemes to private-funded schemes, which also encourages greater flows. The size of capital flows relative to current account flows is therefore larger. Of course for most countries flows are increasing in both directions. Only the net inflows or outflows impact on exchange rates, but these net positions seem to be becoming larger too.

CONCLUSION: TRADE AND CAPITAL FLOW FUNDAMENTALS

News and data on trade and capital flows primarily impact currency markets. The most important measure of the trade position is the current account deficit, usually analysed as a percentage of GDP. This plays a major role in assessing emerging countries (as we shall see), but is sometimes relevant for industrial countries as well, when the deficit is large (3–4% of GDP or more) and persistent. Correcting a deficit nearly always involves a devaluation, a period of slower growth and considerable time (at least a year and usually longer).

With capital flows now so important it is crucial to look at the 'basic balance', which includes both the current account position and long-term capital flows. The difficulty is assessing future trends in capital flows. Any deficit in the basic balance will be made up by short-term flows (banks and speculative positions) or by changes in foreign exchange reserves. Finally, the significance of trade liberalisation should not be underestimated. News that a country will liberalise, e.g. China's decision to join the WTO, is good news for the stock market.

9

International Linkages

The globalisation of trade and capital flows means that countries and markets are increasingly closely linked. The main connections are through oil prices, interest rates and, periodically, policy coordination by the major governments.

IS THERE A WORLD BUSINESS CYCLE?

It is no accident that recessions and booms often seem to come more or less at the same time in different countries. Faster economic growth in one country (especially if it is large) stimulates the exports of another. The rise in exports lifts the whole economy as investment increases and incomes improve. The process also works in reverse. For example, in 2001 the US economic slowdown hurt growth in the rest of the world, particularly impacting countries with substantial trade, including Germany and several smaller Asian countries such as Taiwan and Singapore. Part of the impact comes directly through hurting exports, and therefore incomes and business confidence, in the second country. To this may be added the market linkages and policy coordination linkages discussed below.

But business cycles are not always synchronised. For example, the previous US recession ended in spring 1991 whereas Germany and Japan only emerged from recession in 1994. And Japan saw another recession in 1998. In fact the synchronisation in the recessions of 1974–5, 1981–2 and in the 2001 slowdown was probably due primarily to the world-wide impact of higher oil prices. In the absence of oil shocks, events in the USA clearly impact on other countries, but the effects are unlikely to be major.

The dominance of the USA in the world economy is in steady decline and therefore its leadership role in the world economy, though still very substantial, is dwindling. Forty years ago the USA accounted for two-thirds of world GDP, but the figure is now less than one-third. As Europe integrates further and countries' economies move closer together, Europe's relative weight becomes more important for the rest of the world. Hence we may be moving towards a 'multi-polar' world economy with the USA, Europe and Asia potentially moving separately. We have already seen periods when Europe and Asia were quite strong, despite US weakness, such as in 1991–2. And the USA remained strong in the late 1990s despite Asian weakness.

The more trade that a country has with another the more its economic cycle becomes converged. For example, the impact of the German unification boom in Europe was greatest for those countries already exporting a great deal to Germany, notably Austria, Switzerland, Holland and France, but less important for countries such as the UK which had a smaller proportion of exports going to Germany.

WHY OIL PRICES REMAIN IMPORTANT

Since the early 1970s oil prices have played a major role in the world economy. For the most part oil is moved by long-term changes in supply and demand, although the OPEC cartel was also influential at certain key times, most notably in 1973–4, 1979–80 and 2000–1. In the early 1970s demand for oil had risen to more or less equal the total available supply. When OPEC quadrupled prices in 1973 the rise was sustainable because the oil market was so tight. But for industrial countries the extra money being paid to oil producers amounted to a withdrawal of 2–3% of GDP. Higher oil prices also sent consumer prices rocketing. The result was to plunge the industrial countries virtually simultaneously into a severe recession, with high inflation, thereby synchronising the world business cycle, which had not been synchronised prior to 1973. The re-doubling of oil prices in 1979 had a similar effect.

In the mid-1980s the situation reversed. As a result of the price rises in 1973 and again in 1979, the demand for oil had risen much more slowly than supply, and there was clear over-capacity in the market. In 1986 OPEC was unable to agree on lower production quotas and the oil price responded with an almost 50% reduction in the course of a few weeks. This decline was very important for the continuation of the world economic upswing through the late 1980s. Without the benefit of the downward impetus to inflation from lower oil prices, the central banks in many countries would have brought the 1980s upswing to an end much earlier.

The rise in oil prices in 1990 after Iraq's invasion of Kuwait impacted on business expectations everywhere. In the English-speaking countries recessions were already beginning and the oil price rise converted a moderate downturn into a sharp fall in output. For continental Europe, however, the German unification boom was too strong to be derailed by oil prices.

Finally, oil prices again played a major role in the 1998–2001 period. In 1998 prices fell sharply, touching $10 once again, as the effects of the Asian crisis on demand, combined with dissension in OPEC. This fall helped to keep US inflation under control and delayed Fed tightening, contributing to the asset price bubble of 1999–2000. Then, starting in 1999, OPEC cut production and pushed prices up to more than $30 per barrel — almost tripling the prices from the lows seen in 1998. Even though oil is much less important than before in industrial country energy use, this rise was enough to dent consumers' real incomes significantly and push up inflation to over 3% in the USA and Europe. It played a major role in the world economic slowdown although, unlike in the previous recessions, it was not the only important factor.

INTEREST RATE LINKAGES

Sometimes short-term interest rates are affected by developments in other countries because the central bank is pursuing a formal or informal exchange rate link. Some governments *unilaterally* peg their currencies firmly or loosely to one of the major currencies, usually the US dollar or the euro. This strategy is much less common now than before the Asian crisis in 1997 but it is still practised.

There are two advantages for countries that follow this strategy. First, it provides business with some comfort that exchange rates are not going to fluctuate wildly. (Of course, instead, short-term interest rates may very well fluctuate wildly!) Secondly, by pegging the exchange rate the country often hopes to control inflation. This was important in Europe under the Exchange Rate Mechanism (the precursor to EMU) and was also the reason for Argentina's Convertibility plan which tied the peso to the dollar in the early 1990s.

What Determines the Interest Differential?

Ultimately, if a country is adhering rigidly to an exchange rate policy, then the level of interest rates necessary will depend on overall market confidence in policy. If there is a high degree of confidence that the exchange rate will remain stable, then the interest rate differential can converge to near zero, as occurred in Hong Kong in 2000–1 after an uncertain period in 1997–9 when the territory periodically paid much higher interest rates than the USA. If the markets see the policy as unsustainable and expect that the exchange rate may be devalued, then they will demand a substantial interest differential.

Bond Yields and Exchange Rate Expectations

If a country is known to be linking its currency to another, then bond yields of the weaker currency are linked to the stronger currency and are nearly always higher. Hence in Europe Polish bond yields are watched by the markets as a spread over euro bond yields. If the expectation were that the zloty/euro exchange rate would remain broadly the same as its current level over the long term, then bond yields in Poland would converge on Euroland. This could be either because of the government's determination to maintain a parity or because the market assessment of inflation and competitiveness in Poland is such that there is no need for a devaluation. If, however, markets anticipate a devaluation before Poland links with the euro, then the bond yield spread will continue.

However, even if countries are not trying to link their currencies, this connection between exchange rate expectations and bond yields means that bond yields can diverge substantially between countries. For example, if one country's exchange rate is expected to rise substantially against another's, then bond yields will be relatively lower than they would otherwise be in relation to the other country. In effect bond-holders know that the appreciation in the currency can offset developments in interest rates. This obviously works the other way around too: if a country's exchange rate is likely to depreciate substantially, then the bond markets will require an extra premium to hold those bonds.

Exchange rates could be over- or undervalued requiring an offset from bond yields for a number of reasons. One possibility is that government action on *short-term* interest rates has affected exchange rates. For example, the Exchange Rate Mechanism was maintained by using high short-term interest rates to limit speculation against currencies.

Another example is the UK in 1993. After leaving the ERM the UK government reduced short-term interest rates faster than the Bundesbank, which had the effect of taking sterling to a level that was widely seen as undervalued against the Deutschemark and therefore leaving the possibility of appreciation. In that environment UK bond yields (gilts) could decline relative to German bond yields because the bond market anticipated a possible currency rise.

A final example is where bond yields are pushed up by a particularly strong economy. In 1984 US bond yields averaged 12.5% p.a. against an inflation of 4% p.a. This high real and nominal rate was due to the combination of the US budget deficit raising demands for borrowing, and a strong private sector economy as the USA rebounded vigorously from the early 1980s recession. In comparison, Germany had bond yields of 8% p.a. with inflation of 2.5% p.a. Hence investors in the USA could enjoy real yields 3% p.a. above investors in German bonds. This was enough to take the dollar up substantially in 1983–5, leaving the markets in some degree of equilibrium. Although there was a widespread expectation that the dollar would have to come down, long-term investors in bonds were enjoying the yield advantage.

Bond Yields and Capital Flows

Obviously *nominal* bond yields vary between countries according to their different inflation outlooks and other factors. It is sometimes thought that *real* bond yields, i.e. after inflation, ought to be similar in different countries because international capital flows will equalise

Table 9.1   Correlations between stock markets 1994–9

	USA	UK	Japan	Mexico	Korea
USA	1				
UK	0.59	1			
Japan	0.42	0.42	1		
Mexico	0.53	0.42	0.37	1	
Korea	0.28	0.32	0.60	0.16	1

Source: International Finance Corporation.

them. But, as we have seen, movements in exchange rates to under- or overvalued levels can compensate for different real bond yields, so real bond yields can vary.

However, although they *can* and often do vary there is nevertheless a tendency for them to move together. In the example above, from 1984 bond yields in both the USA and Germany were comparatively high in relation to inflation and either prior or more recent experience.

The key factor linking bond yields (especially real bond yields) is world supply and demand for capital or the perception of it. For example, in 1994 the collapse of world bond markets and the sharp rise in bond yields seems to have been partly due to a perception that synchronised world growth would force short- and long-term interest rates up as the demand for world savings exceeded the supply. Since, in the end, the demand has to equal the supply, interest rates everywhere rose to choke off demand and/or stimulate more supply. Similarly in 2001 bond yields fell everywhere as private demand for capital dropped off in the face of a world slowdown.

STOCK MARKET LINKAGES

There is plenty of evidence that stock markets are linked and to some extent move together. For example, calculations show that 59% of the movement of the UK's stock market index can be accounted for by movements in the US index (see Table 9.1). The remaining 41% reflects other factors including domestic issues and European influences. The reason for these linkages is partly through trade and the business cycle but also the fact that many UK companies make substantial profits overseas. Around half of the profits of the 100 top UK companies in the FTSE index come from abroad.

At times markets seem to fall together. For example, the 1987 stock market crash began in the USA but most markets around the world fell substantially in response. Again in 2000–1 there was a general decline in world stock markets, which helped to spread the weakness in business confidence around the world.

The extent to which stock markets are correlated is an important issue for investors. By holding a mix of different markets, investors can smooth out annual returns and face less risk of a large drop in any one year. Moreover, in time this translates into higher returns, which is why professional investors actively look for shares and markets that are uncorrelated with their core holdings.

POLICY COORDINATION

In the last 20 years policy coordination has generally focused around two problems: currency management and boosting economic growth. In contrast, governments have not tried hard to coordinate when the emphasis has been on slowing economic growth to reduce inflation, seeing that problem as primarily an internal one. Episodes of policy coordination tend to go in fits and starts. Coordination to boost world growth naturally comes up during recession periods, and currency coordination is most prevalent when the dollar is especially weak.

World Coordination to Boost Economic Growth

Often one or more countries in recession want stronger growth elsewhere to help their exports but are afraid of too much stimulation at home in case it accelerates inflation. However, the experience of countries that have helped to supply this growth has been mixed. In the late 1970s Germany deliberately boosted growth to help to support the world economy. Unfortunately this stimulus came just before the second oil price shock and the result was a sharp rise in German inflation and a serious deterioration in the public finances. German officials vowed that they would never do that again.

Japan's efforts to support the dollar and simultaneously boost the Japanese economy in 1987–8 also ended in tears. By 1989 the Bank of Japan was bitterly regretting the asset price boom that followed the monetary stimulus and desperately tried to cool it. The most successful example of one country leading the world has been the USA, at various times including 1983–4, 1993–4 and 1998–9. However this was not policy coordination — the US economy took off on its own due to interest rate reductions. Other countries just enjoyed the ride.

It is doubtful now whether individual countries are prepared to take on the burden of boosting growth unless they are quite sure it fits in with their own objectives and, in particular, does not clash with their inflation objectives. Nevertheless coordination can be important where world business confidence is low. A convincing coordinated move by governments to stimulate across the board can have a significant impact. This has happened several times following financial crises — for example, after the October 1987 stock market crash, again in 1998 after the collapse of LTCM and again in September 2001 following the terrorist attack. In all these cases governments and central banks everywhere combined to stimulate their economies and offer soothing statements in the face of what was seen as the danger of a slump.

CURRENCY MANIPULATION

Since the developed world moved to floating rates in the early 1970s there have been periodic attempts to control exchange rates. However, economists and the markets have been sceptical on whether governments really can control them with market intervention alone.

Scepticism over the ability of governments to control exchange rates stems from three factors. First, we know that the total value of foreign exchange trading is in excess of 1 trillion dollars *daily*. This is about three times the total foreign exchange reserves of the major central banks. Secondly, most economists believe that market prices are determined by fundamentals and so governments, however big they are, are just other players. Thirdly, experience with trying to control foreign exchange trends is not encouraging in the absence of capital controls. Unless governments are prepared to move interest rates and perhaps change other policies, as well as intervene in the markets, then they cannot expect to succeed.

How does Intervention Work?

When a government buys its own currency using its foreign exchange reserves the effect is to reduce the amount of domestic currency in the country. This would normally raise interest rates by reducing the supply of funds, so if the government does nothing else then the currency benefits from the rise in interest rates. This kind of intervention, known as unsterilised intervention, is usually seen as more likely to be successful because interest rates move too.

However very often governments seek to offset the effect on interest rates by sterilising the foreign exchange market intervention. This is done by matching the reduction in local currency resulting from the FX market intervention by buying back Treasury bills or other paper, thereby putting money back into the economy. From the government's point of view this has the advantage that interest rates do not rise. Sterilised intervention is generally not as successful but can still, at times, influence exchange rates by impacting on market expectations. This is more likely to be true if central banks intervene in a coordinated way so that every bank is in the market at the same time.

Another technique, sometimes used in the past, has been to have relatively vague currency ranges, and not to publicise exactly what they are. If a range has hard edges and is known to the markets, then once the exchange rate moves beyond the edge, the government loses all credibility (as was seen with the collapse of the Exchange Rate Mechanism in 1992/3). If, however, the edges are soft then governments can intervene more and more as the exchange rate goes away from the level they want, but there is no single point at which governments are clearly defeated. Foreign exchange markets like to have reasons for picking certain levels for the currency. It makes life easier if they can feel that a currency is particularly weak or particularly strong and that, in itself, sets up factors, that take currency back to the middle.

CONCLUSION: INTERNATIONAL INTERACTIONS FUNDAMENTALS

Oil prices continue to play a major role in the world economy, even though their importance has diminished from the 1970s. At the time of writing prices are probably above their sustainable long-term trend ($15–20 per barrel) so a decline in prices should be expected in the long term, which is good news for the world economy and bond and stock markets.

Stock markets are more correlated than in the past but nevertheless far from completely correlated. Stock markets declined together in most countries during 2000–1, but experience suggests that they tend to rise independently. It is difficult for markets to rise when the US market is falling rapidly; but when the US market is stable, other markets can rise independently and outperform.

Although G7 Finance Ministers continue to meet regularly there has been far less attempt to coordinate policy in recent years than was the case in the 1970s and the 1980s. In part this reflects the failures and difficulties of that period, but it is also due to the strength of the dollar for much of the 1990s. If this changes, past experience suggests that currency coordination will come back on the agenda. Announcements of currency ranges or hopes for particular currencies frequently do have some short-term impact, but only if intervention is unsterilised and, usually, if the authorities and the market are going in the same direction. This will be discussed further in Chapter 14.

If the current world economic slowdown continues for a prolonged period, increased co-ordination to boost growth is possible. The significance of this would be the effects it has on business confidence. If there is a general feeling that governments will stimulate everywhere and successfully lift growth, there is a good chance that business will step up inventories and investment, helping to achieve stronger growth. If, however, the so-called coordination is all talk, it may have little or no impact.

10
Emerging Economies

It would be a mistake to exaggerate the difference between analysing developed economies and analysing emerging economies. Most of the economic fundamentals already covered in this book also apply to emerging economies. Equally, the emphasis placed on structural change in emerging economies to boost growth is too often forgotten as a factor in developed countries' performance. Nevertheless there *are* some major differences in economic structure and performance which investors ignore at their peril.

DIFFERENCES FROM DEVELOPED COUNTRIES

The Need for High Rates of Investment

Emerging countries, by definition, have low levels of income per capita and are trying to catch up with the leaders in economic development, primarily the USA, Europe and Japan. For that they need high rates of investment both in physical capital and infrastructure and in human capital such as education and skills. The success of several Asian countries in generating 8% p.a. or more growth in recent decades required a ratio of investment to GDP of at least 25% (as in Hong Kong) and often at 30% or more. This compares with a ratio of less than 20% in most developed countries. But many emerging countries have inadequate domestic savings and therefore rely heavily on foreign capital. Unfortunately managing the consequent foreign debt creates periodic crises, which can be a major blow for investors in emerging stocks and bonds.

The Need for Structural Change

The catch-up process offers tremendous profit opportunities, since companies do not have to reinvent the wheel. If a plant can be established in an emerging country and run at even half the productivity level of a developed country it will be highly profitable as long as wages are less than half those in the developed country. In many emerging countries hourly wage rates are only one-tenth of those in developed markets. Hence if the opportunities are not blocked by government controls, macro-economic instability or political worries, the prospective returns on capital should be high and therefore emerging countries are capable of growing very quickly indeed. However, most emerging countries need major structural reform to unlock their potential, which can be politically difficult to achieve. Countries' potential for growth tends to be blocked by governments, protecting vested interests. Hence the stress on 'conditionality' by the IMF and World Bank, which means linking finance to policy change. The major forms of structural change will be examined below.

Weak and Volatile Political Situations

The definitional characteristic of emerging countries—low income per head—often goes hand-in-hand with a volatile political structure. The underlying reason for this is that emerging countries tend to have a relatively large percentage of people who have very low incomes, few assets, and are often poorly educated. There is also a relatively small percentage of 'middle class' people. In contrast, developed societies have a greater proportion of middle class who have a major stake in the country's political and economic stability. The middle classes stand to gain from successful economic development and are better able to withstand the occasional period of economic adjustment or structural change. A weak political situation often makes it difficult for countries to implement structural change because of the power of vested interests (typically landowners and existing businesses that survive due to government protection, together with labour groups). It also means that there is a tendency for government management of fiscal policy and foreign debt to be poor.

Vulnerability to World Economic Shocks

Even the largest emerging countries are small in world terms and their economies are often concentrated in a few areas such as particular commodities, e.g. oil, metals or agricultural products, or a narrow range of manufactured goods, e.g. textiles, clothing, electrical or electronics. Others rely heavily on oil imports and are thus vulnerable to fluctuation in oil prices or are dependent on continuing capital inflows. Changes in any of these areas can have major impacts on their currencies (see below for a discussion of the 1997–8 Asian Crisis) and on growth generally.

IDENTIFYING GOOD GOVERNMENT IN EMERGING COUNTRIES

The following discussion is broadly in line with the so-called 'Washington Consensus', a view of the best way for countries to develop as generally agreed among the key development institutions, the IMF, the World Bank and backed by the US Treasury. Of course significant nuances exist between different experts and, to some degree, between the institutions themselves. Moreover, the view itself has evolved over time, with some significant modifications and changes of focus since the Asian Crisis (see the discussion below), but the broad outlines of good government are clear and are based squarely on free market principles.

Sound Monetary and Fiscal Policy

This means keeping the budget deficit low and avoiding excessive money growth, which is bound to lead to inflation. Many emerging countries have a budget deficit of 4% of GDP or more, which is too high. Countries with large deficits tend to have one or more of three problems. First, a government deficit often brings a current account deficit (the twin-deficit problem) which means that the country must borrow abroad. Eventually, when foreign debt becomes too high, that borrowing must be scaled back, which requires a painful adjustment. Secondly, if the deficit is not financed by borrowing, then it will ultimately be financed by printing money, which means high inflation. Thirdly, the financing of the deficit takes resources away from private sector investment, which would probably be more productive for the country as whole. It is for this reason that countries are best advised to reduce the fiscal deficit to zero or even run a surplus.

Minimising the Role of the Public Sector in Business

For most countries this means privatisation, and new privatisation measures have been strongly associated with stock market advances. But it also means minimising regulations affecting companies. For example, India used to have regulations which seem incredible now. In India companies wanting to increase output by more than 10% had to seek government permission! The worst of these regulations were removed in the early 1990s allowing India to accelerate economic growth. But regulation remains one of the biggest problems for business, not just in developing countries. The most damaging regulations (and the most difficult to lift) tend to be labour market rules (for example, restricting hiring and firing) and financial sector rules (for example, requiring banks to lend to 'social sectors').

Maximising the Competition felt Within the Private Sector

For most countries this means opening up to foreign competitors so that companies are forced to adopt competitive practices. Perhaps the single most effective measure that governments can take is to unilaterally reduce tariff barriers. This lay behind the success of Chile in the 1990s, for example. Another important liberalisation measure is to open up to foreign investment. Larger countries may be able to promote competition internally, but weak political institutions and limited market size often means that cartels emerge. In some countries privatisations have led to private monopolies which means that the gains from privatisation are not fully realised.

Investing in Infrastructure and Human Capital

In principle there is no reason why the private sector could not do this. And in many countries it does, investing in long-term projects and providing schools and hospitals that are nearly always superior to any government facilities available. However, in practice, the political and regulatory environment in emerging countries is so uncertain that the private sector finds it difficult to engage in long-term projects except in partnership with governments. This is then legitimately an important area for government activity. It is also a key area for the World Bank and other development banks, both in project work and in support of restructuring government programmes. Unfortunately it also an area where governments sometimes get carried away with large prestigious projects and doubtful returns.

Managing External Borrowing

Exactly how to do this remains an area of controversy, especially since the Asian Crisis. But the important points are to limit the country's vulnerability to a financing or currency crisis in three ways. First, by keeping overall external debt within reasonable bounds. Secondly, by maintaining a healthy level of foreign exchange reserves and limiting the amount of short-term debt taken on. Thirdly, by keeping the exchange rate reasonably competitive.

ASSESSING EMERGING COUNTRIES: A CHECKLIST APPROACH

The assessment of emerging countries is sometimes called country risk analysis or sovereign risk analysis, if the issue is simply whether the government will meet its foreign obligations. Historically the international banks were the main lenders to emerging countries and they developed sophisticated systems of analysis. Multinational companies also developed methodologies often focusing on other issues such as 'confiscation risk' and legal risk. With the rise of the emerging bond market most countries are now rated by the major ratings agencies such as Moodys', Standard and Poors and Fitch-IBCA. Investors in emerging equities need a slightly different approach (see Chapter 16). Nevertheless, there are common elements in all these approaches.

Investors need to assess both the growth prospects of emerging countries and their vulnerability. While there are probably as many ways of doing this as there are investors, a common approach is to use a checklist, including various economic and financial ratios but also more qualitative questions, such as policy trends and political stability. Six questions the investor should ask are given below, with suggestions for data to analyse and points to look for.

How Sound are Fiscal and Monetary Policy?

If there is one single ratio that is most watched in all emerging market analysis it is the ratio of the fiscal deficit to GDP. Although even a surplus here does not guarantee that the country will avoid a crisis, as we shall see later in relation to the Asian crisis, a large deficit is frequently a problem. Deficits are a major cause of slow growth and are frequently implicated in serious crises. A persistent ratio above about 4% is regarded with concern, the range of 2–4% is acceptable but still damaging, while countries with ratios of 2% or less are doing well. Most emerging countries have deficits and are engaged in a perpetual struggle to reduce them.

If the fiscal deficit is large for a sustained period the government is likely to build up a significant debt. In developing countries governments usually borrow mainly short-term from domestic lenders, especially from banks, and from overseas. Few countries have a large long-term domestic currency debt market because of the price they would have to pay given the uncertainties, although a market is starting to emerge in some of the more successful countries. Domestic debt crises have become more common in recent years, though usually in association with foreign crises. The Argentina crisis in 2001 was essentially due to too much government debt. For a developing country the level of debt that is too much is generally lower than for developed countries. A ratio of more than about 70–80% is already extremely vulnerable.

The second area to watch is inflation, together with the rate of growth of money and credit aggregates. Emerging countries are likely to have somewhat higher inflation rates than developed countries because they generally have higher productivity growth. If, for example, half the economy consists of new manufacturing, where productivity growth is 10% p.a., and half is the old agricultural sector with productivity growth of only 2% p.a., then the economy as whole will enjoy productivity growth of 6% p.a., which is high by developed country standards. The rapid productivity growth in the modern sector will tend to lift wages by a similar amount, which of course is not inflationary. But the same wage growth will be seen in the traditional sector too, since ultimately there is only one labour market. However, productivity in this half of the economy is only rising by 2% p.a., so prices here have to rise by 8% p.a., which translates into a 4% p.a. inflation rate for the economy as a whole.

Inflation above about 8–10% p.a. has been shown to be associated with slower economic growth. If money and credit growth are particularly high, the reason is usually either that the government has a large deficit and is 'printing money' to finance it, or that the private sector is experiencing a strong boom, with heavy private demand for money. A popular indicator to watch is the annual percentage growth in domestic credit. Usually persistent double-digit growth is a warning sign that the central bank is allowing money to grow too quickly. Another indicator to watch is the ratio of domestic credit to GDP. This is a measure of the size of the banking sector and tends to be higher the more developed the economy. But if it is high relative to countries with a similar level of development or rising rapidly, this ratio is a sign that the banks are lending at a rapid pace, which may not be sustainable.

How Dynamic is the Economy?

One useful measure is simply the past rate of growth of the economy. The most successful countries in Asia have been able to grow at annual rates of 6–8% on a sustained basis. Others have achieved 4–6% p.a., which is acceptable, particularly if population growth has already slowed down, as for example in eastern Europe. Growth rates of less than 4% p.a. generally mean that the country is only catching up with the industrial countries slowly, if at all. It also means that, given some population growth, per capita incomes are growing very slowly or even falling, which is likely to bring political stresses.

Another measure is the performance of the stock market. A strong performance often means that the economy is doing well and investors are cheered by new policy measures such as privatisation. However stock markets can also be caught up in unsustainable booms, as was seen in Asia in the 1990s. And markets do not always foresee disaster. The Indonesian market, for example, was rising in the first half of 1997 just ahead of its crisis. Also, a rise in the market means that the stock investor is buying at a higher price. It may give the investor in bonds some comfort, however.

There are several more qualitative issues, related to the size of the private sector and the degree of competition that the government encourages or allows. Typically a wave of reform boosts economic growth (and the stock market) for a period but then growth may slow unless there is further reform or new opportunities are opened up. Here there are a number of measures available to the investor. One of the best is the Economic Freedom Index published by a consortium of research institutes around the world.[1] This puts together a range of indicators of the freedom enjoyed by the private sector including tax rates, tariff rates, the cost of setting up companies and others. Countries such as the USA, Singapore and Hong Kong score well, and the index has been found to have a broad correlation with economic growth.

Is the Currency Competitive and are the External Accounts under Control?

Managing the currency has proved to be one of the most difficult areas for governments. If the currency swings around severely, sometimes heavily undervalued and sometimes seriously overvalued, it may have very negative effects on business confidence and investment. Moreover, if the currency is overvalued for a prolonged period the country is likely to be borrowing too much, which will show up in a large current account deficit and a growing external debt.

The size of the current account deficit is a key measure of competitiveness and the sustainability of the external accounts. Any country with a deficit persistently greater than 4% of GDP is probably uncompetitive to some degree. If the necessary financing becomes unavailable for some reason, a combination of a currency depreciation and an economic slowdown will probably follow. The slowdown will also usually cut the current account deficit by reducing imports. Note, however, that a small current account deficit, of the order of 1–3% of GDP, is probably sustainable provided that the economy is growing. A current account deficit is also more sustainable if the financing is through foreign direct investment rather than portfolio flows.

Another measure is the rate of growth of exports. If the country is uncompetitive then its exports are probably growing rather slowly or not at all. For many countries it may be important to look at the type of exports that the country produces since most countries are

---

[1] See www.freetheworld.com

quite concentrated in their output. Also, it is usually best to look at a broad measure of exports to include services or even 'current account receipts' which also includes workers remittances, which is very important for countries such as Egypt and Turkey for example.

Another approach is to try to estimate the equilibrium exchange rate by looking at purchasing power parities (PPPs). It is not a question of comparing the prices of goods across countries because prices are usually lower in developing countries. Rather it is done by finding a prior year when the current account was close to balance and comparing relative inflation trends since then (see Chapter 14).

Is External Debt under Control?

External debt means foreign currency debt owed to foreigners, whether the borrower is the government or the private sector. It is perfectly sensible for countries to borrow overseas to augment domestic savings, but borrowing needs to be kept within reasonable bounds, otherwise at some point lenders may begin to question its sustainability. Then there is a reluctance to lend new money and sometimes an exodus of capital as short-term loans are not renewed and portfolio capital (invested in local bonds and stocks) flows out.

Several measures of debt burden are widely used. With all of these measures there is a level above which debt is certainly dangerously high and there is a level below which debt is not a problem. And then there is the critical range in between, which is more or less worrying depending on other factors such as the type of debt, e.g. whether short or long term, the level of reserves and the rate of growth of the economy.

The ratio of foreign debt to GDP is one of the best measures. Above 50% is dangerous territory while 25–50% is the ambiguous area. Note that a currency devaluation can make this ratio balloon since GDP, when translated into dollars, will suddenly fall. Another important ratio is debt to current account receipts. Above 200% puts the country into the danger zone while below 100% is acceptable. Another good measure is the ratio of interest payments to current account receipts. Above 10% is very risky while 6–10% is in the danger area.

Is Liquidity Plentiful?

By liquidity we mean foreign exchange reserves in relation to trade flows and short-term debt. Traditionally, the adequacy of reserves was assessed in relation to imports. Reserves were judged adequate provided that they were equal in value to three months' worth of imports. However, with the vastly greater importance of debt and capital flows than before, it is better to relate reserves to other measures too. An important ratio is reserves divided by short-term debt (debt maturing in under 12 months). A safe level is over 200% while a risky level is under 100%.

Another useful ratio is to look at reserves divided by the 'financing gap'. The 'financing gap' is calculated as the current account deficit, less foreign direct investment, plus long-term debt amortisation due, plus total short-term debt. This measure is therefore asking how reserves would cope if, in a crisis, the country could not obtain new lending to cover its current account deficit and also could not roll over its maturing short- and long-term debt. Foreign direct investment is subtracted because this tends to be less susceptible to short-term panics. Above 150% is a comfortable level while below 100% is a serious concern.

A final measure is to look at whether short-term debt is at a reasonable level or whether the country is making excessive use of it. Ideally short-term debt is being used mainly for short-term trade financing. Since most trade financing is for three months or so we use, as a rule of thumb, that a short-term debt of three months' worth of imports is a reasonable level. Above that is 'excess' and is probably due to the government allowing, or encouraging, the banking sector to borrow abroad from foreign banks.

Excess short-term borrowing is implicated in most emerging market crises. In part this is due to the fact that, leading up to a crisis, the country finds it more difficult to borrow longer term and the only source of funds available is short-term funds. But if the country borrows too much, even short-term lending eventually stops and goes into reverse. Once it reverses the country is typically in crisis. The reason that short-term funds are available is generally because foreign banks regard this kind of lending as the least risky. While it appears relatively less risky for the individual bank, it is risky for the system as a whole if countries borrow too much.

The attitude of banks is not as myopic as it may appear since experience has shown that there are few losses on short-term lending. The reason is that short-term loans generally flow through the domestic banking system and, even if the government is eventually forced to default on long-term loans, it must keep the banking system afloat and international trade going. Therefore, governments usually do not force losses on foreign banks' short-term lending. Banks are sometimes 'locked-in' for prolonged periods, however, which is why they become nervous and reduce lines when a crisis looms.

Is the Political Situation Supportive of the Required Policies?

Analysis of the economic situation using the ratios and assessment outlined above provides an idea of how well the country is performing. If it is very healthy with fast growth, rapid policy liberalisation, low debt and high reserves then the onset of a period of poor political leadership is unlikely to rapidly create a crisis. It can, however, damage the prospects for the stock market if the government pulls the wrong levers. For example, a rise in the budget deficit or increased regulation as the government tries to buy political support will eventually impact on profits growth and the economy.

If, however, the economic indicators and policy are flashing warning signals the key issue becomes whether the government will be able to implement the necessary adjustment policies. Usually the most difficult area is cutting the budget deficit, since this requires some combination of higher taxes or lower spending. Implementing budget cuts is always painfully difficult, and more so if the economy is weak already. Other key policy changes are reforms such as privatisation and the ending of monopolies.

Cutting the budget deficit makes governments unpopular and may provoke a reaction on the streets. Sometimes it is not easily within the government's power because of lack of control of regional spending or because a fractious coalition threatens to collapse over cuts. Typically at this stage the IMF is heavily involved and sets targets that the government tries to meet. Not infrequently it is the breakdown of an IMF programme, due to failure to comply with budget-cutting targets or backtracking on reform measures, which triggers a crisis.

We look at emerging markets as an investment in detail in Chapter 16. But briefly here, how should investors view this process? Forecasting a crisis or a deteriorating situation is very important. As the situation deteriorates bond spreads over US Treasuries are liable to rise and the stock market is likely to perform less well or even fall. Once the country is in a crisis there are usually plenty of interested investors because they know that bargains may be available. Some may be hoping to buy stocks at the low point; others are looking at the spreads on bonds, which are typically high in the crisis. If the country avoids default the bonds will provide a very good return for the long-term, and if the situation improves in a year or two the bonds can probably be sold at a good profit. Other investors may be expecting the crisis to worsen and may be looking to short the currency or, where possible, short the stock market.

Ultimately the issues involve two questions. How bad is the economic and financial situation? How likely is it that the government will solve it? Of course other factors are important too such as the extent of international support (usually greater if the country is of strategic importance like Mexico or Turkey) and the international environment. 'Contagion' often also plays an important role. For example, some of the countries that suffered during the Asian crisis were not in bad shape fundamentally, but they were dragged down with the rest.

Sometimes economic crises are not caused by government budget problems but by an unsustainable boom in the private sector. The Asia crisis in 1997–8 is the prime recent example and we turn to it now. But more recent crises, including Russia in 1998, Brazil in 1999 and Turkey and Argentina in 2001, did stem from budget problems.

LESSONS OF THE ASIAN CRISIS

The Asian crisis was a major shock and a severe blow to investors in emerging markets. In the first half of the 1990s many investors saw emerging markets, and Asia in particular, as star performers. They had come to believe that rapid and relatively steady economic growth in the region was the norm and foresaw only mild market setbacks. But with the crisis, not only were there excruciating losses on investments, but belief in both the Asian economic model and the attractions of emerging markets were called into question.

Meanwhile the US economy and stock market performed staggeringly well during the second half of the 1990s. Many investors turned away from emerging markets. Others began to ask whether a better way to access the economic growth potential of emerging markets might be to buy the shares of multinational companies with substantial operations in emerging markets, rather than buy local company stocks.

For the countries affected, the crisis was broad-based, affecting virtually the whole economy and financial system, bringing dramatic falls in asset prices, bankrupting the banks in several countries and dominating the political scene. In the three worst-hit countries, Korea, Thailand and Indonesia, the level of GDP dropped between 6 and 14%, the most severe contractions for almost 40 years. Even the economies least affected by the financial turmoil, Singapore, Taiwan and China, experienced a period of uncharacteristically low growth, while the cost of successfully defending Hong Kong's dollar peg was a sharp contraction in GDP. The crisis had its most severe impact on domestic demand, which collapsed in most countries. Investment plummeted in the face of excess capacity and as companies tried to rebuild balance sheets that were unsustainable through high debt burdens. Consumers also cut back spending as unemployment rose and asset prices fell. In some cases car sales fell by 70–80% year-on-year.

The sharp adjustments taking place on the domestic side showed through most vividly on the external accounts. Exports fell, due to the drop in trade financing, lower intra-regional trade, weak commodity prices and the squeeze on the price of manufactured goods caused by excess capacity. However, imports fell even faster, leading to large current account surpluses in countries where previously there had been sizeable external account deficits.

Recessions and the accompanying collapse of the asset price bubbles in the equity and property market led to a vast reduction of credit to the private sector during the course of 1998 and into 1999. Credit collapsed most severely in Indonesia, Thailand and the Philippines, but also fell in Hong Kong and Korea. In many countries the scale of the devastation in the financial sector was severe, with the government forced to close or take over many finance companies and banks.

For investors the crisis brought devastating losses. The Thai stock market had been falling for over a year before the devaluation of 2 July 1997 and was already down more than 70% *before* the devaluation. It fell further in dollar terms after the devaluation. Most other markets had been moving sideways in the year prior to the crisis, while a few, including Indonesia and Hong Kong, had a strong performance in the first half of 1997. But the declines between July 1997 and the lows of October 1998 (after the Russian crisis) were devastating, especially when measured in dollar terms. In dollar terms, during 1997 the stock market index lost 79% in Thailand, 74% in Indonesia and 69% in Korea. Even by the end of 1999, three years later, investors were still down over 50% in Thailand, Indonesia and Malaysia although Korea had bounced back.

Throughout the second half of 1997 and 1998 emerging markets were under pressure. Contagion effects threatened to cause a currency slide in Hong Kong and China, and attention also focused on other countries where fixed exchange rates and weak financing positions might cause problems. The crisis reached its peak with the Russian devaluation and default in August 1998. This triggered a major retreat from risk positions among banks and hedge funds which saw risk spreads widen out dramatically across markets generally. It also precipitated a major move upward in the Japanese yen, as 'carry trade' positions were rapidly unwound, and this helped to stabilise Asian currencies. There followed the bail-out of LTCM (a prominent hedge fund) in August 1998 and a subsequent 75 basis point cut in the Fed Funds rate to calm the financial markets' nerves. Brazil's devaluation in early 1999 was seen as the final global event in the crisis, though its impact proved less serious than expected.

WHY WAS THE CRISIS NOT FORESEEN?

Many investors did expect a Brazilian crisis. Some foresaw a Russian crisis, though others were shocked by the Russian default. However, virtually all investors were taken by surprise by the Asian crisis. Even those who realised that Thailand was in deep trouble prior to July 1997 did not anticipate the virulent contagion effect to the rest of the region. With the benefit of hindsight we can see a number of reasons why the Asian crisis was not foreseen.

First, many investors were complacent because they believed that the lack of a fiscal problem in Asia meant that crises would be avoided. This may be a case of short memories. The Chilean crisis of the early 1980s was caused by a private sector deficit, not a public deficit, while many of the problems in European countries at the end of the 1980s were due to private sector booms and overlending rather than government imbalances.

Secondly, the successful rescue of Mexico in 1994–5 encouraged the view that emerging country crises could be contained by swift IMF action. The unprecedented size and speed of the rescue package and the relatively quick turnaround in Mexico encouraged the view that there was little to be feared. This view may have glossed over the very deep economic and political crisis that Mexico did suffer at that time. It also did not allow for the devastation in the private sector in countries where bank financing (domestic credit), measured as a share of GDP, was much more pervasive than in Mexico.

Thirdly, the extent of the build-up of short-term debt was not fully understood. Short-term debt data for Thailand were available from the Bank for International Settlements (BIS) as well as the central bank and the issue was well-aired in 1995–6. Short-term debt in Indonesia was less well noted since much was in the form of short-term corporate paper and was only issued during 1997, too late to be included in BIS data before the crisis.

Fourthly, the extent of financial fragility was not fully appreciated. In some countries, for example Indonesia, the problems of government banks' weak loan portfolios had been known for a very long time. In others, for example Thailand, the proliferation of finance companies should have been a warning signal. But problem loans ballooned in the second half of 1997 and 1998 with the rise in interest rates and slump in the economy and asset prices.

Finally, and perhaps most importantly, investors were dazzled by the 'Asian miracle'. Growth had been so strong for so long that both local and foreign investors believed that it would go on for ever. Some slowdown might be expected from time to time, but not a major crisis.

THAILAND'S LEADING ROLE

Thailand had maintained a quasi-fixed exchange rate at around 25.5 bahts per dollar from 1987 onwards. Also, starting in 1987, Thailand experienced very high GDP growth rates, averaging 11.6% p.a. from 1987 to 1990 and then subsiding to a still impressive 8–9% growth rate during 1991–5. This rate of growth was seen as a sustainable long-run rate and the emerging bubble in the property sector was not fully recognised. Inflation remained at an acceptable 5% p.a. or so, but clear signs of overheating emerged in the economy during 1994–5 when the current account deficit doubled to reach over 8% of GDP.

Recognising the overheating problem, interest rates were raised to slow the economy. However, this encouraged a further capital inflow, mainly through increased borrowing. With domestic lending rates at over 13% there was a strong incentive for companies to finance with dollar loans. Total foreign debt rose from $43.6 bn in 1992 to $82.6 bn in 1995 but, crucially, short-term debt surged from $18.9 bn to $41.1 bn over the same period. The problem of short-term debt was widely recognised in Thailand (unlike Indonesia) and the government took action to stabilise it, but the level remained high.

Eventually higher interest rates combined with weaker exports, largely triggered by a downturn in the electronics cycle (which affected the whole region), brought an economic slowdown. Investment started to decline as signs of overcapacity emerged. Then, with the current account deficit remaining large but interest rates falling, doubts over the sustainability of the exchange rate began to mount. There were several speculative attacks on the baht in the spring of 1997, which the central bank seemed to be able to fend off with only a small reduction in FX reserves. Indeed the baht actually appreciated in June as the central bank attempted to squeeze the speculators. But, unknown to everybody except the central bank, reserves were effectively down to zero by mid-year because of forward transactions.

Once the central bank left the market the baht abruptly depreciated by about 15% then continued to slide for the rest of the year, reaching a low of 55.5/US$ in early January 1998, slightly more than a 50% overall depreciation. Foreign bank lenders tried to reduce lines, though they were restrained by the IMF and G7 governments. Local dollar borrowers moved to hedge their positions. The baht came back to around the 38–40 level in late March 1998 and stabilised not far from that level for a period, but the damage had been done. The combination of higher domestic interest rates to try to stabilise the baht, a fiscal contraction recommended by the IMF and a collapse of business and consumer confidence sent the economy into a severe recession. GDP fell 8% in 1998.

How far structural factors were to blame remains controversial. Inadequate regulation and supervision of the banking sector was perhaps the most significant structural weakness. The introduction of offshore international banking facilities (IBFs) in 1992 had allowed a sharp run-up in short-term debt, although the central bank started to address this problem well before the crisis. Also the authorities permitted a proliferation of finance companies, which helped to finance the property boom, and did little to restrain them. Linked to this was the problem of so-called 'crony capitalism' where business owners, bankers and government ministers cooperated closely to ensure the flow of licences and lending, though this issue was of greater importance in Indonesia and Malaysia than in Thailand. Finally, exchange rate targeting was certainly one of the main causes of the crisis and this must be regarded as a structural factor.

Contagion to the Rest of Asia

The spread to the rest of the region took place through two main channels. First, investors looked for other countries in the same situation as Thailand, i.e. with a large current account deficit, a fixed exchange rate, substantial short-term debt, weak banks and a slowing economy. Since business and consumer confidence quickly weakened everywhere, this combination soon applied to most countries in the region. Secondly, there was a view that, since Thailand competed with many countries in the region, other currencies would need to depreciate simply to maintain trade competitiveness. Exchange rates per US dollar 1997–9 are shown in Table 10.1.

Table 10.1 Exchange rate per US dollar (end 1996 = 100)

	End 1997	End 1998	End 1999
Asia			
Indonesia	51	30	33
Korea	50	70	75
Thailand	54	70	68
China	100	100	100
Hong Kong	100	100	100
India	91	85	82
Malaysia	65	67	67
Philippines	66	67	65
Singapore	84	84	84
Taiwan	84	85	88
Latin America			
Brazil	93	86	58
Argentina	100	100	100
Chile	97	90	80
Colombia	78	67	54
Mexico	97	80	83
Peru	95	83	74
Venezuela	94	85	73
Europe/Africa			
Russia	93	27	20
Czech Republic	79	91	76
Hungary	81	75	64
Poland	82	82	69
South Africa	96	80	76

Source: IMF

The two other countries with the largest short-term debt problem, Korea and Indonesia, gradually followed Thailand into severe difficulties. Banks tried to withdraw short-term lines, local borrowers tried to hedge their dollar loans and speculators took aim. Reserves eroded and attempts to control the fall in exchange rates with higher interest rates failed when political pressures became too great. Korea's elections took place in December 1997 but the crisis intensified during the weeks just before, in a climate of policy uncertainty. Indonesians turned on President Suharto when the crisis erupted and there followed a drawn-out succession crisis, during which economic policy-making suffered. A key turning point in Indonesia was the decision to close several banks at the IMF's instigation, which triggered a run on other banks, as Indonesians questioned whether the government would, or indeed could, guarantee deposits.

Malaysia suffered significantly too. Although it did not have the short-term debt problem of the others, it did have a huge property overbuild and substantial excess capacity. Taiwan allowed its currency to slip in October 1997 despite large FX reserves, mainly because it wanted to remain competitive. But this put pressure on the Hong Kong dollar because investors reasoned that, if Taiwan could devalue, then Hong Kong might too. The Hong Kong authorities decided not to devalue but the high interest rates needed to defend the currency triggered a major fall in stock and property prices leading to a severe recession. In the absence of devaluation the result was price deflation, worsening the downturn. The Philippines had not enjoyed the 1990s boom like most of the other countries and correspondingly suffered less. Nevertheless the peso declined and the economy suffered a mild recession.

THE RUSSIAN CRISIS 1998

Fiscal problems lay at the heart of the Russian crisis, combined with political upheaval and capital flight. Perhaps the reason why some investors were surprised by the crisis was that they persisted in the expectation that the Russian government would do enough to satisfy the IMF and that the IMF could not 'give up' on Russia. This is a recurrent pattern in crises. Investors are well paid (in the form of interest differentials) to take the risk of government failure in 'last-ditch' crisis management and so are often willing to do so. It was the shock of the failure of that high-risk calculation which led to the reassessment of a variety of risks around the world in the summer of 1998 and the consequent problems for LTCM (Long Term Capital Management).

The Russian fiscal deficit was financed primarily by short-term domestic debt, which rose to some 14% of GDP in 1997. The 1996 liberalisation of the financial markets for foreign participation, combined with high interest rates and a stable exchange rate policy made Russian T-bills (GKOs) attractive to foreign investors. At the same time, Russian banks were borrowing abroad to finance their investment in GKOs (and later in the Russian stock market). Interest rates on state bonds fell dramatically as foreigners' holdings of GKOs reached $19 bn at the end of October 1997, more than the level of FX reserves at that time. By the summer of 1997, Russian banks were turning their attention to the stock market because returns on domestic T-bills were declining.

In the last week of October 1997 the stock market saw the first of several collapses as the Asian crisis intensified and political conflicts in the Russian government worsened. Pressure began to build on the rouble in the final quarter of 1997 and the first half of 1998 as foreign investors, anxious about high short-term debt, poor government revenues and weakening current account receipts began to sell GKOs and capital flowed out of the country. FX reserves fell from a peak of $20.4 bn in June 1997 to $10.5 bn at the end of January 1998, and interest rates jumped. The servicing burden of domestic debt started to rise as a result of higher borrowing costs, while the sharp fall in oil prices cut budget revenues, and planned privatisations failed to deliver required receipts.

In the background, capital flight was accelerating: net resident capital outflows were around $42 bn in 1997, equivalent to 9% of GDP, but the effect on reserves was masked by large non-resident capital inflows until the final quarter of 1997. The current account surplus shrank to 0.8% of GDP in 1997 as a result of falling energy receipts due to low oil prices.

In July 1998 the IMF agreed a $4.8 bn loan to Russia as part of an international aid package worth $22 bn, but by mid-August the flight from the GKO market had become a stampede. Purchases of government and corporate securities had been financed by short-term dollar borrowing, which made the banking sector highly vulnerable to the unstable rouble. The rapid decline in the value of these securities threw Russia's largest banks into distress. Liquidity suffered, forcing default on interbank payments and delay in the return of deposits to customers.

When Rub 4 bn of short-term government debt came due on 17 August 1998, the government, unable to meet payments, froze the local debt market, aiming for conversion into longer-term debt instruments. A 90-day moratorium was declared on rouble-denominated GKO and OFZ treasury bills, worth just under $31 bn, of which around one-third was held by foreigners. The rouble's crawling peg was abandoned and the currency fell from Rub 6.24/US$ at the end of July to Rub 16.1/US$ at the end of September, eventually stabilising at Rub 24.2/US$ in March 1999. In the stock market the Russian Traded Index, which had peaked at 1,032 in October 1997, touched 49 a year later. The aftermath of the moratorium on GKO debt led to the government's effective default, with little prospect for western investors of recovering more than a small fraction of the value of the debt.

The crisis had to a certain extent been foreseen, at least by some investors. However, many foreign investors in GKOs believed that, although the situation was unstable, they would be able to quit the market before the crisis hit. For others, stock market valuations were justified by Russia's huge natural resources potential. Finally, there had been a belief that, with successive governments, the reform programme would deliver on budget revenues and on structural adjustment.

THE BRAZIL CRISIS 1999

The confidence crisis in international markets after Russia's mid-1998 devaluation and debt default showed up Brazil's problems and put pressure on its managed exchange rate system. In the final quarter of 1998 and the early part of 1999, Brazil lost the confidence of international investors. The key factors are discussed below.

Key Factors in the Brazil Crisis

Weak External Accounts

Brazil's current account deficit widened to the equivalent of 4% of GDP in 1997 and 1998. Weak commodity prices and lower Asian demand did not help, but the main reason for the deteriorating trend was the political decision to favour a firm exchange rate to keep inflation low, rather than a weaker exchange rate to help export competitiveness. The Brazilian real was allowed to depreciate in nominal terms by more than the difference between local and international inflation. But in 1998 the real was probably 25% overvalued, and only 6% of this was being clawed back each year under the existing exchange rate regime. Brazil was gambling that markets would allow the further 2–3 years' leeway needed to fully correct the real's overvaluation.

Dependence on Foreign Finance

Foreign debt was large and growing and the Brazilian private sector, like its equivalent in South Korea, depended very heavily on short-term foreign debt. Total short-term debt rose from US$35 bn in the mid-1990s to US$65 bn by mid-1998. This made Brazil vulnerable to a loss of market access, and put a premium on pursuing policies that commanded market confidence.

Budget Deficit Problems

Macro-economic policy in Brazil improved dramatically with the introduction of the Real Plan in 1994, and inflation fell sharply. But most of this improvement was the result of very tight monetary policies. Brazil struggled to tackle its budget deficit, which climbed to 8% of GDP in 1998. Domestic debt climbed to 45–50% of GDP—levels last seen in Brazil in the mid-1980s. On top of the deteriorating trend, the short duration of the debt was also a major problem, with the average maturity only seven months. In the 1980s the debt burden was inflated away. In the 1990s, with the government committed to keeping inflation low, fiscal adjustment was essential to keep down the risk of domestic debt default.

President Cardoso tried to tackle fiscal reform, but progress was very patchy. The problem was politics; the opposition to reform of powerful pressure groups whose interests were institutionalised in Brazil's 1988 constitution (adopted in the flush of populism after the end of military rule). In addition, in an unfortunate parallel with Mexico in 1994, President Cardoso's resolve on fiscal reform weakened in 1998 ahead of the October presidential election. Brazil's fiscal credibility was hurt further by the government's loss of key Congressional votes on social security reform in December 1998, and the January 1999 moratorium on debt payments to the Federal government by the state of Minas Gerais.

Confidence plummeted, capital outflow increased, and interest rates were hiked, making the fiscal position even worse as most domestic debt was at floating rates. With virtually no progress on the fiscal side, an attempt to manage a small controlled devaluation on 13 January 1999 failed. Rather than bolstering confidence, the move had the opposite effect, and the floating of the currency was forced two days later. But the move caused no great surprise, many private sector borrowers had already hedged and there was no threat to the financial system.

The Consequences of Devaluation

Brazilian stocks lost half their value in the six months leading up to the float but then recovered sharply in local currency terms, though continuing to lag in dollar terms. However the overall impact of the Brazil crisis was much less than had been feared and, in a sense, marked the end of the emerging markets crisis as a global event. The real stabilised within three months, inflation stayed low and interest rates came down quickly. The recession proved relatively mild, with growth resuming by the middle of 1999. Following the devaluation the stock market quickly picked up in local currency terms and by end 1999 was at higher levels than before the crisis in dollar terms, though still well below its 1997 highs. The consequences of devaluation were not so bad in Brazil's case for four reasons.

The Private Sector was in Good Shape

Brazil's crisis was a public sector crisis rather than a private sector crisis. Compared to Asia's crisis economies, and Mexico in 1995, the Brazilian banking system was strong and, given the long build-up to the devaluation, most companies had already hedged their foreign currency exposure. The economic slowdown and devaluation undoubtedly caused severe problems for the Brazilian private sector, but there was no repeat of the credit crunches and systemic corporate sector distress which made Asia's recession so severe.

Monetary Policy was Kept Tight

A revamped monetary policy regime, under new Central Bank Governor Fraga, was quickly put in place and interest rates were initially increased very sharply. The hike could not be sustained for long without destabilising the government's fiscal accounts, but was essential to bolster confidence and stabilize the real. The strategy worked, and exchange rate stability was restored more quickly than in Asia.

IMF Support was Already in Place

Brazil still had substantial foreign reserves when it devalued and already had an IMF-led financial support package in place. The package had to be renegotiated, but this was easier than starting from scratch. As a result, a new policy framework was in place much more quickly than was the case in Mexico in 1995, and Asia in 1997–8, bolstering confidence and helping the real quickly to stabilise.

The Regional Contagion was Limited

Countries in Latin America export varied items, with commodities particularly important. This is very different to Asia where many countries export a similar mix of price-sensitive manufactured goods. Therefore, Brazil's devaluation did not produce the leapfrog devaluations which prolonged the crisis in Asia.

ARGENTINA'S CRISIS 2001–2

Argentina's crisis, which culminated in devaluation and default at the end of 2001 has been characterised as the 'slowest train wreck in history'. Many analysts and investors watched mesmerised as the government coasted towards disaster. In the second half of 2001 Argentina paid huge spreads on dollar loans, as lenders feared default, and faced very high interest rates on pesos, as the markets priced in devaluation. This made economic recovery impossible and further reinforced investor belief that policy was unsustainable.

Serious policy errors by the Argentine government made disaster increasingly inevitable during the course of 2001. Ironically, many of the policy errors were implemented by Domingo Cavallo, the man responsible for Argentina's improvement in the 1990s, who was brought back in as economy minister in early 2001.

Under Cavallo, Argentina made four key mistakes. First, the currency board system was changed, by moving towards a currency basket including the euro as well as the dollar. The move was designed to improve FX rate flexibility and competitiveness, but undermined investor confidence in the durability of the currency board, and backfired.

Secondly, Cavallo fatally undermined Argentina's previously strong banking system and independent central bank, two of its main achievements of the 1990s, by replacing the central bank governor, by easing reserve requirements, and by strong-arming local banks and pension funds into 'voluntarily' swapping their government bond holdings for lower-interest loans.

Thirdly, Cavallo appears to have been the person who ruled out full dollarisation in mid-2001. Full dollarisation would not have solved all of Argentina's problems but, by eliminating devaluation risk once-and-for-all, full dollarisation could have brought down local interest rates and, at least until September after which FX reserves depletion had gone too far, could have helped to stabilise the crisis.

Finally, Cavallo is also believed to have been the person who ruled out a formal pre-emptive default during talks with the IMF in the summer of 2001. Formal default and dollarisation in the third quarter of 2001 would still have left Argentina with a painful adjustment, but could probably have headed off the disaster that was to come.

Cavallo's policies eventually undermined the confidence of Argentines and triggered a run on banks and capital flight. The government eventually had no choice but to devalue as well as to default. Capital flight led to capital controls and limits on bank deposit withdrawals which, in a cash-based economy such as Argentina, deepened the recession and triggered the end game; social unrest and political crisis in December 2001. The government continued to make serious errors—for example, proposing to convert domesticly held dollar loans into peso loans at one-to-one, which automatically bankrupted the banking system.

The outlook for Argentina in early 2002 is very uncertain. Default, devaluation and the devastation of the banking system have completely shattered the confidence of Argentinians in their politicians and government. The breakdown in trust is most acute among the middle classes, usually a stabilising influence and the sector of society that helped to stabilise Asia during its crisis. In this environment it will be very difficult to stabilise the currency, and implement the tough reforms and still-tight fiscal policies needed to get new funding from foreign creditors and attract back Argentine capital flight. Argentina therefore appears to be among the worst of the crisis countries considered here, with perhaps only Indonesia in 1998 facing a comparable economic and political crisis.

Underlying Factors in Argentina's Crisis

Analysts differ as to the precise weighting of the underlying factors in the disaster. However, the elements are well understood and familiar from the problems in Russia and Brazil described above. One key element was Argentina's currency board system, called Convertibility, which fixed the peso at one dollar. When established in 1990 it pegged the peso at an undervalued rate and was designed to provide an anchor to bring down inflation. That was successful, but by the late 1990s most analysts (though not all) considered the peso to be overvalued. The economy did begin to adjust through deflation but, at first, the inflexible labour market limited the downward move, certainly compared with Hong Kong. By 2001 wages were moving down sharply in the private sector but it was too late. A flexible exchange rate system would have allowed Argentina to react to a weak economy by depreciating, taking some of the pressure out of the system.

Secondly, the currency board system made Argentina especially vulnerable to external shocks. In 2001 Argentina had to deal with Brazil's devaluation (35% in the first nine months of the year), the strong US dollar (which made the peso strong too and was a particular problem against the euro), the US recession, low agricultural prices and general market risk aversion.

Thirdly, Argentina had a legacy of very high foreign currency debt and had substantial short-term debt. The convertibility system and the substantial dollarisation of the economy (60% of the banking system) had encouraged the government to borrow in dollars even from domestic lenders, which had the effect of linking the exchange rate to the government's solvency. Lenders feared that a devaluation would bankrupt the government.

Fourthly, although the government did succeed in generating a primary surplus on the fiscal accounts (i.e. before interest payments), the surplus was not large enough to convince the markets that policy was sustainable. In addition the Federal government faced continuing difficulties in controlling the spending of some of the provinces. Hence the government was forced to borrow in dollars at interest rates of 15–20% p.a. when GDP in nominal terms was stagnant or falling. This in itself was widely seen as unsustainable, with total government debt already up to 50% of GDP.

Finally, the government was unable to stimulate economic growth. Argentina was in recession from 1999 onwards, reflecting the combination of high interest rates, lack of confidence and inadequate reforms. In the early 1990s Argentina had enjoyed a strong burst of growth based on the economic stability achieved through Convertibility and improved fiscal management, together with important structural reforms. These reforms petered out in the second half of the decade and growth ran out of steam. In general the 1990s reforms failed to create enough competition or enough new jobs, so that unemployment remained high throughout. In the utilities sector private monopolies replaced public sector monopolies.

Perhaps because Argentina's crisis was so widely foreseen, the final devaluation and default had little initial impact on other countries. Indeed, sovereign spreads tightened in early 2002 when it seemed that Brazil was only modestly impacted. Meanwhile Turkey, which had devalued in early 2001 and faced a tough task for several months rolling over its domestic debt, appeared to have pulled through the worst of its crisis by the time Argentina reached a climax.

REASSESSING THE RISKS OF EMERGING MARKETS

The severity of the economic recessions in Asia and Russia and the size of the market declines prompted a major reassessment of the risks in emerging markets. We look first at currency risk and then at various other factors that have received renewed attention since 1997.

Currency Risk

A dominant factor in the Asian crisis, as well as in Russia, Brazil and Argentina, was the dramatic fall in currencies. This is not a new phenomenon; the Chilean crisis of 1981 was similar in many respects, with an unexpected currency collapse having a devastating effect on the private sector. More recently the Mexican crisis of 1994–5 was triggered by a sudden devaluation.

In the Latin American debt crisis of 1982, however, currencies had a supporting role in the drama rather than taking the lead. In that crisis there was a sudden cessation of inflows due to a loss of confidence in Mexico's (and other countries') ability to pay and there was a withdrawal of short-term lines. But the crisis was triggered by the Mexican government's default, which shattered domestic and international confidence. Devaluation came as part of the adjustment process. The big difference was that most lenders had foreign currency obligations and the risk was (primarily) sovereign. Another difference worth noting is that the IMF's role then was usually to urge the necessity of devaluing when currencies were clearly overvalued. In contrast, during the Russian and Brazilian crises the IMF, at least publicly, found itself trying to support a particular parity. The IMF was in a similar position in Argentina in 2001.

Since the Asian crisis investors have regarded fixed exchange rate systems with suspicion. Stock market investors are vulnerable to the market decline if the central bank raises interest rates to defend the currency. They are also vulnerable if a devaluation follows which triggers an economic slowdown and asset price collapse as in Asia. However, devaluation is often good news for stock market investors because it stimulates the economy and therefore profits and also, after a time, may allow for lower interest rates. The Brazilian experience for example was much less damaging for stocks than the Asian experience. In dollar terms the Brazilian market was higher within four months of the devaluation.

These crises set off a major new chapter in the debate over which is the best system of exchange rates. The general conclusion was that if countries want to allow free capital movements they must choose between the extremes of a floating currency at one end of the spectrum and a currency board or dollarisation at the other end. It is more difficult to be in the middle of the spectrum trying to maintain a fixed exchange rate. The success of the Hong Kong peg underlines the importance of credibility if a fixed rate is to be maintained, though when the exchange rate is too high there can be plenty of pain. The floating rate option has now been adopted by most countries in Asia as well as Russia, Brazil and Argentina.

Arguably, if economic policy is sound and political stability is reasonably assured, it may not matter very much which system is chosen. Fixed systems should be relatively easy to sustain while floating rate systems will not be very volatile. In practice, many countries use fixed exchange rate systems to try to compensate for political uncertainty or unstable government finances, which is a recipe for periodic instability. Also the world economy is likely to continue to periodically generate unforeseen shocks which suggests that some form of floating or adjustable system may be superior.

One effect of the Asian crisis has been markedly to reduce inflation rates in most countries. The disinflationary effects of the recession and good monetary policy outweighed the inflationary impact of devaluation. If low inflation is maintained, the risks of investing in these countries should be reduced. In Brazil and even Russia, the inflationary impact of the devaluations has also been contained better than was feared. The outcome in Argentina is not yet clear.

Assessing Currency Vulnerability

Since 1997 there has been a considerable literature on the causes of currency crises and whether they can be predicted. Some studies have found patterns in the data and have argued that forecasting is indeed possible. One study, for example, using a sophisticated technique called logit analysis, found that the most important explanatory variables were foreign exchange reserves, exports and real GDP and, to a lesser extent, portfolio capital flows.

However, other researchers have emphasised that crises seem to vary enough over time that such models cannot be relied upon for future forecasting. A study by researchers at the IMF looked at three forecasting models, estimated before 1997, to see if they predicted the crisis and found that two out of three failed.[2]

One approach to assessing the extent of vulnerability is to look at various risk factors. These can be summarised in terms of two questions. Is a currency overvalued? Can it be defended? It is doubtful whether we can assess the extent of overvaluation with better than a potential error

---

[2] A. Berg and C. Pattillo (1999) 'Are currency crises predictable?' IMF Staff Papers, vol. 46, no. 2, p. 107.

of 10% in the result, which means that we can identify only grossly overvalued currencies (see Chapter 14). But if the recent export performance is poor and the current account deficit is large, that too would indicate that the currency may be overvalued. Whether the currency can be defended depends on two main factors: the level of foreign exchange reserves and whether interest rates can be held high for long enough. The ability to hold interest rates high depends on the strength of the economy, the importance of bank lending in the economy and the political situation facing the government. A strong economy, with low banking penetration and a government far from elections, may be able to absorb a rise in interest rates relatively easily. In contrast, a very weak economy or one with a large financial sector (e.g. Thailand) or a government soon facing elections is likely to try to avoid raising interest rates. Argentina was able to survive high interest rates for a very long time, but it was clear that, in the long run, the government's debt would be unsustainable.

Other Risk Factors

As well as currency risks the Asian crisis also highlighted the risk of private sector excesses, creating problems in emerging markets:

Excess Foreign Currency Debt Accumulation by the Private Sector

The upward trend in short-term debt in the mid-1990s was noted by many observers and there was some nervousness about the implications. The Bank of Thailand, for instance, addressed this problem very actively in 1995–6 and took steps to slow the pace of increase. In mid-1996 it produced a paper for foreign investors explaining the background to the increase and the measures it had taken. Short-term debt owed to banks started to fall from mid-1996, though remained high, at about the same level as foreign exchange reserves.

Excess Leverage in the Corporate Sector

For stock market investors leverage can be a useful way to boost earnings per share. Providing the return on capital is greater than the cost of borrowing, stockholders gain. However, in Asia this may not have been the rationale for the debt-financed growth of many companies. It seems more likely that companies were focused on growth rather than return on capital and may have preferred debt to equity in order to maintain control. However, the return on capital was already falling in most Asian countries well before the crisis, and the currency collapse raised domestic interest rates as well as the cost of servicing foreign currency loans.

Bubble Risks

It has often been said that bubbles can only be recognised after the event. It appears also to be true that some investors recognise bubbles but nevertheless participate, planning to exit before the bubble bursts. Certainly, with the benefit of hindsight we can see the bubble element in several of the Asian countries. The rapid rise in property prices, the frenetic pace of new business openings and the rapid rise in real earnings were all symptoms. Stock prices were not rising much after 1993, except in Hong Kong. In Russia, too, the rise in the stock market in 1996–7 turned out to be a bubble.

Recession Risks

Mild slowdowns or recessions are not necessarily too bad for stock market investors taking a long-term view, but the huge declines in GDP seen in many countries in 1997–8 had a similarly huge effect on stocks. The risk of such a devastating recession was presumably not sufficiently discounted in advance. The worst and longest lasting recessions occur when government policy worsens as a result of crisis, as for example in Indonesia since 1998 and Argentina in 2001–2. Going forward, investors are more likely to include that risk in their thinking.

Weak Banking Systems

In some countries, perhaps most notably Indonesia, the weakness of many banks was known well in advance of the crisis. In others, the full extent only came to light, or was only created, in the crisis. The root of the problem was that, in many countries, deregulation of the financial sector was too rapid and poorly sequenced. Non-bank financial companies, often owned by banks were at the forefront of the problems in some countries. Weak banks, of course, made the crisis worse. For investors, a key problem was that the financial sector was a large part of the investor universe. To take an extreme example, in 1994 the finance, insurance and real estate sectors in just two countries, Malaysia and Thailand, accounted for 6.7% of the *entire* IFCI index (all emerging countries). However, outside the Asian countries the problem for the banking sector has sometimes been a default by the government. For example, in Russia, Turkey and Argentina banks have been in difficulties because of a government debt crisis.

CONCLUSION: EMERGING MARKET FUNDAMENTALS

Assessing emerging economies uses many of the same tools as looking at industrial countries, but also requires a focus on debt, liquidity and politics. Many emerging countries grow faster than industrial countries and should offer good investment opportunities but political instability and periodic crises create serious risks. Since the Asian crisis investors are much more conscious of the potential downside risk for markets, the risk of fixed or quasi-fixed exchange rates, the risk that even very successful countries can suffer major recessions and, finally, the risk of contagion. The worst losses have been suffered in the countries that were the weakest politically, notably Indonesia and more recently Argentina.

Investors have become much more cautious over emerging market investments and there is considerable scepticism about their role in a portfolio. In the author's view this scepticism is exaggerated and probably represents an opportunity for investors. Issues for investors in emerging markets are taken up again in Chapter 16.

Part II

The Fundamentals of Major
Asset Classes

11

Money Markets

We start the analysis of markets by focusing on short maturity instruments such as deposits, money market paper, Treasury Bills and short-term bonds.

The appeal of short maturity investments is that they are liquid and of low risk. As such they are very important for companies and individuals with uneven cash flows who need to have money available at short notice. They are also important for people who do not need the cash today but might need it within a few days, weeks or months. By investing in short-term maturities, as opposed to overnight instruments, investors will usually obtain a slightly higher return. However, if they do need the money before the maturity date and therefore have to sell the instrument there is a chance of selling for less than the original investment.

In the context of long-term investment the main role of short-term instruments is to reduce risk. Short-term investments are less volatile than long-term investments and so the downside risk of a portfolio is reduced by holding more short-term instruments during periods of business-cycle uncertainty. But even within the range of instruments with maturities up to one year, there is plenty of scope for increasing return by guessing the direction of short-term interest rates. The discussion that follows focuses on this issue. There is also scope for increasing return by taking more risk with the issuer, which will be discussed in Chapter 12, in relation to the broader bond market.

WHAT DETERMINES THE SHORT-TERM YIELD CURVE?

The yield curve from overnight to one-year maturities is almost entirely determined by ex-pectations for overnight interest rates — in other words, expectations for the path of rates set by central banks. The level of yields at the other end of the yield curve, on long-term bonds, has only a small impact in itself. Guessing correctly what central banks will do requires an accurate forecast of the economy coupled with an understanding of how central banks will react. We can break this down into four questions.

1. How does Current Inflation Compare with the Target?

This is the easiest question, since we know the latest reported inflation rate and most central banks have explicit inflation targets. The exception is the Fed, but most economists believe the Fed has a range of 1–3% p.a. in mind. There is still some room for ambiguity here because the current inflation rate is sometimes distorted by special factors. For example, large changes in energy and food prices can swing the index up or down so that it may be better to look at a 'core' rate of inflation. Or, occasionally, distortions are caused by changes in taxes. Australia provided a dramatic example in 2000 when it substantially increased sales tax, offset by cuts in income taxes. As a result, inflation jumped to 4.5% p.a. in 2000 compared with 1.5% p.a. in 1999, but then fell back.

Of course central banks aim to be forward-looking so they are really interested in likely future inflation rather than the current rate. But if the current rate of inflation is outside the range or near one end or the other, this will affect their attitude. Obviously if inflation is already above the high end of their target range, or very close to it, the central bank is more likely to respond rapidly to news of stronger growth. Their view of likely future inflation is usually determined by their answer to the next two questions.

2. How Far is the Economy now from Full Employment and Full Capacity?

This question is important because it sets the framework for the way central bankers will react to news. For example, suppose we know that central bankers are very worried about the potential for rising wages because they believe that unemployment is already low in relation to its sustainable level (the so-called NAIRU or natural rate of unemployment). Then news of faster growth is likely to lead to a quick move towards raising interest rates. In contrast, if the economy is just recovering from a recession, news of stronger growth, even if it is well above the long-term sustainable trend growth rate, will be regarded in a relaxed way by central bankers, at least for a time.

Usually we have a fairly good idea of whether or not central bankers think we are near full capacity and full employment because they tell us. It is in their interest to warn about the dangers of overheating in order to justify raising interest rates, which is never popular. However, sometime members of monetary policy committees differ among themselves so that there is a degree of ambiguity. And, of course, full capacity and full employment are not necessarily single points (or the same point), and so there is generally a range of views.

For example, in 2000 US unemployment fell as low as 3.9%, the lowest level since the 1960s. This was widely seen as beyond the full employment level (or NAIRU) for the economy, as was confirmed by the gradual strengthening of wages during 1996–2000. In Euroland, the ECB clearly regarded the 8% unemployment rate reached in 2000 as the critical level. It had argued for the 8% rate several years before, when unemployment was still up at 10% and it regarded the acceleration in wage inflation during 2000 as proof. Hence its reluctance to cut interest rates hurriedly in 2001.

3. How does Current Growth Compare with Trend Growth?

As we saw in Chapter 1, the economy can be regarded as having a trend rate of growth, determined by productivity growth combined with the growth rate of labour force participation. The crucial question is: What do central bankers view as the trend? If actual growth is above trend and the economy is close to full capacity then the central bank is likely to move swiftly to slow the economy by raising interest rates.

The Fed came to the view in the late 1990s that trend growth in the US economy had accelerated to 3.5–4% p.a., up from the longstanding 2.5% trend. The main reason for this view was a belief that productivity growth had accelerated. In contrast the ECB held to the view that Euroland trend growth had not changed and remained at 2–2.5% p.a. Clearly when US growth slowed to only around 1% annualised during the first half of 2001, it was running below trend. But when Euroland's growth seemed to be slowing to about 2% in the same period, only just below trend, the ECB was relatively unworried, particularly with the rise in wages noted above.

We may not know for a few years whether the Fed is right in its new assessment of growth. Certainly growth for the years 1996–2000 conformed to the new rate, but that might not continue, particularly if investment is much slower in coming years. But as long as the Fed believes it, their monetary policy will be based on that. So a return to 3% p.a. growth in 2002–3, for example, will be regarded as still under trend, and therefore not a cause for concern. In contrast, the ECB would find 3% growth in Euroland in 2002–3 a major worry.

4. What is the Current Monetary Stance?

This is probably the hardest question to answer, but is particularly important for the short end of the yield curve. The point is that even if central bankers are worried by the answers to the first questions they also know that they have not yet seen the full results of any moves they made in the last 12 months. So they are always struggling with the question of whether recent moves have already done enough to slow or speed economic growth to the extent they desire. It is rare for interest rates to remain unchanged for more than a year.

There is no definitive way to answer this question; however, remember that in analysing the short-term our problem here is to predict how central banks will answer the question, not whether they have the right answer. (This is not true for other markets of course: whether or not the authorities get it right is crucial for the future of the stock market for example.) But economists within central banks and outside use a variety of techniques to try to answer the question. Most of these are analysed elsewhere in this book (see Chapters 2 and 5 in particular), so I will list them briefly here.

- Analysis of the most recent data on the economy to determine the latest direction. Key data are consumer spending including retail sales data and car sales, investment spending, e.g. durable goods orders, employment trends, etc.
- Scrutiny of leading indicators. The Conference Board's leading index or a similar index produced by the OECD Secretariat are watched very closely. But leading indicators do not always work, they sometimes reverse themselves and each cycle is different so there is always a chance that they are giving false signals.
- Analysis of whether the current level of interest rates is likely to be stimulatory in itself. There are various approaches here, including looking at real interest rates or monetary conditions indices (MCIs).
- Use of the Taylor Rule (see Chapter 5). This is a formula that makes broad sense theoretically and also seems to have matched actual central bank behaviour historically. However, there are different formulations in use and it requires assumptions about exactly which inflation indicators to use. It is also doubtful if the Taylor Rule can be accurate to less than 50 basis points (0.5%) at best, so it may be of limited use for money market players unless the economy is changing very quickly.

MONEY MARKETS IN 2001 IN FOUR COUNTRIES

To illustrate the issue for money market participants, this section looks at the position of four major central banks during 2001 and tries to answer the four main questions posed above.

The US Experience

We start with question 1 above: *How does current inflation compare with the target?* Although inflation accelerated in 2000–1, the core rate remained within the comfort zone (1–3% p.a.) at about 2.5% p.a., leaving the Fed free to cut rates rapidly in response to the economic slowdown.

However, in answer to the second question, capacity use fell sharply during the year, to levels not seen since the 1970s though unemployment remained low, probably below the NAIRU rate and therefore still threatening higher wages. But with GDP growth of only around 1% p.a. in the first half of 2001, and trend growth still reckoned to be 3.5% p.a., there was no need to hesitate in cutting rates during the year. Unemployment was expected to rise above the NAIRU rate. After the terrorist attacks on 11 September fears for the impact on business and consumer confidence easily justified further cuts. In the final quarter of 2001 business cut back more drastically on jobs and investment and gloom descended on the economy. At the same time the National Bureau of Economic Research announced that a recession had begun in March.

The fourth question was the hardest to answer, partly because the effects of the rate cuts made so far had yet to work through and partly because the extent of any further decline in business investment was uncertain. The Fed cut rates by three percentage points in the first eight months of 2001 to 3.5% p.a. in response to the slowdown. After 11 September rates were cut further to 1.75% p.a. Real interest rates were reduced by somewhat less because inflation accelerated, but nevertheless were effectively at zero by the end of the year, similar to the levels seen during 1992–3, when the economy was last weak. Monetary conditions indices suggested that there was rather less easing in 2001 than appeared, because the dollar *rose* in the first half of the year and stock prices fell. Nevertheless, by the end of 2001 it looked as though the easing cycle was over and the markets expected interest rates to begin rising in 2002.

In practice, because of the uncertainty and also because a key part of the Fed's job is to manage expectations, interest rate setting is more a path process than a mechanical calculation. For example, if economic data turn out to be weak in the second half of 2002 the Fed may well cut rates again even if they suspect it may not be necessary. This is because, given the uncertainty, they might rather err on the side of easing too much than too little. Note that their willingness to do this depends partly on their answer to the second question above, namely how far the economy is from full employment and full capacity. But in any case rates could be raised again quickly if the economy seemed to be rebounding very rapidly.

Euroland

Forecasting the ECB's moves has generally been more difficult than predicting the Fed for several reasons. One is that the ECB is new, without a track record. Another is that it is not very transparent because we do not know how policy members voted. A further reason is that the chairman Wim Duisenberg is not as dominant a figure as Alan Greenspan in the USA nor, at least according to some market commentators, as consistent. Perhaps not being such a dominant figure has made it difficult for him to take a lead and give the markets guidance over future policy.

Still, a careful review of the four questions above suggests that the ECB's policy in 2001 was well-grounded. First, inflation in 2001 was above the target of 0–2% p.a., with headline inflation at over 3% p.a. and core inflation of 2.5% p.a. Secondly, the economy was at full capacity and full employment as of mid-2001. And forecasts for much of the first half of the year suggested that growth was headed for a slowdown from an above-trend rate of 3.3% p.a. in 2000 to a growth rate of 2–2.5% p.a., close to trend. Finally, with interest rates of 4.5% p.a. in August 2001, versus inflation of 2.1% p.a. the ECB probably judged monetary policy to be close to neutral measured by real interest rates. Monetary Conditions Indices suggested an easing of policy due to the weakness of the euro. After 11 September the ECB eased further, to 3.5% p.a., reflecting both the new weakness coming from the USA and data showing that Euroland had slowed more than expected (even before 11 September). It gradually became clear that growth was slowing to well below trend, though still short of a full recession.

The UK

The Bank of England (BOE) has the most transparent process of all the main central banks. It has a symmetrical inflation target — in other words, inflation below the target (of 2.5% p.a.) is supposed to elicit an easing of policy, just as much as inflation above target. And the votes of the individual members of the Monetary Policy Committee are published a few weeks after the meeting.

The answers to the four standard questions above appeared to be as follows in 2001: (1) Inflation was just below target, though if the effects of oil and food prices were taken out, inflation would be lower. (2) Unemployment of 3.4% looked to be below any reasonable estimate of the NAIRU and there were some tentative signs of accelerating wages. (3) The economy was, however, moving away from full capacity, due to the weakness in the industrial sector. (4) GDP growth slowed to a 1.6% annual rate in the first half of 2001, somewhat below trend, which was believed to be about 2.5% p.a. Nevertheless, the BOE was concerned about strong government spending, due to the rapid increase in spending on public services. After 11 September there were fears that the economy would slow further though consumer spending remained surprisingly strong and government spending was expected to accelerate further.

The monetary stance was perhaps the hardest question to evaluate. With official interest rates at 5% p.a. in August 2001 and inflation of just under 2.5% p.a. the stance was probably close to neutral. However, house prices were rising rapidly and monetary growth had accelerated. Nevertheless following 11 September interest rates were cut further, to 4% p.a. By the end of the year, with the economy showing signs of picking up again, the markets began to anticipate rises in rates in 2002.

Japan

Japan had been suffering from deflation, i.e. a falling price level, since the late 1990s. The Bank of Japan (BOJ) had a target of stable prices which meant they would be happy to see a stronger economy and deflation going away. The economy had plenty of spare capacity and available labour after 10 years of lack-lustre growth. Moreover although trend growth was reckoned to be only 1–2% p.a. at most, given the slow rate of growth of the labour force, actual growth in 2001 was expected to be negative. The slowdown in Japan's economy was evident well before the slowdown in Europe because of Japan's dependence on regional trade and technology exports.

In the spring of 2001 the Bank of Japan cut rates back to close to zero (0.1% p.a.) in response to the weakening economy. Rates had been raised in 2000 when the economy seemed to be picking up, but now the BOJ bowed to the inevitable. The importance of this level in a deflating economy is that it enables banks to fund their balance sheets at virtually zero cost. Hence they can charge very low rates to their corporate borrowers, many of whom are in difficulties. The BOJ had been uncomfortable with this, because it reckoned that it would be better if the banks called in many of these loans — hence the rise in rates in 2000 despite the anaemic economic recovery at that time. In 2001 the BOJ was pinning its hopes on the government, under new Prime Minister Koizumi, to put more pressure on banks.

With the price level falling, real interest rates were still positive despite the very low nominal rate. The yen weakened in the first half of 2001, helping to ease monetary conditions but in mid-year showed some signs of picking up. To ease monetary policy further, the BOJ gradually increased its use of money *supply* techniques, since it could not do anything more to encourage money demand. This meant buying government paper directly to boost the monetary base. The BOJ had been doing this at a steady but slow rate for some time and it tried to use the carrot of more stimulus to pressure the government to move ahead on reforms. In practice reforms proved slow in being implemented and the BOJ eased policy anyway, with the main impact coming through a weakening of the yen.

MANAGING A MONEY MARKET PORTFOLIO

The key to beating the market (for example, a benchmark index) is to buy longer-term paper when the investor thinks interest rates will fall more than the market expects and short-term instruments when the investor expects rates to rise more than the market expects. For example, suppose 1-month paper is trading at a yield of 4% p.a. and 6-month paper is trading at 4.2% p.a. A fairly flat yield curve like this means that the market expects interest rates to remain fairly stable over the next six months.

Suppose the investor thinks that the Fed will cut interest rates in the next few months. If he buys 1-month paper now, when it has to be rolled over he might only get 3.75% p.a. in one month and, if he sticks to 1-month paper, only 3.5% p.a. in the following month. If, however, he buys the 6-month paper he will enjoy the full 4.2% p.a. yield for the whole six months and only then need to accept a lower yield. In contrast, if he expects interest rates to be raised, it would be best to accept the 4% p.a. yield for one month. In a month's time he should be able to roll over and buy paper with a higher yield.

US INTEREST RATES IN 2000–1

Referring to Figure 11.1 we can see how a manager who successfully forecast short-term rates, ahead of the market, could outperform. At the beginning of 2000 1-month US interest rates (eurodollar rates here, i.e. the interbank interest rates on dollars in London) stood at about 5.7% p.a. with the 6-month yield about 40 basis points higher at 6.1% p.a. At this point the market was expecting a small further increase in rates, hence the upward slope in the curve of about 40 basis points. The best place for the money manager was therefore at the short end of the curve because by May he could buy 1-month paper at 6.5% p.a. and 6-month paper at 6.8% p.a.

Early summer 2000 was in fact the peak for US interest rates. At that point expectations of further rate rises began to fade and 6-month interest rates fell gradually in the second half of the year even though 1-month rates were stable, with the Fed on hold at this time (see the declining spread in the chart). The investor who bought 6-month paper in May therefore enjoyed a yield of 6.8% p.a. while rolling over 1-month paper for the second half of the year would have provided a yield of only about 6.6% p.a.

The real gains though came to the investor who locked in 6-month rates in November, reduced slightly then to 6.7% p.a., but still above 1-month rates of 6.5% p.a. In the first months of 2001 when interest rates began to fall sharply, as the Fed cut rates, 1-month rates plummeted. This meant that an investment strategy of rolling over 1-month paper would have seen the yield obtained drop steadily to only 4% p.a. by the following May (six months on) with an average

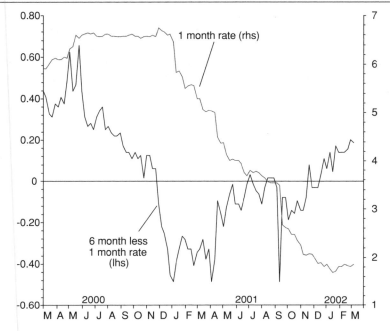

Figure 11.1   US short rates and the yield curve
Source: Thomson Datastream

yield of only just over 5% p.a. But note, too, that if the investor did not lock in the 6-month rates in November, and bought 6-month paper a few weeks later, the advantage was substantially reduced. By early January 6-month paper yielded under 5.5% p.a., less than 1-month paper as the slowing economy convinced investors that the Fed would cut rates much further. The best yields were gained, as usual, by investors who anticipated Fed action ahead of the market.

By the middle of 2001 6-month yields had returned to be nearly in line with 1-month yields, as investors foresaw the end of Fed easing. Hence the yield curve returned to flat, with both 1-month and 6-month yields dropping together at a slower pace. Meanwhile the best returns were enjoyed by the investor who bought 12-month paper in November 2000. He enjoyed his yield of 6.6% throughout the year. Only in November 2001 would he have had to roll over his investment at the lower yield.

CONCLUSION: THE FUNDAMENTALS OF MONEY MARKETS

Outperforming the market in short-term maturities is about correctly anticipating the next moves of the central bank. These moves come in response to the central banks' assessment of the answers to four questions.

- Where is inflation versus the target?
- Where is the economy in relation to full employment and full capacity?
- Where is economic growth going relative to trend?
- What is the current stance of monetary policy?

As we have seen, the last question is often the most difficult to answer, particularly when interest rates have been moved significantly in recent months, because of the lag before interest rate changes impact on the economy. At other times the third question — where is economic growth going? — is typically the most difficult. But investors only have to anticipate what the central bank thinks, not what will actually happen. Of course actual data and outcomes will influence the central bank at its next meeting but it is still their expectations that determine rates.

12
Bond Markets

The word bond covers a variety of instruments but we focus here on its conventional and most common meaning — that is, a marketable security which is sold to investors with a fixed face value repayable on maturity and fixed coupon payments payable periodically during the life of the bond (e.g. twice a year). Bonds are also called fixed income instruments, for obvious reasons. Most other types of bonds are variants on this basic type, although there are some which are really a mixture of equities and bonds, such as convertible bonds. Most of the discussion here is related to government bonds, for example Treasury bonds in the USA or Gilts in the UK. The same basic principles apply to bonds issued by private issuers except that there is then a degree of credit risk involved too.

PRICE IS INVERSELY RELATED TO YIELD

To understand bonds it is essential to know that a rise in yield is equivalent to a fall in the price of the bond and vice versa. The following paragraph explains the relationship between price and yield with an example. Those who are familiar with this concept should move to the next section.

Imagine a new 10-year bond successfully sold to the market at $100, with a face value of $100 (i.e. it will pay $100 on maturity) and a promised interest payment of $10 each year (the coupon) until then. The yield of this bond is 10% ($10 divided by $100). Now suppose long-term interest rates in the market fall and the next 10-year bond issue (also issued at $100 and paying $100 on maturity) can be sold paying a coupon of only $8 each year. We can then say that long-term interest rates or bond yields have fallen to 8% p.a. What will have happened to the price of the first bond issued? Since it still pays $10 p.a. it will be worth more than $100 now since it gives the holder $10 p.a. in income rather than $8. In fact its price will rise so that it too is yielding 8%. The exact price is a precise calculation depending on how long the bond has to run before maturity.

A rise in yield is therefore good news for an investor waiting to buy, because he can buy any given bond cheaper than before and enjoy a higher interest rate. But it is bad news if it occurs *after* he has bought because the price will have fallen. Of course if he holds the bond to maturity he still gets a payment of the face value and he still gets all the coupon payments. But if he wants to sell before maturity the price is lower. Also, if he had waited longer to buy that bond it would have cost him less.

Note that the price at which a bond is first sold to investors is usually not exactly the same as the face value. This is simply because the documentation has to be prepared beforehand, with a fixed coupon payment. And long-term yields are moving around all the time, like any market. Hence the actual price paid, typically through an auction of some kind, is almost the same as the face value.

Figure 12.1 US Treasury yields: the long view
Source: Thomson Datastream

TWO APPROACHES TO ANALYSING YIELDS

Analysis of bonds focuses on the yield (technically the yield to maturity) because this can be related to other interest rates and also the inflation rate and the economic growth rate. There are two ways of looking at a bond yield.

Expectations of Future Short Rates

One approach is to treat the yield as an average of expected future short-term interest rates plus a risk premium. Consider a two-year Treasury instrument for simplicity. Its yield can be viewed as an average of the current 3-month Treasury Bill rate and expectations of where 3-month rates will be over the following 21 months. There should also be a small premium for what is called the horizon risk, essentially the fact that the investor who buys this security is committing himself now and could lose out if short-term interest rates rise unexpectedly.

If short-term interest rates are expected to rise, the yield curve will be relatively steep, with two-year yields significantly above today's 3-month Treasury Bill rates. Sometimes, however, when short-term rates are particularly high because the central bank is trying to slow the economy to control inflation, the markets will anticipate that interest rates will come down so that two-year bond yields will be below the 3-month rates. The yield curve is then said to be inverted (see below).

Real Yield plus Inflation Expectations

The second way of looking at bond yields is to break down the yield into two components, the so-called 'real' bond yield, linked to GDP and the supply and demand for capital, and an estimate of inflation expectations. This enables the investor to take a view on whether bonds are cheap or expensive according to his view on whether the markets are too optimistic or too pessimistic on real yields and inflation.

In several countries, including the USA, the UK, Australia and Canada, a 'real' yield actually exists in the market in the form of the yield on an inflation-indexed bond. These instruments pay a fixed coupon plus an adjustment for the rise in the consumer price index. In principle this allows us to compare the yield of these indexed bonds with the yield on similar dated ordinary bonds to give an idea of expected inflation. In practice tax effects and the limited size of the market (particularly in the USA) may distort the yields somewhat. This type of bond is discussed further below.

In general, however, distinguishing the real yield from inflation expectations is a matter of judgement, arrived at by guessing what the markets expect for inflation. Sometimes analysts use the latest inflation rate for this purpose, but that is obviously flawed since very often the markets anticipate lower or higher inflation than current levels. Another alternative is to use forecasts of inflation, but usually these do not go out beyond one or two years and yet bond buyers must consider up to a 10-year horizon or longer.

Another approach is to decide whether or not the central bank is likely to meet its inflation target over the long run. If the answer is yes, then this may give an idea of the likely outcome for inflation. In principle this should be easiest for the UK, which has a symmetrical inflation target of 2.5%. In practice, on a 10-year view, there are always uncertainties. In the UK's case the greatest uncertainty is whether it will join EMU during that period. For other countries there is always a chance that they may miss the target on the downside, or even go through a period of deflation. Nor can missing the target on the high side be dismissed. For example, the ECB clearly exceeded its inflation target in 2001. It is possible that the ECB will try to undershoot the target on the downside in future years, but it is more likely that it will treat the overshoot as 'water under the bridge'.

The Risk Premium

The expected inflation component of a bond yield can be further divided into the expectations of inflation itself and a risk premium against those expectations being too optimistic. Suppose investors' best guess is that US inflation will average 2.5% p.a. over the long term. They may still require a risk premium of say 0.5% or 1% p.a. (the problem is that we do not know exactly what) to compensate for the possibility that inflation could be higher. The risk premium has almost certainly fallen during the last 10 years, due to the lower rate of inflation and the stronger institutional position of central banks.

Summary

The two components of bond yields, the real part and the inflation expectations, vary according to economic developments. So do short-term interest rates, which are determined by central banks, and expectations for short-term rates, which are determined by markets. The analysis below looks at yields in relation to economic growth, inflation, monetary policy, fiscal policy, and the economic cycle.

BONDS AND ECONOMIC GROWTH

News of faster economic growth generally depresses bond prices, i.e. raises bond yields. This can be seen as reflecting a change in expectations for short-term rates in the future: the markets expect that the government will raise short-term interest rates to combat inflation. Alternatively, using the second approach above, stronger growth can be seen as working partly through expectations of higher inflation and partly through higher real interest rates because of an increase in demand for funds as businesses and consumers borrow more.

However, if the news of stronger growth comes through in the recovery stage of the business cycle or even during the early upswing phase, its effect on raising bond yields will be less. This is because there is less immediate inflation risk and also the central bank may be less inclined to respond with higher interest rates.

Faster economic growth usually also means that the government budget deficit will be smaller because of improved tax revenues and lower unemployment benefit payments. But although this means less bond issuance and therefore should help bonds, the effect is usually outweighed by the negative factors. The reason for this is that the level of bond yields is not just a price at which the market will accept this year's new issuance, but a price that the market demands for holding the *total* accumulated stock of debt. Any one year's issuance is usually small in relation to the total debt outstanding.

BONDS AND INFLATION

News of higher inflation is bad for bonds. If the economy is growing fast, and especially if it is close to full employment and full capacity, then the markets will be expecting a rise in inflation at some point. If inflation is slow to pick up, as it was in the USA in the 1990s for example, the bond markets will be relieved but are unlikely to rally strongly as long as the economy stays strong.

Of course for long-term bonds the inflation rate over the next year or two is only part of the problem since the investor is taking a bet over 10 years or more. The markets have to take a view on where governments and central banks will allow inflation to go in the long run. In the 1970s bond market investors lost out heavily because they failed to appreciate that the authorities would, in the interests of employment and short-term economic growth, allow a major inflation to develop from the rise in oil prices. Between 1972 and 1982 inflation averaged 8.7% p.a. in the USA, 14.1% in the UK and 5.1% in Germany. Bond yields lagged behind inflation for much of the decade, especially in the UK and the USA.

Around 1980, led by the Federal Reserve chairman Paul Volcker and Mrs. Thatcher's new Conservative government in the UK, an altogether tougher approach to inflation appeared. Between 1982 and 1992 inflation was held to an average 3.8% p.a. in the USA, 5.4% in the UK and 2.2% in Germany. In the most recent 10-year period, to 2001, inflation has been even lower, averaging 3.1% p.a. in the USA, 3.2% p.a. in the UK and 2.7% p.a. in Germany.

Many people believe that the new aversion to inflation is here to stay and that the central banks will not allow inflation to return to the levels seen in the 1970s. In recent years central banks have been given more independence in monetary policy. At the same time central bankers themselves have become stronger in their belief that keeping inflation low is the central objective of monetary policy, and indeed, for many, the only objective. The 'ideal' target for inflation still differs somewhat between the English-speaking countries and continental Europe. Whereas the ECB has an inflation target of 0–2% p.a., which perhaps implies they will achieve 1% or 1.5% over the long run, the UK has an explicit target of 2.5% p.a. while the USA also seems to be comfortable with inflation of above 2%.

Still, for the long-term investor, the question is whether this new aversion to inflation will really last. Faced with prolonged slow growth or high unemployment or social unrest, can governments and central banks be relied upon not to stoke the inflationary fires? And the really long-term investor has to take into account the risk of wars, which usually bring inflation. Moreover, so far no central bank has promised to target the price *level* itself, which means that if there is a period of sudden inflation, there is no commitment to bring the price level back down again.

INFLATION-INDEXED BONDS

Government bonds with protection against inflation are now available in several countries, including the USA. Since the early 1980s investors in the UK have had the choice of buying Index-Linked Gilts (ILGs). In 1997 the USA introduced Treasury Inflation Protection Securities, or TIPs. These provide a fixed coupon (the real portion) plus an adjustment equal to the change in the consumer price index. To take a simple example, if a one-year indexed bond is sold with a coupon of 3%, the investor will receive, at the end of the year, this 3% plus the rise in the consumer price index over the same period.

Inflation-indexed bonds are interesting for two reasons. First, they represent, in principle, the perfect risk-free asset since, as opposed to conventional bonds, there is no risk from unexpected inflation. Secondly, their yield can be compared with conventional bonds to derive a view of expected long-term inflation. For example, in early 2002 10-year TIPs were yielding 3.4% p.a. compared to a yield on conventional bonds of 5.3% p.a. This suggests that the bond market is forecasting long-term inflation of 1.9% p.a. The true inflation expectation could be slightly less than 1.9% p.a. because there should be a risk premium on conventional bonds to allow for the risk of much higher inflation. As described above, this risk premium is believed to have fallen over the last decade.

In practice, most analysts are cautious about interpreting US TIPs in this way, because the market is small and relatively new. In the UK, ILGs are a substantial part of the bonds outstanding, around one-fifth, and are watched more closely. Also the UK market has been through two full economic cycles and has seen inflation range from 1.5 to 10% p.a.

Figure 12.2 shows the yield on two British government bonds. The top line is the conventional bond yield showing the decline from yields of around 10% in the late 1980s to about 5% in 2001. The lower line shows the yield on ILGs, which is a 'real' interest rate. Investors in these bonds receive this yield plus an extra amount to compensate for the rise in inflation each year. Notice that the real yield declined between the 1980s and 1990s. Also the spread between the two yields narrowed as inflation declined.

The yield on ILGs (the real component) varies with three factors. First, it goes up and down with the real economy and particularly with the level of short-term interest rates. If real yields generally are high, because the economy is strong, then real yields on ILGs will be higher. Secondly, yields fall if inflation accelerates because these securities become relatively more attractive if inflation is volatile. In other words, their value in reducing inflation risk is higher. Finally, as with all assets the yield can vary according to supply and demand. The long-term decline in UK real yields probably had partly to do with the emergence of a budget surplus in the UK in the late 1990s, which limited the supply of these bonds.

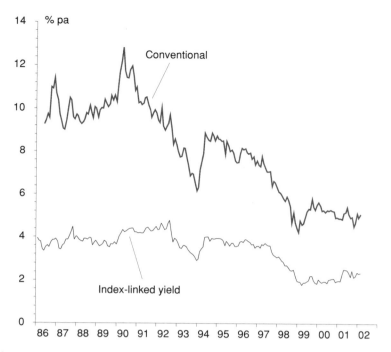

Figure 12.2 UK bond yields
Source: Thomson Datastream

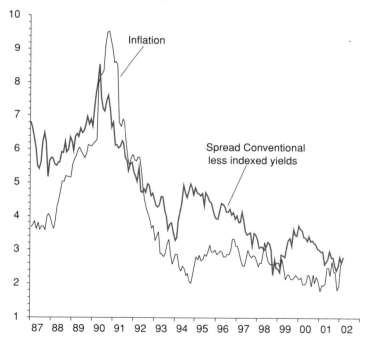

Figure 12.3 UK real bond yield and inflation
Source: Thomson Datastream

In Figure 12.3 the spread between the conventional yield and the indexed yield is plotted against actual inflation as they move down broadly in line. But notice that during the inflation peak of 1990 the spread was less than the actual inflation rate because investors judged that inflation would not stay at that high level and would subsequently decline, given the slowdown in the economy. The two lines converged again in 1998 during the LTCM crisis. Again the market anticipated a possible recession at that time due to the market turmoil, which would have brought UK inflation lower. But in 1994–6, and again in 1999–2000, the spread diverged from actual inflation as the market worried that the strong economic growth at that time could push inflation up again.

Inflation-indexed bonds are not very exciting for investors precisely because they are the ultimate risk-free asset. As such, over the long term they should be expected to provide the lowest return for similar maturity investments. By taking more risk, whether in conventional bonds or in stocks or other assets, investors should hope to make a higher return. Of course they might not and that is the risk. But index-linked bonds are particularly attractive in periods of uncertainty as an alternative to cash, and especially in periods of rising inflation.

BONDS AND MONETARY POLICY

A hike in short-term interest rates has two contradictory effects on bond investors' perceptions. First, it is liable to raise expectations of the future level of short-term interest rates because it implies that the authorities are concerned about the outlook for inflation and could therefore raise rates further. This usually means that the front end of the yield curve at least (say out to three years) will rise.

Secondly, it may lower expectations for future inflation because it is expected to slow the economy. This should help the longer end of the yield curve. But if the rise in short rates is not thought to be large enough to slow the economy, then inflation expectations could rise.

The net result then should be to *raise* the short end of the yield curve but *lower* the long bond yield. In practice, the first effect is fairly reliable but the direction of the long bond yield is much less so. Long bond yields frequently rise in response to a rate increase, though not by as much. One reason is that the rate rise itself indicates central bank concern about the risk of an overheating economy. Since episodes of rate increases often last for a year or more, bond investors sometimes have to revise their view of the likely path of interest rates and this can impact even on long-term bonds. It is particularly likely to do so if the yield curve looks set to go inverted. This is because it significantly affects the attraction of bonds for financial institutions which must finance the bonds out of short-term deposits, and therefore may face a negative 'carry', i.e. the cost of carrying the bonds on their balance sheet.

CHANGES IN THE YIELD CURVE

The yield curve is a chart of the whole range of yields at different maturities. A so-called 'normal' yield curve shows rising yields for longer-term bonds relative to short-term bonds. The reason is that, in order to be prepared to buy long-term bonds, investors need a premium over shorter-term bonds, sometimes called the 'horizon' premium or the 'bond maturity' premium. The exact slope varies during the economic cycle as discussed below and also depends on long-term expectations for growth and inflation. It can also vary according to government policy on the issuance of different maturities of bonds.

The shape of the yield curve is one of the most useful ways to determine both the status of monetary policy and the stage of the cycle. When it is inverted strongly (i.e. short rates well above long yields) then monetary policy is particularly tight. The fact that bond yields are lower than short rates is saying that the markets expect the level of short-term interest rates to slow the economy in time, allowing inflation and interest rates to come down. In contrast, when the curve is particularly steeply upward sloping, with short-term interest rates well below long-term interest rates, this is likely to be a sign of monetary ease (most often seen during recessions or the early stages of recovery). The central bank is trying to boost the economy and the bond markets are concerned that interest rates will have to rise soon.

BONDS AND FISCAL POLICY

Governments issue bonds to finance budget deficits and the relationship between bond yields and government fiscal policy is very important. Generally speaking we would expect that if governments issue more bonds, because public finances are showing a larger deficit, then they will have to offer investors a higher yield to take on those bonds. In other words a large fiscal deficit should be associated with higher bond yields.

However, the fact that governments borrow more in one year than in the previous year does not significantly change the stock of government debt outstanding. Moreover, government deficits tend to be highest just when other borrowings are lowest. Deficits are typically large at a time of recession when tax receipts are down and payments for unemployment benefit, etc., are higher. But it is at just this time that business investment is weak and savings are high (because consumers are saving for fear of unemployment). Hence there may actually be strong demand for government paper.

Also, quite often in recessions, short-term interest rates are low and the yield curve is steeply upward sloping. This makes holding bonds relatively attractive compared with deposits or Treasury Bills, because the central bank is trying to generate recovery. In the US recession in the early 1990s, a substantial part of bond issuance was taken up by banks, taking advantage of the steeply upward sloping yield curve. Hence, in a cyclical time frame, it is not clear that a rising budget deficit leads to higher bond yields. A similar situation has existed for many years in Japan. Very large-scale government bond issuance is snapped up by banks and other financial institutions because Japan continues to generate large savings but the economy is growing too slowly to offer enough investment opportunities.

However, bond yields are influenced by long-run expectations of whether or not the government is running a sound fiscal policy. An unsound fiscal policy may raise the possibility of default in the extreme case. In the late 1990s a number of countries, led by the USA, ran large government surpluses and therefore bought back their government debt. Since many institutions seek long-term risk-free assets the yields on the remaining government debt were pushed down in response to excess demand. In contrast the Japanese government's fiscal position worsened considerably in recent years and some analysts believe it could eventually become a major problem.

JUDGING THE SOUNDNESS OF FISCAL POLICY

In considering whether or not fiscal policy is sound, the best analytical approach is to look at the level of government debt and its trend direction. The maximum ratio of government debt to GDP laid down in the Maastricht Treaty for economic and monetary union in Europe was

60%. As an exact number, this is arbitrary but it has become recognised as a reasonable level to consider as the limit to prudence, at least for developed countries.

Consider the case of a country with a ratio of debt to GDP of 100% (for example, Japan in 1998, though its ratio is now up to over 130%). If the budget deficit is running at 10% of GDP, then total debt will rise by 10% that year. Unless GDP itself, including both the real component and inflation, rises by more than 10% then the debt ratio will rise. For example, if inflation is 3% and growth 2% then nominal GDP will rise by only 5% and in one year's time the debt ratio will be approximately 105% of GDP (110 divided by 105).

It is easy to see that, if debt/GDP is 100%, the debt level will fall as long as the deficit as a percentage of GDP is less than GDP growth (including inflation). In this example, if the deficit is 2% while nominal GDP rises 5% then the debt ratio will fall to approximately 97% (102 divided by 105). Note the temptation here for governments to use higher inflation to control the ratio.

For countries with high debt, lower interest rates are an important factor in reducing the budget deficit. If the average interest rate paid by the government on its debt drops from 10% to 8% then the budget deficit itself, even without any reduction in other expenditures or increases in taxation, will drop to 8% too (still assuming a 100% debt/GDP ratio). This makes it possible for countries to set up a virtuous cycle. If expenditure can be cut and taxes raised then, not only will the deficit before interest payments (known as the primary balance) fall, but interest rates are likely to fall too because of the slowdown in the economy, adding to the decline in the budget deficit. A downside to this situation is that nominal GDP growth may also be weaker as the real component declines and inflation declines too.

In practice, reducing a debt ratio of 100% down to a healthy level like 50% is likely to take 10 years or more. Italy began on this path in the mid-1990s in its determination to join the European single currency. At that time its debt/GDP ratio was 124%. In 2001 with the help of reasonable economic growth, a rising primary budget surplus and lower interest rates (especially since becoming part of EMU), the ratio has been reduced to about 105%. Something to watch is whether, now that Italy is safely in EMU, the fiscal discipline continues or whether Italy slips back into its old ways and allows the debt ratio to rise again. It is committed to reducing the ratio further but an economic slowdown or economic pressures could make that difficult.

Most major countries have a ratio of debt to GDP of nearer 50% and here the arithmetic for controlling the ratio works out rather differently. Consider a country where the budget deficit is 10% of GDP and nominal GDP is rising 5%. At the end of the year debt will be at 60, while GDP will be at 105, giving a new ratio of 57%. Even keeping the deficit to GDP ratio the same as the growth rate of nominal GDP is not good enough. Debt would be at 55 and GDP at 105, which is equal to a rise in the debt ratio to 52.4%. In fact to keep the debt ratio at 50% the ratio of the budget deficit to GDP must be no more than half the rate of growth of nominal GDP. It was this arithmetic which made debt ratios rise sharply in both Europe and the USA in the early 1990s. In general, the problem of government debt is potentially greater in a low-inflation environment.

WHY DOES A HIGH DEBT MATTER?

A rapid rise in debt worries the markets because governments may find it more and more difficult to manage the public finances. In the extreme case bond-holders start to fear that the government will either default (wholly or partially) or deliberately push up the rate of inflation so that the real value of outstanding bonds dwindles.

There is no single level at which the debt ratio becomes critical, but beyond 100% the pressure to reduce it becomes more and more substantial, leaving governments with very few options. Bond markets then have to worry whether the government has the political strength to push through the inevitable tax rises and spending cuts that are implied.

Later in this century most countries will face a serious problem from ageing populations. Commitments to paying state pensions (notably in continental Europe) and to meeting rising demands on health care (particularly in the USA) mean that, as the population of retired people increases in the next 20–30 years, the demands on government spending will rise substantially.

DEBT: THE CASE OF JAPAN

The combination of very slow economic growth, low inflation and high government deficits has put Japan's government debt dramatically higher over the last 10 years. From a ratio of 61% in 1991 gross government debt reached 130.5% in 2001 and is projected to continue to rise. *Net* debt is much lower, at about 57% of GDP but the difference is largely bonds held by government agencies. Unfortunately, as the population ages these agencies will start to run a deficit and will need to cash in those bonds to pay pensions, etc. Hence the gross figure is the relevant one. Some analysts believe that even this figure understates the true liabilities of the state. There seem to be various government agencies not included. Moreover the poor condition of the banking system suggests that banks may require more government funds at some point.

For 2002 the OECD projects that Japan will run a financial deficit of 6.7% of GDP and the debt ratio will rise to 141%. The primary balance is in deficit to the tune of 5.4% of GDP. The difference between the financial deficit and the primary deficit is very small because interest rates are already so low. Nominal GDP is likely to fall with a decline in both real GDP and the price level. So far this high debt level has not caused a crisis. In fact bond yields are at low levels with 10-year yields around 1.5% p.a. The reason is that, with the price level falling, these yields are still attractive in real terms and both households and businesses have substantial savings that they want to put somewhere safe.

Why do Japanese investors regard these assets as safe, given the high level of debt and the prospect that it will rise further? Conventional analysis suggests that there should be a rising risk of either default or inflation. The reason that investors do not expect either is that they are convinced that the eventual solution will be higher taxes and/or lower government spending. The share of taxes in GDP in Japan is just under 40%, higher than the USA but lower than most European countries. And government spending on investment has been very high in recent years, deliberately to spur the economy, so there is room for cutting here. Unfortunately this expectation is so wide-spread that it is one reason why Japanese consumers are fairly cautious about spending. They do not expect high pensions from the government and they fear higher taxes at some point. This makes it more difficult for the economy to pick up.

BONDS AND THE CYCLE

All the linkages discussed above play a role in the behaviour of bonds during the cycle. In the *recovery* phase of the cycle, inflation is likely to be low and falling and short-term interest rates are still low as the central bank is trying to encourage recovery. Bond yields may rise initially when the recovery first emerges but then tend to stabilise or fall a little helped by declining inflation expectations and low real rates. The yield curve is normally upward sloping.

During the *early upswing* phase of the cycle, bond yields usually stop falling and might start to edge up as the market anticipates higher inflation in the near future and real rates rise with increased borrowing in the economy. Also the authorities may be beginning to nudge up short-term interest rates, particularly if they were previously at a low level.

During the *late upswing* phase of the cycle, inflation is rising and the central bank is pushing up interest rates to try to cool the economy down. Real rates too are often high because borrowing reaches a peak. Bond yields will rise but how much depends on how overheated the economy has become and how quickly the markets expect the central bank to slow the economy.

In the fourth stage of the cycle, where the *economy slows* or goes into recession, bond yields are likely to peak and come down. The key point is that, with the economy going into recession, there will be hopes of lower inflation and therefore the expected inflation component should be coming down. At the same time a weaker economy points to lower demands on funds (lower real rates) and also lower short-term interest rates as time goes on. Bond yields will nearly always begin to fall before short-term interest rates. However, in this phase, because the yield curve is typically inverted, with short-term interest rates above bond yields, bond yields may still be constrained from declining. The problem is that although banks or other institutions holding bonds may be looking forward to capital gains, they will have to fund those bonds at a loss through the higher short-term interest rates.

The final stage of the cycle, *recession*, is usually the best period for bond markets. Once a recession takes hold the markets know that it will take some time to work through and will exert strong downward pressure on inflation. The prospect of lower inflation and lower interest rates means that bond yields will be coming down. At this stage, however, the bond markets will be all the time wondering how soon the recovery will come and how low they can expect inflation to fall.

This view of the cycle may appear to offer an easy way to make money. The problems are that it is always uncertain as to how long each phase will last and how intense it will be. The markets will already have factored in all the *existing* news on the state of the cycle. For example, during the early stages of the upswing, it is very uncertain as to whether the upswing will in fact last several years, eventually bringing severe overheating and high inflation, or whether it will be a short upswing with very little rise in inflation.

Similarly, during the recession stage it is very hard to know whether the recovery will happen next month or in two years' time. If it occurs next month, then the low for inflation is only a year or so away. If the recovery itself is still a year off, then inflation will be likely to fall for another year and not reach its low for more than two years. Bond yields can fall further.

In 1994 bond markets suffered a severe crash everywhere and yet, while the US economy was probably moving into the late upswing phase of the cycle, Germany and Japan were only just entering the recovery phase. This demonstrates the uncertainty involved in trying to use analysis of the cycle to time entry into bonds. What seems to have happened in the USA is that a normal two-year bear market was telescoped into a few months. The simultaneous crash in Europe demonstrated the increasing internationalisation of the bond markets.

INTRODUCING CREDIT RISK

Non-government bond issues are a large and growing sector of the market and are of increasing interest to investors looking for higher returns. For investors the attraction is that these issues pay higher yields than on government debt, but have less risk than an equity investment. However, the higher the yield generally the higher the risk and from time to time even well-rated issuers can default. Enron, for example, had been regarded highly until late in 2001, just weeks before it defaulted.

Movements in corporate bond yields can be split into two components: changes in government bond yields and changes in the spread of corporate bonds over Treasuries. We have already analysed the behaviour of government bond yields. Changes in spread are ultimately linked to changes in perception of the risk of default. As with equities this can be approached from the 'bottom up', i.e. aggregating the risk of all the corporate bonds assessed individually. In this book we look at the spread on a 'top down' basis, looking for links with the fundamental macro-economic environment.

RATING AGENCIES

Central to the study of non-government bonds as well as bonds issued by sovereigns other than AAA issues is the ratings provided by the various agencies. The best known are probably Moody's, Standard and Poor's and Fitch-IBCA but there are several others. Moody's and Standard and Poor's have been rating US corporate bonds for many decades and have a substantial historical record of the actual default rates in the various rating categories. These are shown in Table 12.1.

Generally the lower the rating the higher the spread for the same maturity and terms. However, the relationship is not perfect because liquidity varies between different issues and also because the market's view may be different to the views of the rating agencies. On the Standard and Poor's/ Fitch IBCA rating scale, from AAA down to BBB − is defined as 'investment grade' and below that is speculative grade. (Moody's uses Aaa, Aa, A, then Baa, Ba, etc.) But of course ratings can be changed so a bond can go from investment grade to speculative grade if the company deteriorates. This can have important market implications, not just because investors would expect a higher yield if the risk deteriorates, but because many institutional investors have limits or prohibitions on bonds with ratings below certain grades. Sometimes ratings downgrades can also impact on bank lending.

As can be seen from Table 12.1, the chances of default increase significantly below BBB. For example, an investor who buys a BB bond at issue and holds it for 5 years has historically

Table 12.1   Cumulative average default rates* (%)

	Yr 1	Yr 2	Yr 3	Yr 4	Yr 5	Yr 10
AAA	0.00	0.00	0.03	0.07	0.11	0.63
AA	0.01	0.03	0.09	0.16	0.26	0.99
A	0.05	0.14	0.26	0.43	0.64	1.90
BBB	0.27	0.62	0.99	1.63	2.26	5.35
BB	1.29	3.62	6.57	9.35	11.90	21.86
B	6.71	14.08	20.59	25.54	29.12	39.63
CCC	28.76	37.98	43.98	48.76	53.96	60.25
Inv. grade	0.10	0.24	0.40	0.65	0.91	2.33
Spec. grade	5.20	10.27	15.04	18.92	22.08	32.04

* Uses static pools, i.e. original ratings and includes issuers whose rating was withdrawn before default.
Source: Standard & Poor's, Rating Performance 2001, S&P, February 2002.

faced a 12.57% cumulative risk of default over this period. This may not sound too bad but, if default occurs, the investor could face a significant loss. The exact size of the loss varies of course with recovery rates, which differ depending on the type of security. Research reported by Standard and Poor's suggested that across all types of rated instruments the recovery rate for a sample of US corporate debt was 51% (i.e. 49% of face value of the instruments was lost). But this sample includes secured debt and bank debt, both of which have relatively higher recovery rates.

Note that the risk of loss will be reduced by holding a portfolio of bonds rather than a single bond, but then the risk of suffering a default of course increases. For example, an investor holding 10 BB bonds would have only a 51% chance of avoiding a default on at least one of the bonds, assuming the bonds' individual risk could be regarded as completely independent (the probability is 0.8743 to the fifth power).

However, in practice, defaults *are* correlated, and indeed linked to the economic cycle as well as other macro factors (see below). Nevertheless a good portfolio can include different industry sectors as well as different countries and/or currencies in order to obtain maximum diversification.

FACTORS DETERMINING SPREADS

Spreads respond to changes in short-term rates, changes in the economic cycle and changes in equity market volatility. Short rates impact by indicating the direction of Fed policy and therefore the likelihood of an economic slowdown. They may also have a direct effect through their implications for corporate cash flow. Higher interest rates imply a less comfortable environment for companies and vice versa.

The economic cycle is crucial because of its implications for corporate health and cash flows. During the late upswing phase of the business cycle there tend to be more issues of speculative grade debt as risk tolerance increases. During a recession companies are under stress both from more difficult business conditions and, typically, higher interest rates. Sometimes it becomes difficult to borrow from banks or in the commercial paper market and companies can be severely squeezed. Default rates rise during the recession phase and then, for a time, issuance of speculative paper is reduced. Default rates often remain high in the recovery and even in the early upswing phase of the cycle as companies, which had been holding on, finally fail.

Stock market volatility is important because it links to the overall risk of corporate cash flows. Stocks become volatile when investors are anxious about the prospects for the economy and for profits. Naturally this anxiety can pass to bond investors too. In practice stock market volatility is often linked to the late upswing stage of the economic cycle as investors become nervous over how much longer the upswing can continue.

Corporate Spreads in Recent Years

US corporate spreads rose sharply in 1990–1 during the recession but declined during the 1990s upswing (see Figure 12.4, which shows the spread of US BB-rated companies' bonds over 10-year Treasury yields). But in 1998 the Russian government defaulted and the crisis at the hedge fund Long Term Capital Management (LTCM) brought a very sharp rise in spreads. The Russian default, following on from the Asian crisis, raised the awareness of risk and prompted a gradual rise in spreads. When it emerged that LTCM held huge positions on a wide range of bonds and was substantially under water the market sold off further. Given that these positions

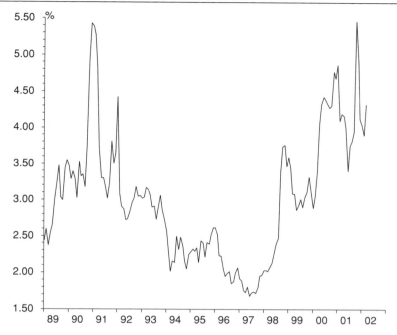

Figure 12.4   US BB-rated spreads over treasuries
Source: Thomson Datastream

were heavily leveraged (i.e. financed with debt) LTCM was in severe danger and only survived because the New York Fed organised a new injection of private funds.

Spreads came down in 1999 but remained much higher than before even though the Fed cut interest rates in late 1998 and the world economy grew very strongly in 1999–2000. Many institutions, including investment banks, and commercial banks, were taking a more cautious approach to risk assets and were running smaller books. In late 2000 and 2001 spreads rose again, to levels higher than seen during previous peaks, as the world economy slowed. This rise was exacerbated by the problems of some telecom companies at the peak of the technology boom in the first half of 2000. When the market soured on the profit outlook for so-called 3-G telecoms, many of these bond issues were downgraded and the spreads widened markedly.

During the first eight months of 2001 spreads started to come down but remained at historically high levels. With the US economy growing very slowly there were fears that the slowdown could still become worse or go on for a long time. Investors were chastened by the collapse of the NASDAQ stock index between the summer of 2000 and spring 2001 and became reluctant to take on risk. Fears also grew over emerging market bonds, where Argentina was drifting towards default and Turkey suffered a crisis early in the year. Meanwhile recorded default rates, particularly on higher-risk bonds, moved up sharply.

Following the terrorist attacks on 11 September and sharply increased fears for the world economy, spreads rose again. Although there were signs of reduced macro-economic risk by early 2002 because of hopes for economic recovery, the sudden collapse of Enron and Global Crossing (a telecoms company) in the USA led to a new widening of spreads.

If the US economy continues to recover in 2002–3 and corporate sector profits revive, spreads will probably come down significantly from the 2001 highs. The best outlook for investors then would be that the US economy (and others) are set up for a few more years of economic upswing during the 2002–5 period, which would provide a good backdrop for corporate bonds. Investors would be able to earn relatively high yields while probably also enjoying a tightening of the spread with Treasury bonds, but the absolute return will obviously depend on the course of Treasury bonds. Treasury yields are likely to be stable or up during the *recovery* and *early upswing* phases.

CONCLUSION: BOND MARKET FUNDAMENTALS

Government bond markets are driven by economic trends, especially the pace of GDP growth and inflation, changes in monetary policy and changes in fiscal policy. Bond prices generally rise (i.e. yields fall) on news of slower economic growth, lower inflation and tighter fiscal policy. The effect of changes in monetary policy on bond yields depends on the market's assessment of the impact on the economy. Sometimes a rise in short-term interest rates can be good news for bonds, though usually not. Other bonds, from municipal bonds through to corporate bonds and junk bonds, follow a similar path to government bonds but with greater credit risk, which is linked to the economic cycle.

Bonds are attractive to hold as a proportion of a long-term capital growth portfolio. They can help to even out the swings in equity portfolios, since at certain points in the cycle bonds will do well while stock markets do badly, notably in the early stages of a recession. In that way they offer investors diversification. The best time to buy bonds, or in the context of an overall portfolio to go overweight in bonds, is when bond yields look high in relation to inflation and there is a good chance of an economic slowdown. As discussed above, timing is always difficult and there are no hard and fast rules. Ultimately the key factor is whether central banks are thought likely to be tough on inflation.

There is a powerful school of thought that for long-term capital growth, investment in equities is much better than investment in bonds. Certainly this has been the historical experience over long periods in the English-speaking countries, though less so in other countries. As we shall see in later chapters this argument is less convincing now that valuations on stocks are at relatively high levels compared to history and inflation seems set to remain low. Moreover the growth of the corporate bond market offers a greater choice of risk/reward combinations than previously.

13

Stock Markets

While stock markets ultimately comprise a host of individual companies, each with their own risks and potentialities, there is a tendency for many stock prices to move in the same direction over time. The focus of this chapter is the fundamental forces that move the market as a whole. These forces can be divided into factors that affect company earnings, valuations, and liquidity.

PROFITS

Structural Factors Affecting Company Earnings

Company earnings, or profits, are the key to stock prices. They provide dividends for investors and most of the finance for investment to boost the company's earnings in the future. Many brokers make forecasts for company earnings to provide the basis for buy, hold or sell recommendations. Forecasts for earnings for the market as a whole are sometimes based on aggregating these forecasts for all the individual stocks, the so-called 'bottom-up' approach, and sometimes based on an aggregate model, incorporating forecasts for economic growth, inflation, interest rates, etc., the 'top-down' approach.

It is useful to separate long-term trend influences from short-term cyclical factors. In the long-term, trend growth in company earnings is mainly determined by the trend rate of growth of the economy. A faster growing economy is likely to show faster average earnings growth. This is one reason for the attraction of emerging markets.

Another long-term trend influence is the effect of a liberalisation of economic policy on the growth of profits. Economic liberalisation — a widespread trend in many countries over the last two decades — involves measures such as reducing bureaucratic controls on investment and bank lending, easing labour laws, reducing tariffs, eliminating prohibitions on imports and freeing prices. For some companies these measures have the effect of reducing margins because of the increase in competition, both domestic and foreign. But liberalisation measures also raise returns on investment and often allow companies to plan using a longer time horizon.

Another significant long-term factor is the behaviour of wages. In countries where labour takes a high proportion of companies' sales revenues, margins are low and profits are limited. This is sometimes a long-run problem in countries where strong labour laws or powerful trades unions prevent the expansion of profits. In the UK, for example, wages amounted to around 68% of GDP in the 1970s, depressing profits and growth. The liberalisation measures of the 1980s, plus a deep and long recession that brought higher unemployment and weakened trades unions, reduced the percentage to 64%.

Finally, among long-term factors, the flexibility that companies enjoy to respond to new circumstances may be a key factor in long-term earnings growth. This flexibility probably comes mainly from easy labour laws, which permit lay-offs or redundancies but it may also be a cultural issue. For example Japanese companies seem to have less flexibility than US companies in dealing with slower growth. The tradition of life-time employment in large companies in Japan reduces flexibility and has been a factor in Japan's long decline. However, in recent years Japan's crisis has significantly eroded life-time employment.

In the last 10 years there is evidence that international competition through trade liberalisation and privatisation is forcing companies everywhere to adopt a tough 'compete or die' philosophy. This philosophy has spread from the USA to Japan and Europe and is likely to bring rewards to the successful, but may also increase the risks for the laggards.

Cyclical Factors Affecting Company Earnings

Company earnings tend to go through a cycle in line with the economic cycle. Years of rapid earnings growth typically occur near the beginning of an upswing while earnings usually fall in recession (see Figure 13.1). Some companies, generally those with large fixed costs and a pronounced sales cycle, are more sensitive to the economic cycle than others, and these are called 'cyclical stocks'. Examples include car manufacturers and chemicals producers.

During the *recession* phase of the economic cycle, earnings are depressed because of reduced sales and margins and therefore lower overall revenues to set against fixed costs. Capacity use is typically low. In severe recessions earnings can disappear altogether for many companies, while other companies, less affected by the cycle — for example food companies — may see very little change in earnings.

In the *recovery* stage earnings are still low, but begin to bounce back as capacity use rises. Interest rates are usually low, which helps corporate cash flow and may also allow an

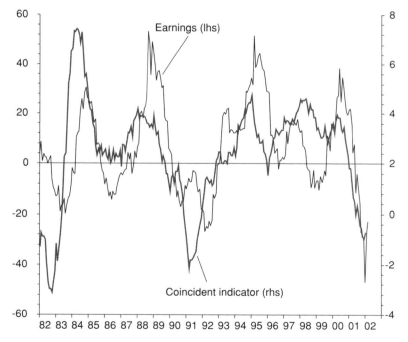

Figure 13.1   US Corporate Earnings and the Economy % change
Source: Thomson Datastream

improvement in balance sheets with longer-term debt replacing short-term debt. Also, companies have usually reduced inventories and cut costs by this stage.

In the *early upswing* phase earnings recover strongly, very often showing rapid growth rates. Remember that after a 50% decline in earnings they must have a 100% rise to return to the starting point! Two factors probably lie behind much of this improvement. First is the rise in capacity utilisation for industrial companies and the fuller use of staff by all companies. Costs, and sometimes margins, remain the same while volume rises, which brings large increases in profits. For the economy as whole this is measured as an increase in productivity, i.e. output per unit of input. At this stage of the cycle wage awards usually remain modest because of continuing relatively high unemployment so that most of the productivity gains flow straight into profits rather than increased wages.

The second factor is often the efficiency gains made during the recession, which do not really show up until output rises. Recessions tend to concentrate management's minds and provide extra discipline on workers, because of the threat of job losses. The result is that some of the 'fat' built up during the growth years, including both obvious waste and 'luxury' projects, are eliminated and a leaner, fitter company emerges from the recession.

During the *late upswing* phase of the business cycle earnings typically do very well because of high capacity use and strong sales. But they may start to be threatened by rising wages and higher interest rates which put pressure on margins. If inflation has picked up, companies gain from stock (inventory) appreciation. But earnings forecasts are likely to be better if inflation is slow to pick up as the late phase of the business cycle will probably last longer.

The final stage of the economic cycle, as the *economy slows* and goes into recession, witnesses the beginning of an earnings decline. Capacity utilisation falls, raising unit costs. Usually wage growth is slow to adjust to the cycle and eats further into company earnings. Lay-offs or redundancies may also be slow to come, but even when they do, they cost money for companies, which reduces so-called *reported* profits, though these charges are often excluded from *operating* earnings. Finally, interest rates are often still high at this point — sometimes penally high — which also impacts earnings.

VALUATIONS

A variety of different measures are used to value stock markets, with the five discussed below being the most common. These measures are best used to compare current values with past historical values for the same country. Using them to compare across countries is more difficult because of the different tax treatments of company earnings and dividends.

Price/Earnings Ratios

This, perhaps the most common valuation measure, is the ratio of a stock price (or a market as a whole) to its earnings and is widely quoted in the newspapers. A high ratio may suggest that the market is expensive while a low ratio suggests it is cheap. Sometimes this ratio is expressed the other way around as an earnings yield. For example, a price/earnings ratio of 20 is equal to an earnings yield of 5%. Fast-growing companies or countries tend to have relatively high price/earnings ratios, and vice versa.

Japan has had extremely high price/earnings ratios for many years, but it is impossible to compare this directly with other countries. One reason is that the different treatment of company accounts means that profits are kept lower than in the USA. Another is that Japanese

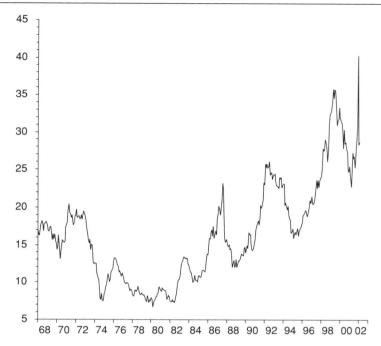

Figure 13.2   US S&P 500 p/e ratio
Source: Thomson Datastream

companies still own each other through a complex web of cross-holdings, though these are now being gradually reduced. This has the effect of exaggerating the number of shares outstanding and therefore depressing earnings per share. For these and other reasons many analysts prefer to look at the ratio of price to cash earnings.

Price/Cash Earnings Ratios

The attraction of this ratio is that it measures cash earnings before depreciation, which is treated differently in different countries. Japan, for example, has a price/cash earnings ratio much closer to the USA on this measure. In the late 1980s when Japan's price/earnings ratio reached 70 or more at the peak of the market, the price/cash earnings ratio was only around 8. However this ratio is generally harder to obtain.

Dividend Yield

This measure is the ratio of dividends to stock prices. Traditionally the UK has had a high ratio, due to high inflation and the tax treatment of dividends while Japan has a very low ratio, in recent years often less than 1%. In the UK, and to some extent the USA, maintenance of this ratio is taken very seriously, even when profits are down, so that the 'pay out ratio', the proportion of earnings paid in dividends, can vary widely. However, some companies, particularly in the USA, do not pay a dividend, arguing that they can use the cash better themselves, investing to develop the business. Moreover, since investors pay income tax on dividends, but in most countries pay a lower rate of tax on capital gains from selling stocks, the tax system biases companies to push up the stock price rather than pay a large dividend. This encourages companies to invest in growth or, failing that, to buy their own stock back with the money, thereby boosting the stock price. In the UK a change in tax on dividends for pension funds in 1998 shifted the relative attractiveness of dividends and capital gains and is beginning to produce a lower dividend pay out and greater use of share buybacks.

Yield Gap or Ratio

This is a comparison of the earnings or dividend yield on stocks with a long bond yield. Most commonly it is expressed as a ratio of the long bond yield to the dividend yield, but it can also be expressed as a difference between the two. Before the 1960s, in a time of low inflation, it was generally expected that the yield on equities would be higher than the yield on bonds to reflect the extra risk involved. But since then, due to higher inflation, bond yields have been higher than dividend yields, and usually higher than earnings yields, giving rise to the so-called 'reverse yield gap'. It is difficult to use this ratio owing to its sensitivity to inflation. Only where the existence of index-linked bonds provides a market for real bond yields, such as in the UK, can we be sure what the ratio means. When the dividend yield or earnings yield on stocks is low relative to bonds, equities are expensive and vice versa.

In the USA the ratio of the bond yield (e.g. the 10-year Treasury yield) to the earnings yield (the inverse of the price/earnings ratio) has proved a relatively good indicator of extremes of valuation. It gave a clear sell signal in 1987 just before the crash and a clear buy signal in 1996. It does, however, mix up the bond yield which includes compensation for expected inflation and the earnings yield which does not (i.e. is a 'real' indicator). Purists therefore question its use for the long term. Moreover, outside the USA, the indicator seems to work less well.

Price/Book Value

This is another commonly used ratio, but is particularly dangerous in cross-country comparisons although it does give some indication of the stock's current valuation in relation to recent history. As the name suggests, it takes the ratio of the price of a share to its book value. Perhaps in years to come the tax and accounting treatment of companies will be standardised across the world but, at the moment, law and practice vary widely.

Valuations and Interest Rates

As we saw above, interest rates affect stocks by impacting on earnings. But more important is their effect on valuations through changing the relative attractiveness of stocks to other assets, especially short-term instruments and long-term bond yields. Generally speaking a rise in short rates and/or bond yields is bad for stocks, but sometimes the effect may be outweighed by strong company earnings growth. Companies such as utilities and banks tend to be influenced strongly by interest rates and are known as 'interest-sensitive' stocks.

Short Rates

The effect on stocks of a rise in interest rates may depend on whether it represents a rise in real interest rates or a rise in inflation expectations. A rise in inflation expectations should mean that forecasts of earnings growth are raised too, so that stock prices are unmoved. However, the experience of the 1970s suggests that this is not always the case. Stocks were generally very depressed during that period, typically selling on price/earnings ratios of 10 or less. The problem is that when investors see higher inflation they begin to worry that the authorities will soon tighten policy, bringing the economic upswing to an end. Alternatively, the rise in inflation causes investors to require a greater risk premium on stocks, which implies a fall in price.

A change in the real component of short-term interest rates means that the monetary authorities have tightened economic policy. Not only does this make an economic slowdown more likely, which would impact on earnings, but it also makes holding deposits (or 'cash') more attractive. This is not to say that stocks will automatically fall in price. The markets could conclude that the rise in interest rates is confirmation of the strong trend in economic growth. They might also decide that the rise in rates will control the economic upswing better and help to avoid an early downturn. But if the markets become convinced that the authorities are determined to end the upswing, to fight inflation, then stocks will be weak (Figure 13.3).

The authorities often speak of their intention to achieve a soft landing, rather than a full-blown recession. In practice managing the economy to achieve this is very difficult because of the uncertainties and lags in policy. Nevertheless, if inflation has not picked up too much the markets may interpret a rise in interest rates as good news because of the chance of achieving that soft landing.

However, as short-term interest rates rise they provide an increasingly high return investment alternative to stocks at a time when the risk of holding stocks seems to be increasing. In the

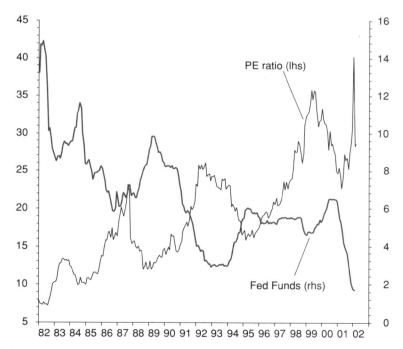

Figure 13.3   US p/e ratio and Fed Funds rate
Source: Thomson Datastream

1970s, although stocks performed poorly, deposits were not a safe haven because interest rates were often less than the inflation rate. Property was then considered to be the best investment. In the 1990s, with central banks more independent and vigilant against the threat of inflation, interest rates on short-term instruments were nearly always above the inflation rate.

The Impact of Bond Yields

A change in bond yields can also have a direct impact on stocks and one measure of the relative valuation of stocks and bonds compares bond yields with dividend yields (see above). As with short rates, a rise in bond yields that is due to a rise in inflationary expectations should not affect stock prices in theory, but in practice often does.

However a rise in the real component of bonds is more likely to be positive than a rise in the real component of short-term interest rates. While it does increase the attractiveness of holding bonds rather than stocks, a rise in the real component of bonds also implies that the economy is strong and earnings growth should be rapid. Hence a period of high real interest rates on bonds can also be a good period for stocks. The early 1980s period was a good example (Figure 13.4).

An inverted yield curve, i.e. when short-term rates are higher than bond yields, might be expected to be bad for stocks, but this also has not always been the case. This may be because it is generally a time of high earnings growth, though an inverted yield curve may also reflect hopes of a soft landing rather than a hard landing.

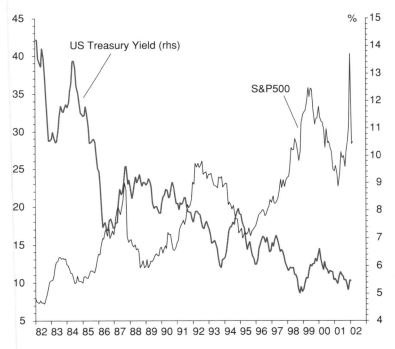

Figure 13.4   US p/e Ratios and Bond Yields
Source: Thomson Datastream

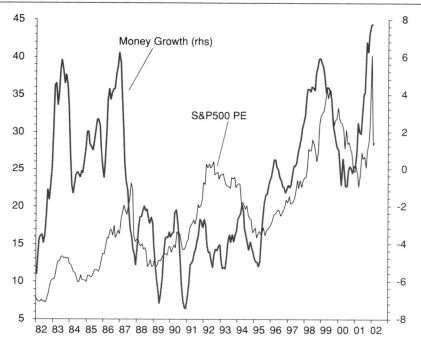

Figure 13.5   US real money growth and p/e ratio
Source: Thomson Datastream

Money Growth

Rapid money supply growth correlates with rising stock markets. This is intuitively obvious in the sense that, if people plan to buy stocks, they need to arrange for money to be available, whether by selling other assets or by borrowing. Many stock market analysts use measures of liquidity, such as the growth in money supply minus the rate of inflation, to measure this effect. Rapid growth in money supply is often associated with low short-term interest rates, because it means that the cost of borrowing is low. For example, the run-up in US stocks in 1999–2000 or the boom in Japanese stocks throughout 1986–9 can be linked to an over-easy monetary policy. However, liquidity can grow fast and if confidence is high enough stock markets can gain ground even with rising interest rates (Figure 13.5).

HISTORICAL PERFORMANCE OF EQUITIES

Most professional investors take the view that a well-diversified portfolio of stocks is likely to be more volatile, but over the long term provide a better return than either bonds or cash. This has generally been the historical experience, notably in the USA and the UK where data go back a long way, but it also makes sense theoretically, since stocks are likely to be more risky than government bonds and therefore should give investors a higher return. They are more risky in the sense that their prices are more volatile and also in the ultimate sense that companies are more likely to go bankrupt than major governments.

However, there have been periods when superior returns from stocks have taken a long time to mature, 10 years or more, and in some countries the historical record is less clear-cut than in the USA and the UK. Extreme cases such as Russian equities from pre-1917 obviously show the risk of investing in any country if the economic system changes.

The worst periods historically for stocks were from 1929 into the early 1930s and again in the 1970s. Between 2 September 1929 and 8 July 1932 the US Dow Jones index declined 89.2%, which is to say that it fell to only just over 10% of its previous value! Contrary to legend this was caused by a long bear market rather than the 1929 Crash. On Black Monday, 28 October 1929, the Dow did fall 12.8%, but by the end of that week, despite falling again on Tuesday, the market was only 8.5% below its level the previous Friday. The long bear market was linked to a catastrophic recession, or depression, which saw US GDP fall by around 30% between 1929 and 1933.

The second major episode of poor stock performance was in the 1970s when a period of relatively weak economic growth coincided with unexpectedly high inflation caused by the quadrupling of oil prices in late 1973. Profits were impacted by the 1974–5 recession but a large part of the stock market decline was due to a collapse in valuations from around 20 times earnings to less than 10 times by the end of the 1970s.

In the 1930s, with the general price level falling, investors would have been better off in deposits (provided that the bank did not fail). In the 1970s deposits and bonds were also poor investments because interest rates were often below the rate of inflation. Holders of long-term bonds were particularly unfortunate. Inflation hedges, such as property and commodities, were generally the best bet.

The 1980s was an extremely good period for stocks, with market indices quadrupling, or more, during the decade. This bull market is explained by the excellent performance of profits, combined with a substantial rise in valuations from depressed levels. Profits rebounded from the weakness at the start of the decade and showed a sustained improvement in growth due both to the strong economic upswing and in some countries, notably the UK, structural changes which brought an increase in the share of profits in output. Valuations improved with the fall in interest rates and inflation, and the lifting of the gloom over the economy that prevailed in the 1970s.

In 1990 stocks were impacted by the recession in the English-speaking countries and the uncertainties of the Gulf conflict. But, outside Japan and later in the decade emerging markets, the 1990s showed another very strong performance for stock markets. Profits recovered and valuations rose to levels rarely if ever seen before. Technology stocks formed a bubble later in the decade but then crashed in 2000–1. A general bear market began in the second half of 2000 as the world economy slowed. Profits fell sharply in 2001 and valuations remained fairly high.

THE EQUITY RISK PREMIUM

Equities are inherently more risky than bonds, especially government bonds. Governments can raise taxes to repay bonds while companies have to compete in the markets to make profits and, if they fail, equity investors are the last in the queue for any money after all the other creditors, including bond-holders. For this reason investors are likely to demand a premium, i.e. an extra return, for holding stocks compared with bonds and this is known as the 'equity premium'.

The only equity premium we can actually observe is the realised return, i.e. the extra return equity investors actually received compared with bond investors. This figure has been calculated as about 5–7% p.a. for the US and UK markets over the last 100 years. Many observers find it a puzzle that the figure is so high. It is true that bond returns are more stable than equity returns over short periods, indeed sometimes up to 10 years, but 5–7% p.a. is a lot for investors to give up, for the benefit of stability. So analysts have searched for other explanations.

One possibility is that investors completely failed to foresee the poor performance of bonds between the mid-1960s and 1981, because they did not foresee inflation. Hence the very low returns on bonds during that period (because yields were too low at the start) bias the equity risk premium up. Another argument is that the calculated equity risk premium is too high for statistical reasons. There is always a danger in these calculations of a distortion in the numbers from what is called 'survivor bias'. For example, equity indices are frequently changing as declining companies drop out and rising companies are included. Using equity indices to calculate investors' returns may overestimate what can actually be achieved in the real world. Moreover, the cost of transactions may be higher in stocks than in bonds which could subtract further from the apparent premium.

The final argument is that investors were indeed too pessimistic, due to the bad experiences of the 1930s and 1970s and also the world political uncertainty during the Cold War. According to this view there is no reason for a large premium in future because all the evidence of the last 100 years or more shows that a well-diversified portfolio of stocks has eventually always outperformed bonds and therefore investors would be irrational to expect hugely higher returns from stocks. Once this is realised, according to the argument, investors will buy stocks until they reach such high levels that their future likely return is reduced to being only just above or even to equal to bond yields. This argument has been used to justify the high valuations reached in the 1990s.

Most calculations suggest that the expected equity premium on US stocks has been falling since the 1950s and may now be down to around 2–3% compared with 6–7% in the past. This view is reinforced by some historical studies which suggest that the equity premium was in the 2–3% range in the nineteenth century and right up to 1929. On this view the period from 1929 to the late 1950s was the unusual period.

Another argument, however, is that the relative risk of stocks to bonds or deposits has been re-rated by investors. The experience of the 1970s showed the dangers of holding bonds and now the slightest whiff of inflation sends bond yields skywards. Meanwhile the ability of institutional investors and mutual funds to diversify stock holdings means that the risk of holding a stock portfolio can be reduced.

A low equity risk premium has two implications for investors. First, if it can be maintained, it is good news because the relatively high price/earnings multiples of recent years may be sustainable, contrary to the view of some pessimists. Secondly, it means that investors should not expect to gain as much as before from being in stocks rather than bonds. An equity risk premium of 2% means that returns on a diversified stock portfolio should, over time, return 2% p.a. more than a long-term government bond portfolio. This is much less exciting than before, though, of course when this difference is compounded over many years it will make a considerable difference.

CONCLUSION: STOCK MARKET FUNDAMENTALS

Stock markets rise with economic growth, because of the consequent growth in company earnings. Recessions, higher interest rates and political uncertainty are usually bad for markets. However, sometimes higher interest rates are taken as a good sign, indicating strong economic growth or a central bank that is in charge. Stocks tend to be more volatile than other asset classes such as bonds. Stock markets typically have one or two years in the economic cycle that show much of the rise for the cycle and one year with a major correction. The major rise often happens in the middle of the recession or early in the recovery phase when the markets suddenly anticipate an upturn. The downturn often happens when valuations are stretched and the markets suddenly anticipate an economic slowdown or are upset by a political 'shock'. It would be wonderful if investors could time the market to miss the down-year, but the risk is always that they will miss the good years! This is especially true because good performance of equity markets often starts at a time of the greatest uncertainty over the economic outlook.

Experience and theory both suggest that, for long-term capital growth, stocks should form a substantial part of an investor's portfolio. While most investors would like to be able to time the markets — for example, anticipating recessions and avoiding bear markets — this is very difficult. Being out of the market is almost as dangerous as being in it, because of the possibility of missing a strong rally. Most professional investors trim or add to their stock portfolios only at the margin during the economic cycle and concentrate more on individual stock picking to add value.

14

Currency Markets

Academic economists argue that the currency markets (like other markets) are 'efficient' in the sense that they include all the available information (see Chapter 19). In fact since the markets in the major currencies are so liquid and enjoy very low transaction costs they are believed to be the most efficient of markets. This implies that exchange rates are impossible to forecast. Most professional investors do not fully accept the 'efficient markets hypothesis' but would certainly agree that exchange rates are very hard to forecast.

The problem is that currencies seem to behave differently at different times. In the 1980s monthly US trade reports were the key to fluctuations in the dollar. At other times interest rates have been the key factor, themselves driven by relative economic growth rates. In recent years long-term capital flows seem to have played a decisive role in the strength of the dollar. There have been still other times when the markets appear to have been gripped by so-called 'fads or fashions', taking exchange rates to dizzyingly high or stunningly low levels.

There are a number of forecasting models available but they only work if other variables are correctly forecast and sometimes not even then. For example, in 2001 there was general agreement that news of a strong US economy would boost the dollar because it would make further cuts in US interest rates less likely. It followed that, if investors could successfully predict the turnaround in the economy, they could forecast the dollar. For most months that would have worked, but not every month. Sometimes a weak economic report strengthened the dollar.

Many investors use charts to forecast exchange rates. Although chartists are all looking at the same picture they often give different predictions. Still, if enough people believe that, for example, a move above euro 0.9620 means that the euro will move to 1.08 (a typical chartist prediction based on past patterns) then it could quickly become a self-fulfilling prediction.

Most investment managers take a longer-term view, ignoring the day-to-day fluctuations of the markets. This still requires forecasting trends in the economy but arguably can give a better perspective. Others treat currency movements as a variable to be avoided and use hedging techniques including futures and options to eliminate or reduce their exposure. Nearly all investors treat currencies very carefully and with great respect, partly because they are so difficult to forecast and partly because they can make such a large difference, particularly to short-term returns.

KEY CONCEPTS

Before looking at the various forecasting approaches there are three important concepts that are useful to understand: 'covered interest parity', 'real exchange rates' and the related concept 'real effective exchange rates'.

Covered Interest Parity

This concept simply states that the difference between the forward exchange rate and the spot exchange rate is always equal to the difference between the interest rate in the two countries over the same period. If it were not, then investors could quickly make money by borrowing in one currency, converting into another and entering into a forward contract to the first currency. It means, of course, that the currency with the higher interest rate will have a forward rate below its spot rate (and vice versa).

Sometimes the difference in interest rates is referred to as the 'cost of hedging', but strictly speaking this is incorrect. For example, the US dollar based investor who decides to buy some Australian dollar bonds may choose to hedge the currency so that he is not exposed to the risk that the Australian dollar falls. But if Australian dollar one-year interest rates are 1% above US rates, our investor will immediately lock in a 1% 'loss' over a year since the forward exchange rate for Australian dollars will buy 1% less US dollars than the spot rate. The reason that this is not strictly a cost is that a 1% decline in the Australian dollar is the market's best expectation and that expectation will also be factored into the yield on Australian bonds. Strictly, the cost of hedging is only the spread paid to the broker or market maker.

The Real Exchange Rate

The concept of the real exchange rate is linked to the purchasing power parity (PPP) theory discussed below. As with other 'real' concepts in economics the intention is to take inflation out of the equation. Real exchange rates are quoted as index numbers. For example, let us suppose that the dollar/euro rate was 100 on 1 January 2002 and the movement over the following three years in *nominal* terms took the dollar down 5%, which would be measured as 95 on a nominal exchange rate index. The dollar would apparently become more competitive. But if

Figure 14.1   US$ Nominal Effective Exchange Rate
Source: Thomson Datastream

we suppose that inflation in the USA had been higher each year, say 3% p.a. higher, adding up to a cumulative 9%, then the real exchange rate index would be approximately 104, showing the US dollar to be less competitive. In effect the 9% higher price level has not been sufficiently compensated by the 5% devaluation.

The 'real effective exchange rate' is the same idea, except that instead of being simply calculated between two countries it takes all the countries with which the country trades and weights them according to the size of trade. This is a concept to which the central banks pay particular attention in setting monetary policy. It is the best way to determine whether the exchange rate overall is depreciating in real terms (i.e. becoming more competitive), which would be a stimulus to the economy, or appreciating, which would be a contractionary force.

The nominal effective exchange rate (Figure 14.1) is an index of movements in the exchange rate with trading partners, weighted by the size of trade. However, it does not take account of different inflation rates. With inflation almost everywhere down to low single digits now, this index is good enough for most investors. Swings in exchange rates, especially because of the increase in capital flows, tend to overwhelm the relatively small differences in inflation rates.

FOUR APPROACHES TO FORECASTING

There are four broad approaches to forecasting exchange rates, though most forecasters probably use a combination of them all. These are: (1) approaches based on identifying a fundamental or equilibrium exchange rate; (2) approaches based on the relative strength of different economies, which will be evidenced in different interest rates, or different trends in monetary growth; (3) approaches based on assessing overall current and capital flows; and (4) approaches based on assessing the savings–investment balance in countries.

Fundamental or Equilibrium Exchange Rates

The oldest theory of what determines exchange rates is the so-called 'purchasing power parity' theory. This theory is rooted in the idea that exchange rates are basically changing to keep trade in balance. Suppose for a moment that there was no international investment flow and that the only currency transactions were US importers buying yen to pay their suppliers in Japan and US exporters changing their yen earnings back to dollars.

Then, if prices in Japan rose faster than in the USA, Japanese imports would not be able to compete so well in the US market and volumes would probably fall. At the same time US exports would rise because US products would have become more competitive. This would mean less demand for yen and more for dollars, so that the dollar would rise.

On this view then, the exchange rate should change to keep different countries broadly competitive with each other. If it did not change then trade surpluses and deficits would become large, which cannot occur in the absence of capital flows to finance them. Another way of explaining PPP is to say that exchange rates will tend to move to keep the purchasing power of the same amount of money constant. Thus if inflation is rising faster in the USA than in Japan, the US dollar would be expected to depreciate over time.

There are a number of problems with this theory. First, we know that, in practice, the size of currency transactions far outweighs the size of world trade. Total *daily* foreign exchange transactions in just the three largest markets, London, New York and Tokyo, amount to well over $1,000 bn or $1 trillion, when world trade in a whole year amounts to about $18 trillion. Secondly, since there are increasingly large investment flows we know that large trade deficits can be financed for long periods so there is no reason for the exchange rate to adjust quickly. Thirdly, experience shows that exchange rates do indeed move very substantially over time, and far more than price trends would suggest. Finally, there are serious practical problems with estimating the PPP.

Calculating Purchasing Power Parity

There are three approaches to calculating purchasing power parity, though each inevitably contains a considerable margin of error. One is to try to compare the prices of goods in different countries. Note that the goods to be compared should be so-called 'tradable goods' since there is no reason why the price of a haircut or a McDonald's hamburger should be the same in two different countries. Of the price you pay for a McDonald's hamburger only a small proportion is actually a traded good, i.e. beef or wheat or tomatoes, the rest is 'non-tradable', e.g. transport costs, restaurant space or unskilled labour.

The second approach to measuring purchasing power parity, which is the one more commonly used, is to take a long period, 10 years or more, and work out the average real exchange rate over the period. Then provided that the PPP theory works over the long term, that real level must be the PPP.

This approach faces a problem over which price index to use. For example, use of the consumer price index would include a large number of goods and services prices that are not traded. Use of the export price index would look at goods that are actually exported and not necessarily things that *might* have been exported at a different exchange rate. More commonly economists use the wholesale price index, but again this might not be a true reflection of the prices of tradables.

The third approach is fairly similar except, rather than taking an average over a long period, the analyst selects one year when the exchange rate seemed to be in equilibrium judging by the current account being in balance, and then looks at relative inflation since then. So, if the US dollar/Euro was in equilibrium in 1997 we can deduce what the equilibrium is now by allowing for the difference in inflation since then.

With all these methods in use and different price indices being employed, it is not surprising that estimates of PPP vary quite often by as much as 10 or 20%. Realistically, therefore, we can only estimate the PPP within a wide range. For example, most economists would agree that the euro/dollar PPP *for traded goods* is between euro 1.10–1.25, and the yen/dollar 100–120.

The Yen and PPP: Why Tokyo is so Expensive

Visitors to Tokyo often find living so expensive that they conclude that the yen must be massively overvalued on any kind of PPP comparison. Attempts to calculate PPP based on general consumer prices arrive at a level of 140 or weaker. Yet Japan has enjoyed a current account surplus for many years despite a much stronger currency.

The answer to this paradox is that Japan is very efficient at making so-called tradable goods but generally very inefficient in many non-tradable areas. For example, in areas such as cars and electronics, Japanese companies are extraordinarily efficient at producing very high quality items at low cost. But much of Japan's service sector, including distribution networks and shops, are highly inefficient by US standards and also face the high costs arising from shortage of space in a crowded country. For this reason economists focus on the PPP for traded goods.

Why PPP is still Relevant

Hardly anyone believes that PPP is a useful guide to the direction of exchange rates in the short or even medium run (up to three years or so). But it is still important for several reasons. First, in broad terms it does seem to work in the very long run, meaning 5 years or longer. This may be important for investors taking a long-term position. Secondly, governments and central banks do take PPP very seriously in their approach to exchange rates because they know that periods of under- or overvaluation may lead to sudden currency instability or be destabilising for business. It may therefore influence interest rate decisions as well as provoke direct interventions.

Thirdly, calculations of PPP are often a key factor in considerations by both governments and markets as to whether a particular fixed (or controlled) exchange rate can survive. For example, most analysts argued (and the Bundesbank seemed to agree) that when sterling entered the European Exchange Rate Mechanism in 1990 the central rate chosen, DM 2.95, was too high. This view contributed to the strength of the speculation against the pound and may also have been behind the Bundesbank's unwillingness to help to defend it. If the UK joins the euro, a key issue will be at what rate, and the authorities will base their approach to this on PPP considerations.

Finally, there are times when PPP factors do seem to matter to the markets and dominate other factors. This usually happens when a large current account deficit is opening up and the markets question whether a growing deficit can be financed. Then they focus on the currency level that is needed to correct the deficit.

Relative Economic Strength

This approach focuses on currencies from the point of view of investment flows rather than trade flows. It says that currencies strengthen if their interest rates move up relative to other countries because investors switch into that currency to obtain the higher yield. This works best if the economy has plenty of spare capacity and there is therefore no immediate inflation threat. News of a rise in official interest rates will probably have the same effect, though not if the markets judge that this rise will actually slow the economy and may soon be reversed.

Which interest rate is the most relevant? The answer is probably that both short- and long-term rates matter but bond yields are the most important. It is the bond market that is really telling us more about the state of the economy and therefore the likely direction of interest rates beyond the immediate term. Strictly speaking it should be the *real* bond yield differential to allow for differences in expectations of inflation.

Combining PPP with Relative Strength

The relative strength approach tells us the response to news on the economy but does not tell us anything about the *level* of exchange rates. The PPP approach indicates the level of exchange rate that can be regarded as a long-term equilibrium. These two can be combined to generate a more complete theory.

When interest rates are high in one country a flow of capital moves into that country, tending to raise the exchange rate. Even if investors begin to see the exchange rate as overvalued in some long-term sense, they may still be content if they feel the extra yield compensates for that. However, once the exchange rate reaches an excessive level, they will question whether the high yield is enough to justify the likely exchange rate depreciation.

For example, during the first major episode of dollar strength, in 1984–5, investors were content with a DM/$ exchange rate in excess of DM 3 because yields on bonds in the USA were around 4% p.a. higher than in Germany. Even given the likelihood that inflation would be higher in the USA investors still enjoyed a real yield pick up of 2–3% in US bond yields compared with German bond yields. This would be enough to justify a 20–30% overvaluation. Note, however, that this model broke down in 2000–1 when the dollar remained very strong against the euro despite having bond yields only marginally above euro yields.

What of the role of short rates? There is little question that short-term interest rates can influence exchange rates but primarily in the short term. The level of short-term interest rates influences the extent to which speculators are willing to bet against a currency. If interest rates in a particular country are especially high, speculators are less likely to go short because the currency needs to move further. Similarly, very low interest rates on Japanese yen in recent years have periodically encouraged investors to borrow yen to fund other investments (the so-called carry-trade).

Assessing Capital Flows

Some capital flows may be comparatively unaffected by relative interest rates, either short- or long-term rates, because the instigators choose not to take a view on possible exchange rate changes. This is likely to apply mainly to foreign direct investment flows and some long-term equity investments. (The difference between the two is a matter of degree, but FDI occurs when the investor acquires control rather than just part ownership.) From 1999 onwards there was considerable focus on this issue because of the surprising strength of the dollar versus the euro. This coincided with a clear increase in long-term flows from Euroland to the USA, including especially FDI and, until 2001 at least, purchases of US equities.

Sophisticated investors with easy access to hedging techniques, may choose not to take a view on the exchange rate either because they see the investment as very long term, or because they believe their investment possesses a natural hedge. There is an argument that, for the long-term equity investor, it is better to ignore currency changes, since they will be insignificant eventually. A natural hedge could arise if a European company took over a US company with substantial exports to Europe. Then, a fall in the dollar versus the euro would result in higher sales and higher margins on those exports.

The importance of long-term capital flows may have the effect of reversing the usual relationship between short-term interest rates and the currency, because a cut in short-term rates would be expected to boost economic growth and the stock markets, thereby making these long-term investments more attractive. In this environment central banks face a dilemma. Whereas they might want to respond to a weak currency that is threatening to stimulate the economy too much and raise inflation, by *raising* interest rates the effect may actually be to push the currency lower. Hence the effectiveness of monetary policy is much reduced.

This appeared to be a problem for Euroland at times during 2001 when the ECB's reluctance to cut interest rates as the economy slowed, because of rising inflation and a weak currency, seemed to make the currency weaker. Similarly the Fed's aggressive cutting in the first half of 2001 pushed the dollar higher, reducing the impact of lower interest rates in stimulating the economy.

Savings–Investment Balances

This approach integrates the three methodologies described above by explaining currency movements in terms of domestic savings–investment balances and their consequences for the exchange rate. Although it is not easy to use for forecasting, it can sometimes help us to understand why currencies seem to depart from equilibrium for long periods.

Suppose that an economy suddenly begins to expand rapidly, driven by a new government budget deficit or bullish entrepreneurs. If domestic savings do not change there will be excess demand for capital, as investment tries to exceed savings. Investment can only exceed savings if foreign savings are used, but this requires a deficit on the current account of the balance of payments, as a matter of definition (see Chapter 8). A country cannot have a net capital inflow unless it has a deficit on the current account.

Where does this deficit on the current account come from? Some of it may arise simply because imports are strong, due to the buoyant economy or because exports are weak as companies focus on the domestic market. But if that is not enough the answer is that the exchange rate needs to rise. If capital flows are attracted to the country, either due to high interest rates (which ties in with the relative economic strength approach above) or due to attractive expected returns on investments (the third approach above), then the exchange rate will indeed rise as needed.

However, since trade takes time to adjust, the exchange rate will frequently depart from generally accepted equilibrium rates for prolonged periods, typically 2–4 years, as it forces the current account deficit to open up. Eventually the currency will achieve the necessary current account deficit and may start to decline from its peak. Of course it needs to stay strong as long as domestic investment exceeds savings. Only if the economy slows suddenly so that investment weakens, is the currency likely to weaken sharply.

If the economy becomes weak enough at this point and domestic investment intentions no longer exceed domestic savings, then the currency also needs to weaken. To generate a current account surplus the exchange rate may need to move to a level well below its equilibrium rate and there is then a risk that the currency will swing back sharply to an undervalued position.

THE WEAK EURO 1999 —

The euro was first established as a currency at the beginning of 1999. However, to the surprise of nearly everybody it proved persistently weak, falling from about 1.18 per dollar to a low of 0.82 per dollar in late 2000. The principal explanations put forward are in line with the four approaches above:

1. The long-run equilibrium level of the euro–dollar, originally thought to be in the region of $1.20, based on the past performance of the DM/dollar rate, is much lower, perhaps 1–1 or even less. Proponents of this view point to weaknesses in the basic structure of EMU (see below) and what they see as the fundamentally superior performance of the US economy in terms of productivity growth and returns on capital. This view is closely linked to the 'new economy' enthusiasm for the US economy discussed in Chapter 4. According to this view the limited reaction of the dollar to the economic slowdown in early 2001 was due to expectations that it would be temporary and quickly reversed.
2. The dollar's strength has reflected the faster economic growth rate in the USA than elsewhere and consequent higher interest rates. However, this view ran into trouble in early 2001 when

the US economy slowed abruptly and interest rates fell sharply. The dollar did weaken for a while but then showed renewed strength. Proponents of this approach refocused on *expected* relative growth. The dollar's renewed strength in 2001 was explained by expectations of an early rebound in the USA, combined with continued weakness in Europe.

3. The dollar's strength has been due to long-term inflows into the USA where investors naturally do not hedge. This view is supported by the sharp increase in foreign direct investment into the USA from Europe during the late 1990s and early 2000s. This partly reflected the optimism on the US economy discussed above. It may also have been due to the greater openness of the US economy to foreign acquisitions, in contrast to many countries in Euroland where legal and regulatory barriers remain, as well, perhaps, as language and cultural barriers. However, there is no doubt that direct investors as well as stock investors do, at times, hedge their investments. Hence there is no guarantee that we will not see, at some point, a sudden rush to hedge these long-term positions if there is a widespread change in perceptions. In 2001 most of the long-term inflows were actually into US bonds, where opportunistic hedging is even more likely.

4. The dollar's movements can be explained in terms of the savings–investment balance in the USA. During 1997–2000 the US economy grew very rapidly with pressure to reduce domestic savings and increase investment. Households reduced savings because they were encouraged to do so by low and falling unemployment and the rise in the stock market. Businesses cut savings because they saw major new investment opportunities. Some also felt a pressing need to invest in technology, particularly in computers, to beat the Millennium Bug and in web-sites to fight off the new internet companies. Meanwhile government saving did increase as the surplus widened, but not enough to offset the pressure from the private sector.

The result was a soaring US dollar, against all currencies, though the euro was the real loser. Japan was not unhappy to see a weaker currency given its slow economic growth and deflation. This soaring dollar achieved the necessary effect of widening the US current account deficit from 1.7% of GDP in 1997 to 4.2% in 2000. In fact US exports did rather well during this period (except for a slowdown during the Asian crisis), reflecting the prevalence of technology exports. Most of the adjustment took place through fast-growing imports.

Why did the US dollar stay strong in 2001 despite the economic slowdown and fall in interest? The answer seems to be that the savings–investment picture was still under stress. Although business investment fell, household spending held up strongly and the personal savings rate fell. At the same time the government surplus fell (i.e. less savings from the government) due to the slower economy and an expansionary fiscal policy.

At the time of writing the dollar is still relatively strong (in the 0.85–0.90 range). The reader will know what happened next! If the US economy, and particularly investment, bounces back strongly during 2002–3, then the savings–investment balance will remain under stress, keeping the dollar relatively strong. However, there may be no need for the current account deficit to widen further, in which case the currency has no need to strengthen any further and could give up some of its gains. This, perhaps, points to a euro–dollar range of €0.90–1.0. If, however, the US economy grows only slowly the savings–investment imbalance may fall back. This would require a weaker dollar, suggesting the euro–dollar moves above parity, to a range of €1.0–1.10. A 'double-dip' US recession, implying much weaker investment and higher private savings (though partly offset by a larger government budget deficit) could point to a dollar at €1.10–1.25 (Figure 14.2).

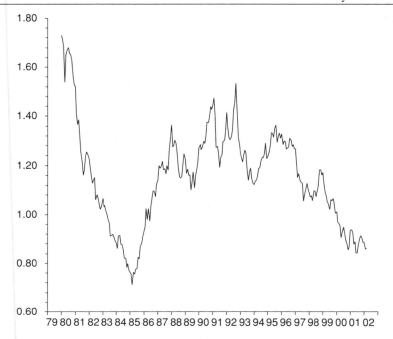

Figure 14.2   US$/euro rate
Source: Thomson Datastream

DOES INTERVENTION WORK?

Governments periodically intervene to support currencies. The usual approach is to buy the weak currency in the spot market, making as much noise about it as possible. Such interventions can be and have been on a large scale though they will inevitably be dwarfed by the potential size of private capital movements.

Intervention, therefore, only works if governments can persuade private investors that it will succeed, and this depends on a number of factors. Sometimes, especially if investors are already not sure how much further the currency can fall, government intervention can be enough to stop the move fairly easily. Obviously a great deal depends on the credibility of government intervention at that particular time.

In the mid-1980s the markets regarded central bank intervention with scepticism, and often treated it as a chance to make money. By the end of the decade, however, intervention was being treated with much more respect. The authorities had learnt to use some clever tricks (or perhaps re-learnt, since many of these tricks were used extensively in the 1970s). The 'bear squeeze', for example, is where a currency is allowed to fall to low levels, luring speculators into a trap, and then very heavy intervention deliberately pushes the exchange rate a long way very quickly so that many speculators are forced to close out with a loss. Perhaps the most important technique, which has been used very extensively, is closely coordinated intervention. On occasion a dozen or more central banks would intervene together within the space of a few minutes.

Exchange rate theory suggests that if governments intervene in the FX market but do not allow interest rates to move to support the intervention, then they are likely to be unsuccessful.

If governments do not allow interest rates to move the intervention is called 'sterilised' while if they do allow rates to move it is called 'unsterilised'. However, even with sterilised intervention the evidence since 1985 suggests that governments can sometimes move a market. In particular they may be able to create a view among investors of where the exchange rate might go in the long term even if the market takes the exchange rate outside that range in the short term. Hence G7 actions may act to reinforce the idea of a fundamental exchange rate (or PPP) to which it must return in the long run. This is not altogether surprising since the G7 countries rely on sophisticated versions of purchasing power parity as their main indicator.

In the 1990s there was much less intervention in the major currencies. Periodically the Japanese yen was supported or pushed down, but European currencies, first the Deutschmark and then the euro, were generally left to themselves.

EMU AND INVESTORS

In 1999 most of the members of the European Union fixed their currencies 'irrevocably' and entrusted monetary policy to the independent European Central Bank, the ECB. In 2000 Greece joined and, over the next few years, more members may join including several so-far reluctant countries such as the UK, Denmark and Sweden and several central and east European countries, waiting to join the EU itself. Nevertheless, despite the enthusiasm of many countries, EMU does create some economic problems which can affect markets. It also solves other problems and opens new opportunities.

EMU: The Advantages for Investors

EMU offers practical advantages to investors in that the money, bond and stock markets in Europe are now broader and more liquid than before. In particular, the foundation of EMU has unleashed a boom in non-government bond issuance in euros, and investors do not have to consider currency changes within Europe. Equally significant, however, is the potential for greater economic growth and consequently profits growth in Europe as a result of EMU combined with the single market, which would lead to an improved stock market performance.

In principle EMU can boost GDP growth in several ways. Least important are the savings made by eliminating the costs of changing money. This is represented by the jobs eradicated at banks, *bureaux de change*, and by the time saved in businesses and households from not having to calculate exchange rates and hedge against changes.

Much more important for the long term, however, is the impact of a single currency on company behaviour. Exchange rates are probably as much a psychological barrier as a real barrier to economic integration and probably impact mainly on small and medium size companies that previously did not consider selling, or sourcing, directly overseas (rather than through agents). Married to the practicality of the internet, Europe is likely to see a much faster development of the single market, which was proclaimed in 1992 but has been emerging only slowly.

There is a psychological change for companies in countries outside the euro zone too. Imagine if Canadians faced 12 different currencies in the USA. Is it not likely that they would be less likely to do business south of the Canadian border? Of course there remain substantial other barriers to the development of the single market in Europe including language, culture and remaining legal restrictions. The EU still has some way to go in creating a single market in the financial area for example, allowing companies to offer financial products freely across borders. Nevertheless these barriers will gradually be pulled down.

The result should be greater competition and therefore more dynamic development of companies, though the failure to agree a Takeover Code in 2001 was a major setback. Despite this there is likely to be an extended process of consolidation over the next decade as more large Europe-wide companies emerge, able to match the scale of US companies and reap the economies. One result of this should be downward pressure on inflation. This is good news in itself but also means that the path of interest rates is likely to be lower than it would otherwise be. This should support investment and economic growth, which is good for stocks. It also means lower bond yields and also higher valuations for stocks, which should make both bonds and stocks more attractive for investors.

EMU: The Risks for Investors

One concern for investors is that, since the new ECB wants to establish its anti-inflation credibility, it may be overcautious on inflation, risking a deflationary shock to the economy. Alternatively, and perhaps paradoxically, investors may look at the possibility of new members from central and eastern Europe and conclude that this will keep the currency weak because the new voters on the committee may be more willing to risk higher inflation than the existing committee.

Another concern is the uncertainty created by a new and untried central bank. There has been considerable doubt about its approach to policy, for a number of reasons. One is that the ECB is not transparent in its voting, nor does it publish minutes of its meetings. The rationale for this is sensible enough. If the votes of all the members were public knowledge there could be pressure on them to vote for the interest rate that would suit their own country rather than what is best for the euro zone as whole. Critics argue that the reverse is true, particularly since the votes are not actually conducted by secret ballot so insiders may well know how members lean. Reportedly, meetings aim for consensus but that may mean that interest rates are adjusted rather slowly rather than proactively.

One Size Fits All?

The major concern about EMU, however, is whether it can withstand the political consequences of the divergent economic performance of countries, given that all countries must have the same interest rate and there is no possibility of devaluation. In any currency union, e.g. the USA or the UK, particular regions, periodically and sometimes chronically, are weaker than others. Incomes are low, unemployment is low and they may be depressed for years or even decades. Usually the initial reason is the decline of a particular industry or sometimes simply that new industries emerge elsewhere leaving that region behind. One way to solve the problem would be for that region to devalue its currency to remain competitive. While this is certainly not the whole solution it may be a faster way to attack the problem than waiting for wages to adjust downwards. But a currency union of course makes devaluation impossible. The political consequences of a depressed region within a country may be manageable, not least because there is likely to be emigration from that area to a more thriving area. But what happens if, for example, the whole of France is depressed?

Imagine a situation where some of France's strongest industries are in difficulties. Perhaps agriculture is suffering because of world oversupply combined with attempts by the EU to cut back on the Common Agricultural Policy subsidies; or luxury goods are in decline because of a world slowdown or a change in tastes. Imagine, too, that France has just enjoyed a few good years with a tight labour market so that wages have risen and house prices have surged. But now France is moving into recession while the rest of Europe is still growing. France is really hurting because unemployment is rising, house prices are falling and there is downward pressure on wages. The unions are calling strikes in protest against redundancies and wage cuts and the government is bitterly resisting cuts in subsidies while farmers blockade the ports. At the same time the government needs to cut back on its growing budget deficit or else seriously breach the Stability Pact on fiscal policy which requires countries to keep their deficits to less than 3% of GDP.

What can the ECB do? If the rest of the Euroland area is still strong and inflation is in danger of breaching the 2% ceiling it would probably do nothing on interest rates and simply add to the chorus of opinion arguing that France needs to make significant structural change. Needless to say, EMU would not be popular in France and neither would the EU. France would probably be arguing for financial support from other countries, but this would be resisted.

This scenario is a real possibility in Europe precisely because Europe is not as integrated either in political or economic terms as, for example, the USA, or for that matter Germany. Imagine if California were in the same depressed situation. The US Federal government would be much more willing to provide fiscal help. In any case there would be a natural change in flow of funds to California from Washington as Californians paid less federal tax, due to higher unemployment and lower incomes while still receiving the usual transfers. Also Californians would be much more likely to leave California and move east than French people would be to move to another country in Europe. And, since US monetary and political union is not an issue, there would be no serious political argument for establishing or re-establishing the old currency.

For investors this scenario in France would be a worry for three reasons. First, if it began to appear that there was a real possibility that a country would actually leave EMU, its bonds and other paper would begin to have a currency risk premium. In other words, the spread on that country's bonds would widen out relative to other euro spreads. Given the political commitment of most European countries to union this would seem to be highly unlikely at present but it cannot be ruled out. Secondly, tension and disagreement within the euro zone could paralyse the political process. If this meant that further progress on opening up the single market was put on hold investors would be disappointed. Finally, the risk of this scenario raises the danger that a country might go through a serious recession and be unable to pull out for a prolonged period. This could impact on companies in that country, affecting their stock prices. It could also mean that public finances deteriorate, with debt rising, so that fiscal sustainability becomes an issue.

To minimise the risk of this scenario governments are under pressure to complete the single market and to harmonise on tax policies. There is also pressure for some coordination of fiscal policy and perhaps more facility for regional transfers to depressed areas. The Stability and Growth Pact also recognised this problem by encouraging countries to run a balanced budget in upswing years, in order to allow room in a downturn for the automatic fiscal stabilisers to work and perhaps even an active fiscal policy stimulus. However, European governments ran a relatively loose fiscal policy in 1999–2000, continuing with deficits despite the upswing. The result was that in 2002, with slow economies, Germany and Portugal were perilously close to the 3% deficit limit in the Pact. Meanwhile it will take decades for Europe to approach the degree of integration seen in the USA, or within any individual country. Therefore the risk of the one-size-fits-all policy, leading to a political crisis threatening EMU, will remain.

At present some analysts worry that Ireland is the country most at risk. In recent years it has enjoyed a very strong economic boom with rising incomes and house prices. If it faces a period of slower growth and house prices fall, Ireland might suffer a prolonged new downturn. However, this would not seriously threaten EMU. The only countries that could throw EMU into turmoil would probably be France or Germany, if they were in prolonged decline. Germany did suffer badly in 2001 but is expected to pick up in 2002. Italy could be another possibility, but as Italy is the country with the greatest popular support for EMU, this seems unlikely at present. Another could be the UK, if it enters EMU less than wholeheartedly. The UK economy is less integrated with Europe than, for example, France so there is perhaps a greater danger of it being out of step. On the other hand, the UK has the freest labour markets in Europe so perhaps would be the most able to adapt.

What should investors look for over the next few years as signs that EMU is working? First, more progress towards a single market and indications that companies are increasingly becoming European rather than national. Secondly, increased 'federalism' with more money going to and from the centre. At present Brussels only handles about 1% of tax money in Europe and this does not look likely to increase very much. It may take a crisis of some sort to increase the role of the centre. Thirdly, measures to free up labour markets so that there is more flexibility. Recent developments have been mixed. A number of countries have introduced new contracts for new employees (while often leaving existing employees on old protected contracts). On the negative side, there is a continued flow of new worker 'protection' legislation aiming at reduced hours, greater maternity and paternity benefits, and stronger workers' councils, etc.

CONCLUSION: THE FUNDAMENTALS OF EXCHANGE RATES

For international investors exchange rates represent both risk and opportunity since, over short time periods, movements in exchange rates are frequently much greater than gains or losses in individual bonds or stocks. Exchange rates can often be explained by relative inflation trends (through changes in so-called purchasing power parities), by relative economic strength (through changes in real interest rates), by changes in capital flows, or by careful analysis of the savings–investment balance. But forecasting, as opposed to explaining after the event, is not easy.

The analysis suggests several guidelines for dealing with currencies, though these are not hard and fast rules. First, given the difficulty of currency forecasting, the investor would be wise to be cautious in taking currency risk and in deciding whether or not to hedge risk. Secondly, the investor should not assume that because currencies have been responding in a particular way to particular news, that they will continue to do so indefinitely. Thirdly, investors need to be wary of government attempts to support overvalued exchange rates. They may succeed for a time, sometimes a long time, but nearly always eventually fail. Fourthly, investors should expect G7 government intervention aimed at supporting weak currencies or selling strong currencies to succeed.

15

Property Markets

Investing in property has been extremely profitable in many countries in recent decades, though not without periodic major downturns. Property prices in most countries are a multiple of their level of 20 or 30 years ago. However, investors often spectacular gains were not simply a by-product of the general price inflation of the last three decades. Rather, they were possible because of the prevailing low real interest rates of much of the period, combined with rapid growth in rents (*see Appendix for a fuller explanation*). The rapid growth in rents was due partly to economic growth, together with population growth and partly due to government planning (or zoning) restrictions which limit the supply of new buildings.

WHAT CAUSES GAINS IN PROPERTY PRICES?

Property provides a return to investors in the form of capital appreciation and rents. Investors usually assess the current value of a property by looking at the rental yield, i.e. the rent divided by the value of the property, expressed as a percentage. Quotations of yield are usually for gross yields, which is before all costs. For the investor, net yields are the relevant consideration, i.e. after subtracting all the ongoing costs involved such as rental agents fees, management fees, depreciation and repairs. The net yield is usually substantially lower by, typically, 2–5 percentage points.

To analyse property further it is helpful to consider the gains from investing in a building or land in addition to the gains from the benchmark risk-free investment of an index-linked bond. Index-linked government bonds are the investment with no credit risk (except the sovereign risk taken to be the lowest available in most countries) and no economic risk from higher inflation, recession or any other shock. The gains from property investment above the index-linked return can be divided into three components. The final return is calculated from these gains less the cost of buying and selling the property.

1. Gains arising because the net yield on the property is greater than the real rate of interest.
2. Gains arising because the price of the property rises faster than price inflation.
3. If the property is mortgaged, gains because the increase in property prices is greater than the nominal interest rate.

We will discuss these components in turn.

Net Yield Greater than the Real Rate of Interest

Suppose for a moment that property prices are not rising faster than general inflation and there is no mortgage on the property. Then, if the net rental yield is (say) 4% and the real rate of interest is also 4%, it is evident that the owner is making no gain in addition to an interest-bearing asset. He is simply receiving the same return as if he put his money into the index-linked bond. If, however, the net rental yield is above the real rate of interest, there is a genuine gain, and vice versa.

Property Prices rising Faster than General Inflation

Most people buy property in the hope of making a capital gain, or in other words hoping that property prices rise faster than inflation. Over the long term, property prices will normally achieve this, i.e. go up in real terms, for several reasons. First, the cost of new building tends to rise faster than price inflation because it is closely related to wage inflation, which itself rises faster than price inflation as living standards rise. Of course if labour productivity in building houses rose at the same pace as wages then costs would not rise. But the productivity growth that drives general wage growth tends to be in manufacturing, while building workers must still be paid more as wages rise generally. Hence the cost of building tends to rise faster than general inflation. That is also why it is much cheaper to build a house in, for example, Thailand than in the USA.

Secondly, rising wages means rising rents, and property ultimately derives its value from the stream of expected future rents (rather like a stock's valuation depends on future dividends). Thirdly, good locations will always command a premium. So city centres, inner suburbs, beach-fronts, or in the case of commercial properties, convenient locations, will do well. As populations, and particularly cities, expand under the pressure of population growth, the value of these locations increases. Fourthly, planning restrictions limit the supply of good locations.

Gains because the Percentage Increase in Prices is Greater than the Borrowing Cost

This is the power of leverage. The really great fortunes from property over the last 40 years have been made because borrowing costs were lower than the rise in prices. Of course, if the location is good enough this can happen even with a prudent central bank, keeping real interest rates in the normal range of 2–4% p.a. above consumer price inflation. Anyone who bought property in London in 1980 will have done well, because even though real short-term interest rates have averaged 4.3% p.a., London's growth as a world city has been much faster.

But gains at certain times and in various places have been even greater than this, because interest rates were actually very low in real terms. This was true in most countries in the 1970s for example. A more recent example was Hong Kong up until 1997. Because the Hong Kong dollar was pegged to the US dollar, interest rates were set at or close to US interest rates. But wage and price inflation was relatively high, reflecting the strong productivity growth in the territory, so real interest rates were negative for much of the period. As a result, property prices rose an average 19.7% p.a. between 1983 (a cyclical low) and 1997, the high. Even in 2001, after falling around 50% from the peak, the gain from 1983 onwards amounted to an average 10.2% p.a., ahead of consumer price inflation averaging 7.6% p.a. The investor who borrowed money, even at the relatively high mortgage spreads for much of the period, did very well. A similar example is Ireland during 1997–2001, following Ireland's entry to the euro, which left interest rates in Ireland well below the general inflation rate.

HOW TO ASSESS PROPERTY VALUATIONS

The attraction of commercial property as an investment is assessed by looking at rental yields. Some investors may simply be looking for a high yield, compared with interest rates. Others, seeing a high yield will expect it to decline, i.e. prices to rise. Residential property can be looked at in terms of yield too, though it is commonly assessed also in relation to average earnings.

The yield is the rental income as a percentage of the value of the property and gross yields usually range between lows of around 2–3% and highs up to about 15%. Strictly, however, we should look at net yields after subtracting all the costs of maintaining the property and generating the rental income. These costs include depreciation (since in most markets newer property is worth more than older property), agents fees, management charges, voids (i.e. periods between lets), repairs, insurance, etc. This total is unlikely to be less than 2% p.a., properly assessed and, where management costs are high or depreciation is substantial, may be 5% or more.

A Useful Property Pricing Formula

We can analyse yields using the following simple formula.

The price of property should move over time to make the net yield equal to the real rate of interest, plus the risk premium attached to property, less the expected increase in price above ordinary inflation.

A numerical example may be helpful. Suppose the current gross yield on a property is 8% p.a. and the investor calculates that annual costs are about 3%, giving a net yield of 5%. The real rate of interest (taken from index-linked bonds) is 3% p.a. and the risk premium is assumed to be 5% p.a. Then the implied expectation for property price increases is 3% p.a. The investor can then judge for himself whether a 3% p.a. increase in prices is a reasonable expectation. Obviously every building is unique and investors need to assess its particular characteristics and prospects. In this discussion we focus on the overall market fundamentals.

Given this formula we can then see the impact of changes in the components. For example, if real interest rates rise, the yield has to rise. Since a rise in real interest rates will not usually automatically raise rents, this means that the price of property is likely to fall. Similarly, if the risk premium rises, perhaps because of an economic downturn which makes tenants more difficult to find, the yield also has to rise. Finally, using the numerical example above, if the economy starts to grow rapidly and investors start to believe that a 3% p.a. increase in prices is too cautious they will push up prices, driving down yields. These factors are considered in more detail below.

The Four Factors Driving Yields

Rents

In money terms yields are obtained from rents which will go up and down in line with the economy, unemployment, real wages, etc. Over the long term rents will tend to rise faster than nominal GDP in any location where supply is limited, either by geography or government. Given rents, we are interested in how property prices vary, changing the yield; but, other things being equal, higher rents will mean higher property prices. In the case of housing, 50–75% of the market in most countries is owner-occupied. In practice the demand from owner-occupiers is driven partly by the same economic factors as rents. It is also influenced by expectations for house prices since, particularly during the boom period, households tend to focus on the potential gains from property.

Real Interest Rates

As we have seen, real interest rates are set in the short term by the government but longer term by the strength of the economy. So, during the *late upswing* phase of the cycle property yields will be under pressure when real interest rates rise because the central bank is trying to slow the economy. Yields will also be under pressure if real interest rates are high due to heavy government borrowing, so-called crowding out. Finally, if the economy is growing very strongly, that is also likely to raise interest rates because of pressure on capital. But, in this environment, strong economic growth is likely to be generating high expectations for property price inflation and perhaps also a low value for the risk premium.

Property Price Expectations

Key macro-economic factors driving property prices are the rate of growth of the economy and the rate of growth of population. In countries with very fast productivity growth, wages will be rising much faster than prices and therefore gains in property prices will be relatively faster. Similarly, if natural or government restrictions apply to new properties being built in the same location, prices will rise on scarcity value. There is also probably a tendency for people to extrapolate past movements, thus extending price upswings and deepening downswings. This kind of overshooting is a feature of most markets.

The Risk Premium

This is the risk of buying property versus buying a safe investment. The risk premium for a bond (not index-linked) is the risk that inflation moves up unexpectedly. Or the risk of buying a stock is that its earnings perform much worse than expected. In Chapter 12 we suggested that the risk premium on bonds now, in an era of low inflation, is quite low, probably less than 1% p.a. The risk premium on stocks (Chapter 13) is also believed to be lower now, perhaps only 2–3% p.a. Many people regard property as a relatively low risk investment. Certainly it is protected against inflation. Of course prices could go down if there is general deflation, but the investor without a mortgage would not actually lose anything unless prices go down faster than goods price inflation. The investor with a mortgage may have more difficulty with deflation since real interest rates tend to be high.

But there are nevertheless a number of risks with property. First, expectations for the real interest rate or for property prices could prove wrong. It is sensible to attach at least some probability to that. For example, if the investor could buy an index-linked bond yielding 3% p.a. and thought that the most likely long-term return from property was 4% p.a. he might not think that the extra 1% p.a. was enough to justify the risk that he is wrong. Secondly, there are considerable specific risks associated with an individual property, just as there is with an individual stock. It may not be possible to rent it for long periods. Or the tenant might default, perhaps leaving the owner with substantial legal costs to obtain possession. Or the government might suddenly decide to build a motorway past the property, hurting its value without adequate compensation. Investors buying stocks can reduce the impact of risks to an individual stock by buying a broad portfolio. With property, much larger investments are needed for full diversification and few investors are able to do so. They may, however, be able to buy a property mutual fund or, in the USA, a real estate investment trust (REIT) to obtain diversification.

The other major issue with property is its lack of liquidity. A stock or bond can usually be traded virtually instantaneously, but a property cannot. If the investor changes his mind, or circumstances change, it will take weeks or months or longer to sell a property. If any of the other risks materialise, therefore, the investor cannot move quickly to avoid them. Moreover there are usually substantial costs involved in buying and selling a property including taxes, refurbishment costs, vacancy periods and agents fees. These costs are unlikely to be less than 5% of the value of the property. If the investor wants to sell quickly for whatever reason, there is a risk of loss. Overall then, the risk premium is likely to be at least as high as for stocks, and perhaps higher.

THE PROPERTY CYCLE

Property prices typically follow a cyclical pattern, lagging the economic cycle compared with stock markets. In periods of high inflation this means that price inflation varies between slow and fast. However, since 1990, with the major economies experiencing very low inflation or even deflation, property prices in many countries have shown periods of outright decline. The property cycle is driven by the interaction of changes in rents, changes in expectations of price increases and interest rates.

Residential demand is driven by confidence about employment and growing incomes, which reaches a high during the *late upswing* phase of the economic cycle. Also people are frequently seduced by rising house prices and want to participate in the apparently easy gains. They therefore buy houses larger than they really need, thinking of it partly as an investment. Expectations of future price gains are high and the risk premium is low. Rental yields decline despite rising rents.

When the *recession* bites, demand falls sharply and house prices start to slide. In most markets house prices adjust relatively slowly and this slide often continues through the *recovery* phase of the cycle as well. After a severe recession consumers will still find jobs hard to find right through the *early upswing* phase. Moreover, they no longer believe that housing is such a good investment and therefore are interested in buying only if they need the space. But many people already have enough space because they overbought during the previous upswing. Also, the risk premium is high at this point, particularly if house prices are still substantially below their peak and some owners face 'negative equity'. Only when the economy moves into the *late upswing* phase of the cycle, and unemployment is low, do prices start to rise again significantly.

Commercial property follows a similar pattern. During the *late upswing* phase demand for property is particularly strong and rents rise. Demand is strong both because of the buoyant economy and also because companies are doing well and frequently seek new, more prestigious offices. They also expect to grow so look for offices and factories with room to expand. Demand for retailing space is strong too because consumers are spending heavily and new stores are starting up in large numbers. At this point developers start to build new property at a relatively rapid rate. Land prices rise as the supply of new land with permissions to build declines.

When the *recession* comes, all this goes into reverse. Companies retrench staff and are content with smaller, less impressive space. New start-ups are less common. Consumer spending growth slows and there are fewer new retail stores while some of the old ones fail. Often demand falls just as new property planned during the upswing phase comes on stream, driving rents sharply lower. Property prices inevitably follow, but fall even faster so yields are driven up.

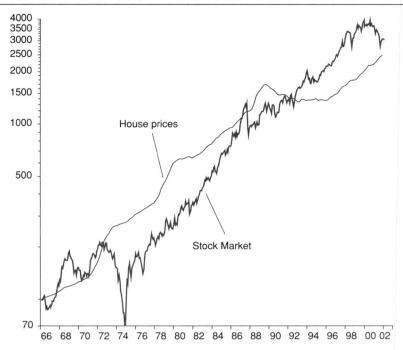

Figure 15.1   UK: Stocks versus houses
Source: Thomson Datastream

THE UK EXPERIENCE WITH HOUSE PRICES

The price of the average house in the UK increased by 25 times between 1965 and the end of 1991 according to the Nationwide House Price Index. A typical house worth about £100,000 now, would have sold for £4,000 in 1965. The UK stock market has increased by somewhat more, 35 times, from 1965 to the end of 2001. Stocks outperformed during the late 1960s but then, after the collapse in 1973–4, took 10 years to return to the same performance as houses. Since about 1990 stocks have outperformed (see Figure 15.1).

This comparison is simply of the *price* index for stocks and houses. A full comparison would need to take into account dividends and rents (or imputed rents for owner-occupiers). However, it is probable that this would not change the result that the stock market, overall, has outperformed. The stock market return index for the UK shows that if an investor reinvested all dividends (and assuming no transactions cost), he could have turned an investment of £100 in 1965 into about £21,000 by the end of 2001. This 210-fold increase is much greater than the increase in the price index, reflecting the fact that, until recently, average dividend yields in the UK were relatively high, at about 5% p.a. For an investment in housing to have achieved the same return would have required a net rental yield of just over 6%. A more plausible average net rental yield would be 4–5%, which over such a long period would represent a substantial underperformance.

Over the same period the consumer price index increased about 12 times, which means that real house prices have slightly more than doubled. However, real house prices have followed a clear cyclical pattern with the three most recent cycles shown in Figure 15.2. These correspond

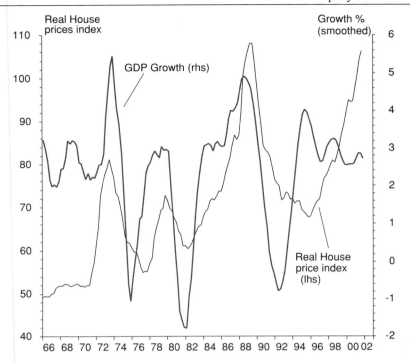

Figure 15.2   UK real house prices and GDP growth
Source: Thomson Datastream

to the UK business cycle. In the recessions of 1975 and 1980 nominal house prices did not actually fall because underlying annual inflation was relatively high, 24% in 1974 and 18% in 1980. In 1990, by contrast, inflation was only about 9% p.a. and it quickly fell to under 4% p.a. by 1992. The result was that the correction to nominal house prices, in the aftermath of a severe recession, was a painful 20% from the peak in Q3 1989 to the low in Q1 1993. House prices overall then began to rise again in 1996 and have shown a new strong upward move in recent years.

The four major cycles in house prices since the mid-1960s are illustrated in Figure 15.3 in relation to average earnings. During house price booms the ratio rises to over 4 times earnings and then typically falls back to the 3–3.5 times range during the downswing. In the mid-1990s the ratio fell to an unusually low level, only 2.8 times, reflecting the widespread reluctance to buy houses after the substantial decline in prices in the early 1990s. Expectations for future house price increases were very low and the risk premium particularly high. Since 1996 the ratio has climbed again but is, so far at least, less exposed than in previous cycles.

One of the key drivers of the cycle was real interest rates which were frequently negative during the 1970s (see Figure 15.4). This was not the case in the 1980s, however, and the substantial gains in house prices during that period were due to the prolonged economic upswing of the time. There were also important tax changes in the late 1980s which encouraged increased buying. Since the mid-1990s real interest rates have been significantly lower than in the 1980s. At the same time the economy, particularly in the south of England, has been relatively strong. A key driver has been the rapid expansion of London's economy which has

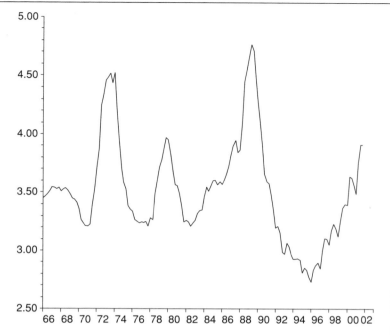

Figure 15.3   UK: House prices/average earnings
Source: Thomson Datastream

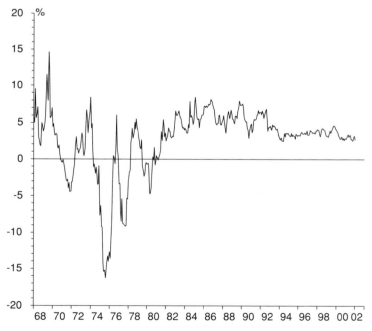

Figure 15.4   UK: Real interest rates
Source: Thomson Datastream

encouraged high rates of immigration. With the acceleration in prices from about 1995 onwards the risk premium gradually fell.

The Outlook for UK House Prices

House prices have been rising strongly in recent years, albeit from low levels in relation to earnings. As of early 2002, with prices still buoyant and interest rates low, the much-watched ratio of house prices to average earnings has reached relatively high levels, though not as extreme as in 1973 or 1989. Commentators derive some comfort, however, from the fact that this average is high partly because the ratio is particularly high in the southeast of England, boosted by the buoyancy of the London-based service economy, allied to very tight planning controls. Outside the southeast prices are generally more reasonable in relation to earnings, though rising fast.

We can analyse the position today using the tools outlined above. In the mid-1990s rental yields on prime London flats were generally at or above 10% p.a. but expectations for increased prices were low and the risk premium was high, following the pain of the price declines in previous years. Rents rose during the second half of the 1990s, buoyed by immigration and economic growth. Owner-occupied demand also increased as unemployment fell to levels not seen since the 1970s and real wages grew strongly. Nevertheless property prices increased significantly more than rents or average earnings so the rental yield fell to 5–7% p.a. for prime London flats.

In 2001, however, signs emerged of a weakening of rents in London, partly due to the shake-out in the financial sector. Generally the world slowdown had little effect on the UK property market because the economy continued to grow moderately, boosted by government spending and households were encouraged by the cut in interest rates, which took real short-term interest rates to unusually low levels.

Real short-term interest rates are likely to rise in 2002–3 assuming the world recovery continues, though real bond yields, the preferred benchmark, will probably remain at about 3% p.a. Expectations for house price inflation appear to be relatively strong. Published forecasts by the Halifax and Nationwide Building Societies (the main providers of data on the market) point to continuing house price increases over the next year, though at a reduced rate. Anecdotal evidence suggests that consumers are still expecting further gains though some are sceptical and remember past cycles. A key phenomenon that has driven flat sales in recent years is the growth in 'buy-to-let' purchases as wealthier individuals invest in property. However, there are signs of declining rents in some areas where a large number of flats have been purchased for rent.

The risk premium at this point should be high, given the run-up in the market. However, all the evidence suggests that it is not high, but low. Anecdotally there is a widespread opinion that although prices may not rise much further they should not fall very much, given current economic conditions. The risk premium could rise sharply, however, if there was a 'double dip' US recession or a new geopolitical shock.

If we look at how the current market is valuing property in terms of yields, the gross rental yields on prime flats in London of 5–6% p.a. implies net yields in the range of 2–3% p.a. With real interest rates at about 3% the market is pricing property with expectations of continuing strong price appreciation, at least 5% p.a. if we take the risk premium to be 3–4%. This is not an unreasonable view given wage growth of 4–5% p.a. and expectations that London will continue to grow strongly. But it would be rudely upset if real interest rates rise and/or the economic outlook worsens. Moreover with yields historically low and the house price/earnings ratio relatively high (particularly for London) the upside potential is naturally much more limited than it was five years ago. And the risk of a fall in prices is high.

CONCLUSION: PROPERTY FUNDAMENTALS

Gains from investment in property arise from three scenarios: first, if the net yield is greater than the real rate of interest; secondly, if the price of the property rises faster than consumer price inflation; thirdly, if the property is mortgaged, because the annual increase in property prices is greater than the nominal interest rate.

Property can be assessed by analysing the net rental yield and determining its direction in the future. Expectations of a fall in yield imply a capital gain unless rents are expected to fall. The four factors driving yield are money rents, real interest rates, property price expectations and the risk premium. Property prices tend to follow a cycle, linked to the economic cycle, but usually with a lag of one or two years.

APPENDIX: WHY INFLATION IN ITSELF DOES NOT GENERATE GAINS

Suppose an investor buys a building for $100,000 in a period of 100% p.a. inflation. After one year it is worth $200,000, but this is of no more value than before in real terms since everything else has also gone up 100%. We can ignore the rent for a moment because the investor would have received that anyway, even without the inflation. Of course, a year later the rent should have doubled, but it is worth no more in real terms. Clearly, in this extreme example, inflation has not helped the investor.

Is the situation any different if the investor uses a mortgage to help to finance the property? The answer is that it depends on the rate of interest. If the rate of interest was equal to inflation (i.e. a zero real interest rate) and the investor borrowed $70,000, then at the end of the period he has a building worth $200,000, as before, an interest bill of $70,000 (i.e. 100% p.a.) and a debt due of $70,000. In short he has $60,000 net, exactly double his initial outlay and therefore worth the same. Note also that had he put the $30,000 in the bank and earned the 100% rate of interest, he would also have $60,000.

At first sight it might seem that if we extend this example one more year the investor would make money because the interest rate is fixed to the original sum borrowed, which is fixed. But this is not so. After two years the property is worth $400,000 (another 100% rise), the debt is still $70,000 and the new interest payment is still just $70,000. So, if he sells the property and pays off the $70,000 mortgage he has an asset worth $330,000 and has paid out only $140,000. So, net, he has $190,000.

A good return? Actually, no. No more than he could have obtained by banking the money, assuming he could also have earned an interest rate of 100%. His initial $30,000 would have become $120,000 and the first $70,000 he paid in interest in the first year would have earned an additional $70,000, so the total he would have is $190,000, exactly the same. Again, inflation as such is of no help to the property investor.

But suppose the rate of interest is less than inflation, say only 90%. (This is another way of saying that the real rate of interest is negative 10%.) Then, in the 70% mortgage example, the asset is still worth $200,000 after one year, but interest costs are only $63,000 so, after selling and paying off the mortgage, he has $67,000 instead of $60,000. This is worth $33,500 in 'old' money so he has a gain of 12%.

If he held the property for two years the gain builds up very rapidly. After the second year the property is worth $400,000 as before, but the total interest paid is only $126,000. So after repaying the mortgage and subtracting the $126,000 paid he has $204,000. This is $51,000 in 'old' money, a gain of 70%. The reason for this substantial gain is the negative rate of interest.

Note that, with a negative rate of interest, buying property is a much better investment than putting the money in a bank. After two years the property is worth $400,000, so the investor has not gained in real terms. But if he put the money on deposit at 90% he now only has $361,000. In old money this is worth $90,250, so he has lost nearly 10% of his wealth.

These examples show the crucial importance of property price inflation being greater than the rate of interest. Otherwise the investor who borrows to buy property has to rely on rental income being high to generate a good return.

16

Emerging Markets Investments

In the late 1980s and early 1990s, emerging markets were seen as 'hot' investments. Asian markets performed spectacularly well in the early and mid-1980s and Latin American markets rose strongly in the late 1980s and early 1990s. The best year of all was 1993 when the MSCI emerging index climbed a remarkable 66%, while the US S&P 500 index managed a modest 7%. Many individual markets doubled in value in just two or three years. If investors could ride these spurts, returns could be very impressive indeed.

As emerging stocks became more and more fashionable most global investors began to include them in their portfolio. International brokers opened offices in exotic locations in search of information and clients and funds under management climbed. For many countries this international interest proved very helpful in developing their stock markets and enabled more private issuance of stocks as well as new privatisations. Unfortunately for investors, the market performance since 1993, and since 1997 in particular, has been extremely poor, both in absolute terms and in relation to the US and European markets (Figure 16.1). Between February 1994 (the peak of the boom) and February 2002, the IFC global emerging index fell 38%. Asia performed the worst, declining by 50%.

For investors the questions are: (1) Does this poor performance reflect merely a weak economic performance, which might be reversed? (2) Is it due to the bursting of a bubble? (3) Is it due to fundamental problems in investing in emerging stocks such as lack of protection for minority shareholders or excessive volatility in business conditions? If it is the first, there may be an excellent opportunity for investors in coming years simply because emerging markets are now so much out of favour. But this will be true only if emerging countries can perform better.

EMERGING STOCK INDICES

There is no single accepted benchmark for emerging stock market data though three are widely available: the S&P/IFC indices, starting in 1985; MSCI, starting in 1988; and ING Baring indices, starting in 1992. The IFC publishes a Global index (IFCG) and an Investible index (IFCI), the latter confined to stocks where there is sufficient liquidity and availability for foreign investors. MSCI publish the MSCI Free indices, with the same aim. However, different indices give widely varying results due to differences in weighting and coverage. For example, the IFC builds its indices from companies with the greatest market capitalisation, MSCI stresses industry representation and Barings focuses on liquidity.

The indices can also be relatively unstable over time because of large changes in composition as countries come and go. For example, in 1995 the addition of South Africa to the IFCI index took its weight from 0% to 25% overnight and other countries were reduced accordingly. Similarly, the effective closure of the Malaysian market in 1998 had a dramatic effect on indices.

Despite these problems most fund managers do compare their performance with particular indices and there is no way of looking at the sector as a whole without using indices. The IFCI is clearly preferable to the IFCG for most purposes, but data go back only to 1988.

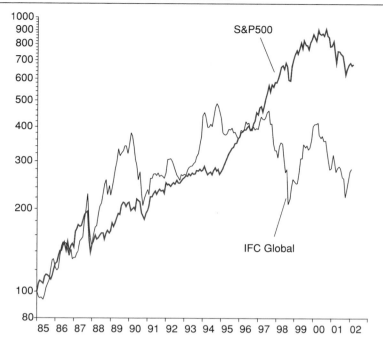

Figure 16.1   S&P/IFC Global Emerging Index and S&P 500 (log scale)
Source: Thomson Datastream

At the beginning of 2000, publication of the IFC indices was taken over by Standard and Poors.

Many investors include Hong Kong and Singapore in their concept of emerging markets because so many of the companies on the Hong Kong and Singapore exchanges are directly involved with emerging markets. However, due to their high per capita income levels, they are not included in the IFC emerging market indices.

WHY INVEST IN EMERGING MARKETS?

The case for investing in emerging markets rests on five key propositions.

Emerging Countries can Grow Faster than Developed Markets, Provided that They Adopt Market-oriented Policies

Given good economic policies, emerging markets are expected to grow relatively quickly for several reasons. First, as they are catching up with the industrial countries they are not limited by technical progress. The first industrial country, the UK, is estimated to have grown at around 2.25–2.5% p.a. throughout the 200+ years since the Industrial Revolution in the late eighteenth century. Germany and the USA, catching up in the nineteenth century, managed growth rates of 4–5% p.a. for long periods. In the twentieth century Japan, South Korea and others enjoyed long periods of growth of 8% p.a. or more. The key is to be able to mobilise sufficient capital for investment by generating a high domestic savings rate, and then to use those savings efficiently (see Chapter 2 for a detailed discussion).

A second reason for expecting emerging countries to grow rapidly is that they should be able to attract capital, management and technology from the developed countries. Foreign direct investment brings all three, while foreign purchases of stocks and bonds brings capital. Increasing globalisation, powered by the end of the Cold War and progress on world trade liberalisation, is expected to reinforce this trend.

Finally, emerging countries mostly have fast growing populations and even faster growing labour forces, given the relatively young population and increasing participation of women. This is in stark contrast to Europe and Japan (where both populations and workforces are growing very slowly). Most emerging countries are also seeing faster labour force growth than in the USA despite the latter's high rate of immigration. Rapid labour force expansion can permit faster economic growth, by helping to provide a continuing labour supply and home market.

Countries will Increasingly Adopt Market-oriented Policies in the Current World Environment

Probably every country in the world has been adopting more market-oriented economic policies over the last 20 years, even including the laggards such as North Korea and Cuba. This has been driven partly by the success of 'early-adopters', which then became development models for others. In Asia the four original 'tigers', Hong Kong, Singapore, Taiwan and Korea, led the way though they also looked to Japan for inspiration. In Latin America the success of Chile was crucial in motivating Argentina and Brazil and others in the 1990s. In Europe the European Union countries are the inspiration for surrounding countries.

Another major factor has been the discrediting of socialist models of development following the failures in the Soviet Union and Yugoslavia (where a worker–ownership model was tried in the 1960s and 1970s). All the remaining communist regimes, such as China and Vietnam, are moving towards more market-centred forms of organisation.

A supporting factor here may be the increased popular knowledge of what is going on outside people's home country, through the greater penetration of TV, increased travel and more recently the internet. Whether or not a government is democratic, the political pressure to deliver the good life, in the form of material comfort, is more intense than ever. Only a few governments—for example, in Iraq or North Korea—seem to be able to ignore this, although even then not completely.

However, politics can be a short-term business, with irreconcilable pressures preventing progress on structural change. To tackle this problem the IMF and World Bank link their loan programmes to compensate governments for the short-term political pain of implementing structural changes. Without such compensation governments may be unwilling to tackle change. Emerging stock markets tend to rise when IMF and/or World Bank programmes are announced.

One very important area is privatisation. Annual privatisation revenues in developing countries climbed from \$2.6 bn in 1988 to \$25.4 bn in 1996, according to a study published by the Centre for Economic Policy Research.[1] The same study suggested that privatisation has played a crucial role in emerging market development and is associated with excess returns in stock markets. Privatisation, of course, adds to the stocks available on local equity markets but also tends to boost the whole market. The CEPR authors argue that 'the process of privatisation itself, whenever implemented rigorously and consistently, leads to a progressive

---

[1] E.C. Perotti and P. van Oijen (September 1999) Privatisation, political risk and stock market development. CEPR Discussion Paper 2243.

resolution of regulatory and legal uncertainty and thus to a resolution of uncertainty over future policy'.

Sometimes major structural reform is pushed through by undemocratic governments, for example in Korea in the 1960s, Chile in the 1980s or China today. However, there are also plenty of recent examples of democracies achieving radical change, e.g. Argentina and Peru in the 1990s. Newly elected governments usually have 4–5 years to prove themselves before the next election, which can often be enough to reap the benefits of change. In contrast, a weak undemocratic government may not be able to risk political unpopularity for that length of time.

A final factor which needs to be remembered, particularly in taking a long-term view, is the role of the international environment. Reasonably strong growth in the industrial countries and openness to trade are crucial supports for emerging market success. The problems in east Asian countries in the late-1990s, though partly self-generated, were also linked to Japan's chronic recession and the consequent weak yen. If all the industrial countries were in recession at the same time, as occurred in the 1930s, the prospects for emerging markets would be much more uncertain.

Companies in Fast-Growing Emerging Markets will be able to Generate Matching Profit Growth

This is the weakest proposition of the five. In some countries profits have performed well but in others results are poor. There are several reasons why profits may not grow as rapidly as expected. First, many emerging country companies appear to have followed growth strategies rather than profit strategies. The emphasis has been on growing in size rather than in earnings. This has long been the Japanese approach to development and companies in many other Asian countries, in particular, seem to have followed the same path.

Secondly, there is concern that, in some cases, publicly quoted companies are run in parallel with privately held companies, often with inadequate transparency in the relations between them. This may mean that earnings are limited in the public company as majority owners transfer them to their private companies. On occasion even, assets have been directly transferred between them contrary to the interests of minority share holders. Worries about these two points have made some fund managers argue that it is better to participate in the faster growth of emerging markets by buying the stocks of multinational companies with a large emerging market involvement.

A further problem with investing in emerging markets is that the mix of stocks may not reflect the economy very well. In particular, the fastest growing areas of the economy may not be well represented. If that is the case then it becomes much more difficult to argue that investors can tap into fast country growth by buying a portfolio of the country's stocks.

Emerging Markets have Acceptable Risks

The volatility of emerging markets equities indicates that risk is higher than for major markets. The standard deviation of returns on global emerging markets' indices is usually around 20–25% p.a. compared to 10–15% p.a. for major markets. Broad regions such as Asia or Latin America are higher still, while individual countries frequently show standard deviations of 40–60% p.a. or more.

Until the Asian crisis there was a general perception that risks were receding. Broad country risks seemed to be reduced after the collapse of the Soviet Union and with the spread of globalisation and the widespread adoption of market-friendly policies. More specific risks of investing in emerging markets seemed to be dwindling as liquidity increased, settlement improved and moves were made to increase transparency in many countries. There was also a view that by investing in a wide range of emerging countries investors could diversify away much of the risk. This latter point is indeed supported by the statistics, though investors were surprised by the contagion effects unleashed by the Asian crisis.

Emerging markets were recognised as a high-risk investment, but in investment theory 'high risk' implies that you can expect high returns, so this appeared to be an attractive proposition especially for the long-term investor. The decline in interest rates in the industrial countries added to that attraction in the 1990s. However, the actual returns in recent years have dented that expectation. Not only has a 'buy and hold' strategy of emerging markets proved extremely unrewarding, but the general decline in emerging markets in 1997–8, and again in 2000–1, left little scope for even an active manager to make money in this asset class.

Emerging Market Stocks have Relatively Low Correlations with Major Countries

The data suggest that correlation has increased over time, so some analysts argue that emerging markets are no longer as attractive from the point of view of diversification. IFC data suggest that the correlation between the composite emerging stock index and the US S&P 500 index rose from 49% in the five years to 1994 to 68% in the five years to 2000. Nevertheless, even a 68% correlation means that, according to investment theory, there are potential gains to be had. Emerging markets are influenced by domestic issues to a considerable degree, particularly broad issues of economic policy and country risk. However, emerging markets are also influenced by world economic growth, world trade and US liquidity, for example, which does link returns in emerging markets with major markets.

WHAT DRIVES EMERGING STOCK MARKETS?

We can identify six key drivers of performance. These are based on past historical performance and, as always, this is no guarantee of future performance. Also, there is tremendous variation in the performance of different countries within the total picture.

1. *Countries that* **accelerate** *economic growth enjoy stock market gains.* Countries with rapid economic growth do not necessarily produce better investment returns than countries with slower economic growth. However, countries that achieve an *acceleration* in growth do show stock market spurts. This accounts for the stellar performance of many countries in Asia in the early 1980s and also in 1992–3. It also accounts for the strong performance of Latin markets in the early 1990s. Chapter 10 showed why an acceleration in economic growth typically requires an improvement in policy such as restoring fiscal and monetary stability, significant privatisations or major liberalisation of domestic markets or foreign tariff structures. Very often markets will move on this news, even before the results are seen in economic growth and this is why no direct relationship is observable between the growth itself and stock market performance.

2. *Countries with more rapid economic growth tend to have higher valuations* (e.g. price/ earnings ratios). Again this is not too surprising and indeed is partly a consequence of the first point. Markets rise when investors believe growth is going to accelerate, and that takes price/earnings ratios higher. Hence we observe, when the growth comes through, relatively high valuations. Historically countries growing rapidly (e.g. 6–8% GDP growth annually) have enjoyed 20- to 30-fold price/earnings ratios. However, this is not much use to the new

investor since it is principally the *news* of an acceleration or deceleration of growth that moves markets.

3. *The link between GDP growth and profits growth is not strong.* This is a surprising and disappointing result that suggests that it is wise to treat emerging markets with some caution. There may be a number of reasons for it. At the macro-economic level, although we would expect profits to broadly rise with GDP, we also know that the share of profits in GDP can itself vary. Another way of looking at this is to say that the return on capital can vary. There may be a tendency for the share of profits in GDP and the return on capital to fall during a period of strong GDP growth. Alternative explanations focus on the firms themselves. Perhaps individual firms are unable to capture increased profits even as the economy grows. This could be because new firms are the gainers. Or it could be the problem that the people who control publicly quoted firms divert the main profits into their privately owned firms, through transfer pricing and other methods.

4. *Emerging stock markets frequently outperform during periods of Fed easing.* Unfortunately there is no simple relationship here, not least because falling US interest rates usually go along with weak US GDP growth which is a negative for emerging markets. Nevertheless, periods of Fed easing such as 1992–3 and 2001 saw emerging markets outperform. The reason is the increased liquidity held by investors and the greater willingness to take on more risky investments.

5. *Emerging stock markets perform worst during the slowdown phase of the US economy.* This is partly a reflection of high interest rates and partly due to expectations of slower economic growth as export markets slow down and commodity prices start to weaken.

6. *Emerging markets do well when commodity prices are rising.* Since many emerging economies are dependent on commodities this is not surprising. Of course, oil cuts both ways since some countries are major importers and suffer from higher prices.

PRACTICAL ISSUES FOR INVESTORS

Emerging markets are at the frontier of stock market investing and present greater risks and costs than investing in major markets. There are three broad areas of risk[2]:

1. *Settlement and operational risks and costs.* There are considerable risks that a party will default on payment or delivery obligations. If trades fail and the settlement system does not ensure that shares are only delivered versus payment (DVP), then investors are exposed to counter-party risk. According to the World Bank, most emerging markets do not conform to DVP. Delays in trades and erratic payments of dividends are common.

2. *Legal and custodial risks and costs.* A key problem is fraud: for example, securities may not be recorded in the legal registry or certificates may be counterfeit (the World Bank cites instances in India, Indonesia, Malaysia and Turkey). Another major problem has been investors' rights as minority shareholders. Many emerging market firms are closely held and managed by majority shareholders and there may not be sufficient protection in the legal system or in effective enforcement for minority shareholders.

3. *Informational and regulatory risks and costs.* Information is scarce due to lack of good accounting information. Regulatory systems are generally weak, which contributes to the unreliability of the information and can also allow substantial insider trading.

---

[2]World Bank (1997) *Private Capital Flows to Developing Countries: The Road to Financial Integration.*

Taken together these risks translate into extra costs for investors because of the expense of counteracting and dealing with them, and also because of periodic losses. Linked to this is the low liquidity in many markets (i.e. relatively low turnover) which means that investors may not be able to change their positions quickly to take advantage of market conditions or new information. This becomes a particular problem for large funds. Since 1997 turnover has fallen in many markets.

In all these areas progress has been made over the last 20 years, partly at IFC and World Bank instigation. But changing laws does not always change practices, especially in countries where enforcement of property rights is often difficult. And these issues remain a major concern to investors, particularly now that the perception of likely returns in emerging markets is less positive. For most investors collective funds are likely to continue to be the best way to invest in emerging markets. An alternative is American Depositary Receipts (ADRs) which are offered for many of the larger emerging market stocks and trade in the USA.

EMERGING BOND MARKETS

Many emerging countries issue foreign currency bonds and this has become a significant asset class over the last 10–12 years. A strong impetus for the growth of this market was the issuance of so-called Brady bonds (named after the then US Treasury Secretary), starting in 1989. These bonds were issued by a number of countries, mainly in Latin America but also the Philippines, in exchange for international banks' old rescheduled loans dating from the debt crisis of 1982. The banks took a 'haircut' of 20–30% in most cases but the new bonds were partially backed by US Treasury bonds. During the 1990s these bonds were increasingly sold by the banks and became widely traded. Over time they were gradually replaced by other bonds without any backing, when countries were able to borrow at more advantageous terms.

As well as Brady bonds there have been many other foreign currency issues from governments of developing countries. Many governments tap the international bond markets because they want the money to boost reserves or help finance development. Some do it primarily to provide a benchmark issue for private issuers from their country. There are also issues by private companies based in developing countries which put domestic credit risk (see Chapter 12) on top of emerging market sovereign risk.

The most widely used index of performance is the J.P. Morgan Emerging Market Bond Index Plus (EMBI+). J.P. Morgan's first index was the EMBI, which included only countries with Brady bonds. EMBI currently includes 11 countries but is dominated by Brazil, Russia and Mexico. As of 31 July 2001 the index covered bonds with a face value of $83 bn and market value of $58 bn. The EMBI+ includes 18 countries, adding, among others, South Korea and Turkey. Face value stood at $213 bn with a market value of $164 bn at the end of July 2001.

J.P. Morgan also publish an index called the EMBI global, which includes more countries, and the EMBI Global Constrained, which limits the amount in certain countries, effectively reducing the importance of Latin America. Other firms, for example, Lehman and Salomon, also publish emerging market bond indices.

ANALYSING EMERGING BONDS

Emerging bonds are analysed by separating the yield into two components, the US Treasury yield and the spread over US Treasuries. Obviously the US Treasury yield will move up and down affecting these investments. But typically movements in the spread component are far

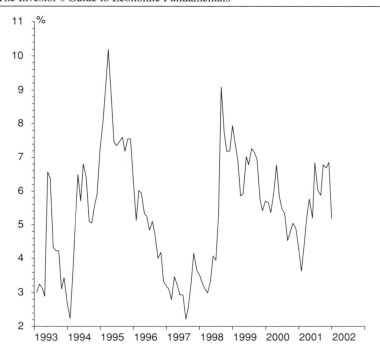

Figure 16.2   Yield differential on Brady bonds (spread over 30-year US Treasuries)
Source: Thomson Datastream

greater than changes in US Treasury yield as countries are buffeted by changes in country
risk. Some professional investors eliminate the impact of changes in Treasury yields by selling
short US Treasuries.

The primary influence on spreads is perceptions of country risk in the country or countries
concerned. Problems in one country often impact on spreads in other countries through forms
of contagion. But spreads are also influenced by the overall willingness to take risk in world
capital markets and, probably, the level of interest rates. Since the early 1990s the yield spread
has moved through three waves of panic: in 1994, following the Mexican devaluation, in 1998
before and during the Russian crisis and in 2001, due to the Argentina crisis (Figure 16.2).

Causes of Widening Spreads

1. *The breakdown or suspension of an IMF programme*. At any given time a large number of
   major borrowers are involved in an IMF adjustment programme of one sort or another. And
   usually one or two others are 'critical' in the sense that the country is in poor shape and
   yield spreads are already high, reflecting the perceived risk.
2. *A change in the sovereign rating*. By one of the main ratings agency's ratings (e.g. Moody's,
   Standard and Poor's or Fitch-IBCA). The agencies have sometimes been criticised for being
   slow to react to events and, in effect, following the market. However, this is not always the
   case and ratings changes frequently are regarded as news by the markets, thereby creating
   a market reaction. Also, there are certain key ratings cut-offs that trigger a market reaction
   because they affect some funds' ability to hold paper in their portfolio. These funds face
   restrictions either on the minimum ratings for investments or on the proportion of a portfolio

below a certain rating. Hence a rating downgrade can trigger sales and reduce the amount of funds able to buy that paper. The two major cut-offs are a downgrade from Investment Grade, e.g. from BBB− to BB+ or a downgrade below B− to CCC.

3. *A new political development in a country*. The key to successful adjustment policies is usually to maintain the political consensus behind the necessary austerity measures. Any development which appears to threaten this, such as a disagreement within a coalition government or a dispute between a Prime Minister and Finance minister or serious popular resistance such as strikes or demonstrations, puts this at risk.

4. *Poor economics news*. This could be news of slower growth in the country, which threatens budget targets and perhaps also political cohesion. Or it could be news of the budget itself, or sometimes news of export performance, which affects the perceived sustainability of the currency. Sometimes it could be bad inflation performance.

5. *Poor local market news*. This may be news of a disappointing domestic debt auction, with higher spreads demanded than expected. Or it could be a fall in the stock market, indicating that confidence is worse than expected.

Contagion Effects

As well as these internal factors there are major 'contagion' effects when problems in one country affect the spreads in others. These can arise in several ways:

1. *Devaluation*. Thailand's devaluation on 2 July 1997 was the trigger for the Asia crisis. Fears of Argentina devaluing undermined the Brazilian real during 2001 although, when Argentina did finally devalue, the reaction was small because it was so well anticipated. Sometimes the link is direct because a devaluation in one country would affect the exports of another unless it devalues too. Sometimes, however, it reflects market reassessment of the risk of devaluation in another country by questioning the economic model. The latter was the case for several Asian countries in 1997–8. However, very few countries now have fixed exchange rates.

2. *Default or the threat of default*. Countries that default, either on domestic obligations or on foreign obligations, usually face a period of economic and political trouble, because of the difficulty of obtaining new finance. Hence the determination of most governments to avoid default. Nevertheless, whenever a country does call a moratorium or miss payments, or is apparently at risk of doing so, investors become nervous that other countries could either choose or be forced to do the same. This is particularly likely to be true if the country depends not just on rolling over existing finance but also needs new finance. Worries over the risk of Argentine default, together with the impact of the world slowdown hit emerging debt during 2001. Again, however, when Argentina did finally default, the news impact was very small.

3. *A sudden economic slowdown in one country*. Sometimes this can impact on a neighbouring country by affecting trade. Alternatively the markets may judge that the slowdown is coming from an external source, e.g. a fall-off in export markets or a loss of domestic confidence which could affect other countries.

CONCLUSION: FUNDAMENTALS OF EMERGING MARKETS

Emerging stock markets perform best when domestic economic policy or higher commodity prices promises faster economic growth or when world liquidity and growth conditions are particularly favourable. Emerging stocks tend to be more volatile than the major markets. The performance since 1993 has been terrible, with composite indices down substantially. One view is that this reflects inherent structural weaknesses in these economies and/or in their markets. Another is that this has become an unpopular asset class, ripe for rediscovery.

Emerging bonds performed poorly in 2001 primarily because of fears of default in Argentina. Argentina's eventual 'meltdown' with both default and devaluation had surprisingly little impact, with contagion very limited, perhaps because it was so well anticipated. And in early 2002 emerging bonds performed well. Emerging market debt is likely to remain as an important asset class. For investors the key is to understand the country risk.

17
Commodity Markets

Investors in commodities have two broad routes. One is to buy the stocks of companies owning commodities or a mutual fund focusing on this area. These companies will do well depending on their efficiency in the market and their ability to generate productivity growth. They will also do well, usually, if the price of the commodity goes up. The second approach is to use the commodity futures and options markets to speculate in commodity prices going up or down.

Every individual commodity has its own story based on its specific fundamentals of supply and demand. Nevertheless there are general fundamentals as well, which affect broad indices of commodity prices. These include economic growth trends, inflation and interest rates. Notice that the different commodity price indices commonly used (see Figure 17.1) vary somewhat because of their different composition and weightings. A crucial factor is their differing weightings of energy. *The Economist* commodity indices, for example, do not include precious metals while the Bridge/Commodity Research Bureau (CRB) index in the USA is aimed mainly at commodities traded on US exchanges. One of the best overall indexes is the Goldman Sachs Commodity Index (GSCI) because it weights commodities according to world production.

COMMODITIES AND ECONOMIC GROWTH

Fast economic growth, especially when it is simultaneously fast in a number of countries, as in 1994–5 or 1999–2000, means strong demand for commodities. This is especially likely if industries such as cars and house-building are strong, because of their heavy use of raw materials such as copper and timber. Still, strong economic growth only has a major impact on prices if stocks are low and commodity producers are near capacity. This tends to happen in the *late upswing* phase of economic cycles, e.g. 1972–3, 1978–80, 1988–90 and 1998–2000, though oil prices sometimes move out of phase with the economic cycle. The biggest commodity price boom of recent decades was in the 1970s. It came after years of strong economic growth, but supply conditions were also very tight, not only for oil but other commodities as well. The boom was fuelled by increased use of commodities as an asset class, to try to hedge against high levels of general inflation and low or negative real interest rates.

In the 1980s commodity prices were generally weak as capacity developed in the 1970s came on stream and the world suffered slower economic growth. Commodity prices rose in 1988–90 at the peak of world growth but then fell back until 1993. In the early/middle 1990s, as US growth accelerated and Europe recovered from recession, commodity prices started to pick up again. However the peak came in 1997–8, with the Asian crisis triggering a new decline, led by oil prices. In 1999–2000, as world growth accelerated sharply, oil prices rose strongly again, from lows of around $10 seen in 1999, taking commodity indices higher once more. However, most commodities showed only a meagre response and then fell again with the world slowdown in 2001 (Figure 17.2). At the time of writing, commodity prices are just rising from their lowest levels for 25 years, having been in a flat or descending channel since 1979.

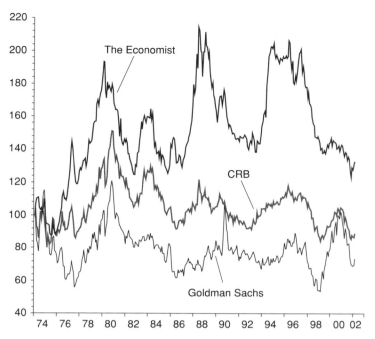

Figure 17.1 Commodity price indices (1974=100)
Source: Thomson Datastream

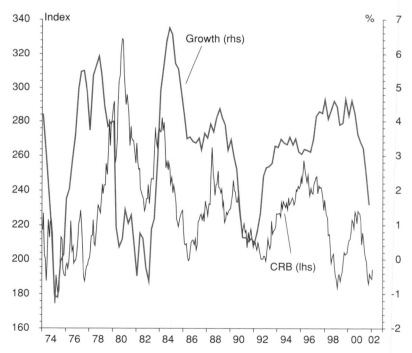

Figure 17.2 US GDP growth and the CRB Index
Source: Thomson Datastream

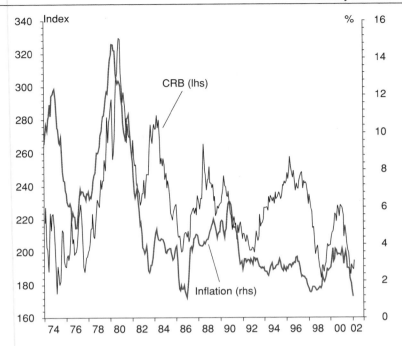

Figure 17.3 Commodity prices and US inflation
Source: Thomson Datastream

COMMODITY PRICES AND INFLATION

Commodity prices respond to inflation partly because all prices tend to be dragged up by inflation and also because, for many investors, commodities are one of the best hedges against inflation. The reason that US inflation matters rather than world inflation is that commodity prices are generally analysed in dollars. Of course inflation is usually a sign that the economy is starting to overheat and that goes alongside strong demand for commodities as inputs, so that it is difficult to separate the two effects (see Figure 17.3).

It should be stressed, however, that all the signs are that commodity prices *decline* relative to wages or consumer prices over the long term (see below). In the world of very low inflation or even deflation that we see now, commodity prices will probably show an actual decline over the long run, rather than cycling about a flat or declining trend, as has been the case in the last 25 years.

COMMODITY PRICES AND INTEREST RATES

It is primarily US interest rates that matter since commodity prices are measured in dollars. Commodity prices and interest rates tend to move in the same direction (Figure 17.4). Interest rates move up when either the economy is strong or inflation is rising, both positive influences for commodities. Similarly, when interest rates are moving down the reason will be falling inflation or weak growth.

However, there is also a link with real interest rates. Low short-term interest rates, especially low real interest rates, tend to support commodity prices for two reasons. First, they make it

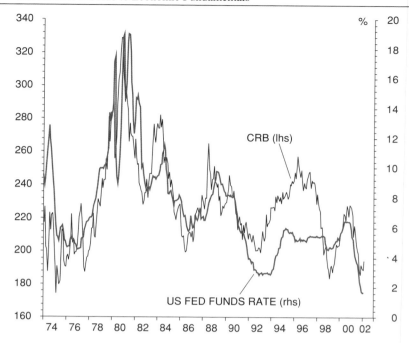

Figure 17.4   Commodity prices and interest rates
Source: Thomson Datastream

cheaper to speculate in commodities, which of course pay no interest. Secondly, low interest rates may be taken as a sign of expansionary monetary policy, which sooner or later is likely to boost growth and inflation and commodity prices. Similarly, high real interest rates have the opposite effect. Speculation is expensive and high rates may be a prelude to an economic slowdown.

PRECIOUS METALS

Some investors insist that, to be complete, any portfolio should have a small portion of gold. The reason is that not only is gold an inflation hedge but it also benefits from political uncertainty. Moreover, what makes gold important for some investors, mainly in countries that may not be politically stable in the long run, is that it is portable. In parts of the Middle East and Asia gold is very widely used as a store of value, particularly by poor people and women. There is some evidence that gold has maintained its real value over the long period, in contrast to most commodities which have a long-term trend to a decline in real value.

While investors see gold as something that might hold its value in times of inflation or political uncertainty, economists tend to be dismissive of gold partly because it has very little use-value. There are a few small industrial uses and, of course, it is used in jewellery but gold's value to investors is primarily that everyone agrees that it is the money of last resort.

In the nineteenth century and into the early years of the twentieth century the gold standard was used to peg national currencies, giving gold a central role. Under the Bretton Woods

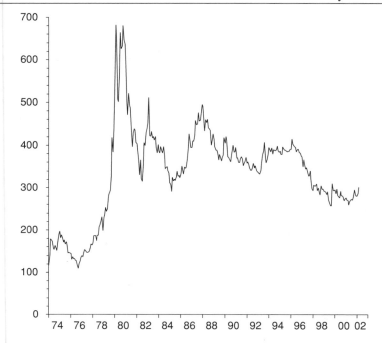

Figure 17.5 Gold $ per ounce
Source: Thomson Datastream

system (1945–71) there was an official gold exchange standard which meant that, although not every dollar was necessarily backed by an amount of gold, the US Treasury was committed to provide gold to any other government in exchange for dollars on demand.

With the breakdown of the Bretton Woods system in the 1970s this guarantee was abandoned. As inflation took off, gold soared in relation to dollars, reaching (briefly) a high of over $800 per ounce in 1980 (Figure 17.5). Most governments still have substantial reserves of gold though several have sold some in recent years with the gold price being so lack-lustre.

A few economists cling to the idea that, one day, gold will be restored to the heart of the monetary system, but this looks highly unlikely. While a gold standard can provide a discipline against inflation it also means that the general price level is linked to the supply of gold. In the event of a rise in the supply of gold, as occurred in the sixteenth and seventeenth centuries following the Spanish and Portuguese development of South America, the general price level tends to rise. If supply is restricted, as seems to be the case this century, the use of a gold standard might force a general decrease in the price level as output increases.

One factor that is unique to precious metals is that the total outstanding of these commodities dwarfs the annual production. This means that the price is much less affected by world economic growth and by partial or temporary supply interruptions due, for example, to strikes. Instead prices are affected primarily by expectations for inflation and interest rates and by political uncertainty. However, in recent years the gold price has shown little life, trading within a relatively narrow range.

FUELS

Oil prices have played a central role in the economic history of the last two decades, and it is difficult to overestimate their importance in affecting investment returns over the last 30 years. This importance reflects a number of factors. For example, in terms of value, fuels including oil account for around half of all commodities produced. A rise in oil prices therefore has a far more pronounced effect on the industrial countries than a rise in, say, the prices of industrial metals Oil can therefore be a very important inflation hedge because it directly impacts the general price level.

Another reason for oil's importance is that a substantial amount of supply comes from the Middle East, which has frequently proved politically unstable. The first oil crisis in 1973 was linked to the Yom Kippur war and the Arab oil embargo while the second, in 1979–80, was linked to the Iran–Iraq war. In 1990 the rise in oil prices after Iraq's invasion of Kuwait was a key factor in the US recession. The 2000–1 world economic slowdown was partly triggered by the rise in oil prices then, as OPEC restricted supply to try to control the market.

OPEC's grasp of oil prices has never lasted very long. Briefly, in 1973–4 there were restrictions on oil shipments but the big rise in oil prices at that time, and again in 1979–80, was mainly due to the very tight oil market (Figure 17.6). In 1986, when the excess supply developed, OPEC was unable to agree sufficient production cuts and lost control of the market. Later in the decade and through much of the 1990s both the USA and OPEC aimed for a modest long-run price of about $18 a barrel.

In 2000 a new period of OPEC power dawned, as Saudi Arabia and Iran buried their differences and began to follow a much more aggressive and elaborate scheme to control prices. They were helped in this by the relative tightness of the oil market following the collapse in

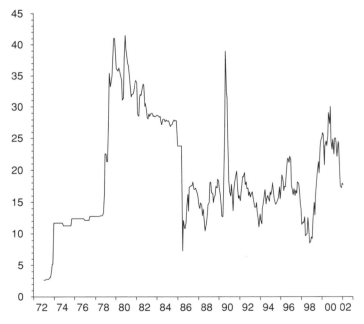

Figure 17.6   Oil price $ per barrel (Saudi Light)
Source: Thomson Datastream

prices in 1998–9 which had cut production in some countries, as well as the period of strong growth in the US economy during the second half of the 1990s. However, as before, most of the periodic cuts necessary had to come from Saudi Arabia. Moreover OPEC's target price range of $22–28 looks high against the generally accepted marginal cost of $15 for new oil production. At the time of writing the oil price has fallen below OPECs target range and it therefore appears doubtful whether the cartel will be able to maintain this range for the medium term.

For the poorer OPEC members, especially the smaller ones, there is frequently a tendency to 'cheat', i.e. produce more than agreed quotas because of the need for revenues and the limited impact of a small extra supply on the price. In contrast the rich Gulf countries, several of them relatively large suppliers, notably Saudi Arabia and Kuwait, have a strong incentive to keep prices moderate for two reasons. First, as very low cost producers with decades, if not hundreds of years worth of reserves available, they have an incentive not to see prices too high which would choke off demand in the long term. Secondly, given the strong economic and security links with the USA, they have an incentive not to disrupt the industrial countries too much. The more aggressive approach taken by Saudi Arabia from 1999 onwards may reflect the change in leadership.

But OPEC has also been influenced by the painful consequences of periods of very low prices. In 1986, when OPEC was unable to agree on new quotas, the oil price plunged sharply to only $10 per barrel. This fall came as a huge surprise to many people because for most of the early 1980s it had been assumed that oil prices could only go up. Economic forecasters routinely assumed that oil prices would rise by 3–5% p.a. in real terms, i.e. after inflation. In fact since 1986 oil prices, although up somewhat, have remained weak in real terms (Figure 17.7).

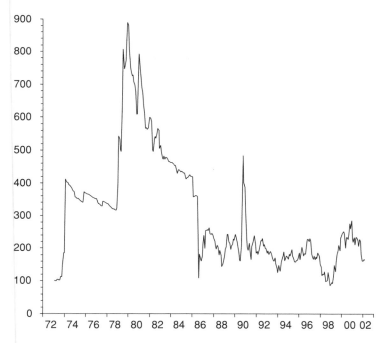

Figure 17.7   Oil price in real terms
Source: Thomson Datastream

More recently, the plunge in prices in 1998 was a wake-up call to OPEC and probably accounts for its relative cohesion in 2000–1 and its greater determination to control the market. The fall in 1998 was due to the impact of the Asian crisis, which sharply reduced Asian demand, just at a moment when the oil market had appeared to be tightening. Many of the smaller Asian countries, such as Korea, are heavy users of oil.

From the cartel's point of view, production cuts of 10% increased prices by 150% (to $25) and therefore the gains were clearly worth while, at least in the short run. The difficulty that could arise in coming years is that a similar cut will have only a marginal impact on price because as long as OPEC tries to hold the price too high it is providing a wonderful incentive for non-OPEC producers, such as Russia, to increase production. Exploration in the USA increased dramatically in 2000–1 when it became clear that OPEC would try to maintain the overvalued price.

INDUSTRIAL RAW MATERIALS

This category covers a variety of individual commodities including the metals, copper, iron, zinc, lead, etc., and agricultural raw materials such as timber, cotton, etc. Each has its own story but economic growth, and especially growth, of the industrial sector, is the most important demand-side influence. In a strong economic upswing as in 1987–8, 1994 or 1999, especially if there are worries over inflation, some of these commodities, especially the metals, are liable to rise as a result of speculative pressures.

FOODS AND BEVERAGES

In this category are both seasonal foods (i.e. they cannot be stored for long) and non-seasonal foods. Prices of the former are very dependent on the weather but, by their nature, there is little scope for speculation except in the very short run. The latter include products such as coffee and orange juice where markets are very active, again often in response to weather or other supply conditions. The most famous supply-side factor is frost in Brazil, which periodically devastates the coffee crop. Demand is much less influenced by world growth. Although it will rise with growth it does not show wide swings with the business cycle.

LONG-RUN TRENDS IN COMMODITY PRICES

The view was prevalent in the 1970s that commodity prices would inevitably be on a long-run up-trend because the world has limited resources and the easy sources of minerals and other commodities would soon be used up, forcing producers to dig deeper or otherwise spend more money on extraction. The experience of rising commodity prices through much of the 1970s seemed to bear out this view. It is still heard from environmentalists periodically.

Prior to the 1970s the prevailing view was that developing countries were in fact doomed to poverty if they persisted in exporting only raw materials because of a tendency for industrial goods prices to rise faster than raw commodity prices. For much of the twentieth century this had indeed been the case, the main reason being improved technology in finding and extracting minerals or, in the case of agricultural commodities, in growing and harvesting.

From the perspective of 2001 it is clear that the traditional view was more accurate than the 1970s' view. Production costs for most commodities have fallen in real terms and there is little evidence that supplies of commodities are dwindling. New discoveries in new regions or at greater depths continue. Also, the cost of extraction continues to fall, despite reduced accessibility, due to improving technology. So, although proven reserves of most commodities, including oil, are often only a few decades, there is no doubt that new sources will continue to be found and generally at a declining real cost.

The 1970s' experience in fact showed the market in action. A prolonged world upswing in the 1950s and 1960s ended with a rapid boom in the early 1970s, leaving limited capacity in many commodities. But the higher prices of commodities soon produced cutbacks in demand, new sources of supply and alternative products, so that by the 1980s there was widespread overcapacity.

The generalised tendency for a rise in commodity prices in the decades leading up to the 1970s and then for a fall since then seems to fit in quite well with the Kondratieff long cycle (see Chapter 2). A strict interpretation of this cycle emphasises that it is a price cycle, not a growth cycle. With commodity prices and general inflation on the decline since at least 1980 on some indices and 1973 on others, the Kondratieff cycle would predict a long-term low soon, followed by the beginning of a new generalised price upswing, likely to last decades. Unfortunately such analysis, even if it turns out to be true, generally cannot place the turning point with an accuracy better than several years or even a decade. In other words, even if we are approaching a low, it could come very soon or might occur at any time within the next 5 or even 10 years.

CONCLUSION: THE FUNDAMENTALS OF COMMODITIES

For investors, commodities play the role of an inflation hedge. There is historical evidence that a small proportion of commodities or commodity company stocks in a diversified portfolio can lower the overall risk because commodity prices tend to move up when bonds and stocks are weak. But the view, widely held in the 1970s, that there would be increasing shortages of raw materials and therefore commodity prices would show a long term up-trend, has been discredited. The prices of commodities are mainly determined by the supply and demand for each individual commodity. Seasonal factors, political upsets and labour disputes play a significant role as well as long-term trends for that particular commodity. The key economic fundamental influences on commodities are world economic growth, US inflation and US interest rates. Generally, commodity prices rise with stronger growth, higher inflation and lower interest rates. Gold is seen as a hedge against inflation and political instability.

For investors there is no inevitable up-trend in commodity prices, and there could be an inevitable long-term down-trend. Making money therefore depends on timing the cycles. There may be a very long cycle, the Kondratieff (55-year) cycle, but this is likely to be of little use for investors. Generally it will be the shorter-term business cycles that matter. Commodities can be a useful hedge against inflation but are unlikely to be a major part of a portfolio. One effective way to invest is through a fund that invests in the shares of natural resource companies. This provides a stake in commodities themselves but will also do well if the company is successful in reducing costs or finding new resources.

Part III
Summary and Conclusions

18

Summary: Economic Fundamentals and Market Performance

This chapter provides a summary of how economic events impact on markets and also looks at likely future market returns. Chapter 19 describes the various different approaches to investment and how economic fundamentals are used in the investment process. Finally, Chapter 20 discusses how the economic fundamentals have changed over the last 10 years and looks ahead to likely developments in future.

MARKET RESPONSES TO ECONOMIC EVENTS

This book has shown in detail how economic fundamentals such as changes in economic policy, the phases of the business cycle and events or 'shocks' impact on the economy and on asset markets. Table 18.1 summarises the most frequent economic events and indicates the most likely response of different asset markets. Of course the investor can only profit from this if he can identify these coming events *ahead* of the market. If they are already anticipated the market will not necessarily move at all; and if they are not anticipated the market may move very quickly to incorporate them, as market-makers immediately adjust their bid/ask prices, leaving little time for investors to react.

Some of these events can arise suddenly, in the form of an announcement of some kind — for example, a change in short-term interest rates or new government budget measures. Most of them, however, emerge gradually from the noise of regular data releases. For example the first sign of the coming end of a recession could be that industrial production falls only (say) 0.1% month-on-month, better than larger falls in previous months and better than the expected decline. The markets will probably treat this as a sign of approaching economic recovery, pushing up stocks and hurting bond prices. Similarly, news of an acceleration in inflation and a tightening labour market will lead investors to anticipate a rise in official interest rates. The actual move, when it comes, may be largely discounted. The prize then is to forecast the emerging economic environment and correctly anticipate the central bank's reactions ahead of the rest of the market.

Market-makers (institutions which hold inventory of securities ready to sell) rely heavily on knowledge of the information in the table because they need to know which way to mark prices when news releases first appear on Reuters or Bloomberg screens. These instant movements mean that investors are unlikely to be able to benefit once the event has occurred unless they feel that the immediate market move is not enough. Generally investors must rely on superior analysis and forecasting so that they can identify these moves ahead of the market.

LONG-TERM ECONOMIC 'HOLDING PATTERNS'

In addition to the fundamental events listed in Table 18.1, it is quite common to find countries fixed in 'long-term holding patterns', sometimes favourable and sometimes not. Japan, for

Table 18.1   The effects of fundamentals on major asset classes*

Event	1–3 year bonds	Long-term bonds	Stocks	Property	Commodities
Business cycle phases					
Recovery	−	−	++	0	+
Early upswing	0	0	+	+	+
Late upswing	− −	− −	+	++	++
Slowdown	+	++	− −	+	−
Recession	++	+	−	− −	− −
Higher inflation	−	− −	0	+	++
Cut in short rates	++	0	+	+	+
Fall in real rates	+	+	+	++	+
Rise in real rates	−	−	−	− −	−
Devaluation	−	−	+	+	+
Increased political uncertainty	−	−	−	−	0
Increase in productivity	0	+	+	+	0
Rise in oil prices	−	−	−	0	+
Pro-business government measures	0	+	+	+	0
Rise in budget deficit	−	−	+	+	+

* The event is assumed to take place *after* the investment is purchased. Scoring is from ++, highly positive to − −, highly negative with 0 as neutral.

example, has been stuck in a series of recessions, weak recoveries and slowdowns since 1990, without ever enjoying an *early upswing* phase of the cycle of any length let alone a *late upswing* phase. In fact it might be better to regard Japan as in a state of structural paralysis, or lack of adjustment.

This is quite a common problem in emerging countries too. After an economic slowdown some countries take years to prepare for a new vigorous upswing and show a long period of underperformance. This happened in many countries in Latin America in the 1980s and has afflicted some Asian countries since the 1997–8 crisis. Again, the basic problem is lack of adjustment so that the full upward business cycle cannot get underway. The country becomes mired in too much debt and a weak banking system. Business is reluctant to invest because of too many uncertainties or lack of opportunities.

A much more pleasant holding pattern is the prolonged *late upswing* phase seen in some countries. The USA enjoyed a prolonged upswing during the 1990s helped by disinflationary events elsewhere, together with the improvement in productivity growth. A key part of this pattern is usually strong investment which keeps the economy going and also, by increasing capacity, helps to keep inflation at bay. Another holding pattern linked to the prolonged upswing phase is the asset price boom. This can last a surprisingly long time because of the feedback from higher asset prices to stronger spending, and therefore stronger growth and inflation, thereby justifying higher asset prices. However, it may be storing up trouble for the future.

A final holding pattern is the country with a borrowing or debt crisis. This can apply to local currency or foreign currency debt or both. Many emerging countries become stuck here for years. The problem is that, once debt has built up to high levels, it takes years to bring it down again. Moreover, the reason for the rise in debt is typically a weak fundamental political situation so that the government relies too much on borrowing. Every government can get away with this for a while, as investors are willing to lend up to a point. Then, at some stage, the weight of debt or perhaps some new crisis makes it difficult to continue borrowing. To reverse the build-up of debt governments struggle against an unfavourable political situation and are frequently unable to do more than react to the worst crisis. This may stabilise the immediate outlook but, once the crisis is past, there is not enough political cohesion to really improve the situation.

MARKET PERFORMANCE: THE HISTORICAL RECORD

Table 18.2 shows returns (in US dollars) in major markets since January 1990. With the major exception of Japanese stocks the long-run performance has been good for investors. In fact in a long-run perspective it could be said to be an excellent period. Stock market returns in the USA and Europe have risen considerably faster than GDP and profits, which is another way of saying that valuations have risen. Bond returns have also been greater than bond yields, which means that there has been a downward trend in yields over the period as inflation subsided. Neither of these trends can be sustained indefinitely.

Taking a very long-term view, since 1900 on average, US stocks have returned 6–7% p.a. above inflation, and government bonds have returned about 1% more than inflation, slightly ahead of Treasury bills. Similar numbers can be found in the UK. However, it should be noted that these are long-term averages and there have been long periods of divergence from them. Bonds performed particularly badly for many years in the 1970s while stocks performed badly in the 1930s and again in the 1970s. In Germany bonds outperformed stocks for more than 15 years in the 1970s and early 1980s. Nevertheless, taking the very long run, these are the exceptions.

Table 18.2   Bond and stock market returns

Annual % returns, end year to end year, USD basis	1989–94 5 year annual average	1994–9 5 year annual average	2000	2001
Fixed income				
Cash/near cash	6.7	6.5	7.9	8.3
US$ bonds	7.5	7.4	13.4	6.7
European bonds	10.3	5.7	−1.0	0.5
Japanese bonds	15.2	5.5	−9.1	−10.0
Emerging bonds	16.6	17.5	14.0	1.9
Equities				
US large cap	8.7	28.6	−9.1	−11.9
US small cap	8.3	15.1	−4.2	1.0
Europe	3.8	19.9	−9.7	−21.2
Japan	−4.2	1.3	−28.5	−29.9
Emerging (total)	17.4	2.1	−31.8	1.8
Emerging Asia*	17.1	−1.3	−36.3	−5.9
Emerging LA	31.5	5.6	−14.7	−2.0
Emerging Europe/ME	na	na	−28.2	−12.4

* includes Hong Kong and Singapore.
Sources: Salomon 1–3 years, Salomon SGBI, Salomon Brady, S&P 500, Russell 2000, MSCI and IFC (for emerging except Asia). Asia emerging includes Hong Kong and Singapore.

FUTURE MARKET RETURNS

What should investors reasonably expect from different asset classes for the future? Of course the near future is full of uncertainty but we can talk about the long-term, 5 or 10 years or more. This is not intended to be a forecast, more a 'rule-of-thumb'.

It is reasonable to expect that, over the cycle, companies should be able to generate profit growth in line with the growth of nominal GDP. If we take the USA, assuming trend GDP growth is 3.5% p.a. and inflation over the long run will average 2% p.a., this implies that profits will grow at 5.5% p.a. Profits of large companies may be able to grow slightly faster if they are increasing their market share or are able to enjoy rising margins due to monopolistic advantages (the so-called 'power of brands'). Also they could grow faster to the extent that they expand overseas and take greater market share there or participate in faster-growing economies. Few people are willing to push expected profit growth beyond about 7% p.a. for the long-run however, and some believe that that is too optimistic. We will assume 6.5% p.a. In addition we may assume that companies will pay a dividend of around 1% annually on average and also use cash-flow to buy back shares equivalent to a further 0.5% annual dividend. In total then, a reasonable long-term expectation for returns from stocks may be approximately 8% p.a., or 6% p.a. in real terms. This is before transactions costs and management costs.

The sensible best expectation for bonds is the current yield, which for US and European government bonds is 5.1% for 10-year bonds at the time of writing. This is a real yield after inflation of about 3%, which is at the low end of the long-term average. Of course if yields fall further then the investor today will enjoy better than 5.1% returns. Government bond yields in Japan currently are below 2% and bond yields in other countries could clearly fall much further too if inflation falls further or the price level declines. Notice that the implied equity risk premium, i.e. the excess return on equities compared with bonds, is approximately 3% p.a.. This is lower than the historical risk premium for the USA and UK but, arguably, does represent a reasonable extra return to compensate for the risk. However, it does assume a continued good economic and political environment to allow p/e ratios to stay at around 20 times earnings, higher than the twentieth-century average of about 15 times. If valuations contract in future years, because of a worsening environment or a rise in interest rates, average returns would be much lower.

What of property? If the current yield is regarded as sustainable then investors should enjoy a return equal to that yield plus a rise in property prices equal to nominal GDP, less expenses and depreciation. For example, the London residential property market currently has a gross market yield of 6% p.a. If we assume that prices will rise in the long-term at the same rate as nominal GDP growth of 5% p.a., and expenses and depreciation combined are 4% p.a., then property returns should be about 7% in nominal terms or 5% p.a. in real terms. This would place property returns in between bonds and stocks. Optimists would argue that London property could rise at a faster pace than the UK GDP. Pessimists would note that the current 6% yield is historically low. If yields need to rise back to the average of past levels then returns will be lower.

The returns for the various markets suggested above are broadly in line with the very long run (up to 100 years or more) experience in the US and UK markets, where data are available. They may appear disappointing, however, to many investors because they are well below the returns seen over the last decade or more. In fact if mean reversion occurs, we should expect US returns to be lower in coming years than in past years, merely to restore the long-run trend in returns. Perhaps the best returns over the next 10 years will come from the laggards of recent years, Japan and the emerging markets!

19
Economic Fundamentals and the
Investment Process

This book is about how economic fundamentals affect markets. But different investors incorporate economic fundamentals in different ways into their investment decisions. While a full discussion of the investment process is beyond the scope of this book, in this chapter we outline the various approaches to investment and show where economic analysis fits in.

A CAUTION FROM FINANCE THEORY

First, however, a word of caution. Since the 1950s there has been a growing literature on how markets work and whether clever investors really can make money through 'beating the market'. The key debate has been whether markets are 'efficient' in the sense that they incorporate all the information available. If markets are 'efficient' the theory suggests that it is not possible to persistently outperform the market by using publicly available information or even by using a better theory than other people. Of course some investors do, but it is argued that this is luck rather than judgement.

A strict belief in this view means that almost any form of active investment management is unlikely to generate above-average returns. Instead investors should confine themselves to choosing a portfolio of assets based on their appetite for risk. Stocks will outperform bonds over the long term, but with greater volatility, so low-risk investors will hold more stocks and vice versa. Investors would also be wise to avoid significant trading of a portfolio since this adds costs without being likely to add to returns.

However, efficient market theory has come up against behavioural finance theory over the last decade or so and the two are often incompatible. For example, the basis for the efficient market theory is that investors are rational, yet behavioural psychologists have shown that people do not behave strictly rationally when it comes to risk. Experiments have shown, for example, that people are influenced by others around them, or influenced by the most recent performance they have seen. Given these behaviour patterns it can be shown that markets tend to overshoot in both directions and that market bubbles and slumps can occur.

PRACTICAL LESSONS FROM THEORY

Academics are now trying to reconcile behavioural theory with finance theory but this is proving difficult and the two are often uneasy partners. So where does all this leave the investor? A number of practical conclusions can be drawn from the insights of both theories.

First, traditional finance theory demonstrates the importance of understanding the relationship between risk and return. Generally speaking, investments that are likely to provide a higher return are likely to have more risk, which is reflected in greater volatility. That means that they will have years that are worse than other investments and years that are better. Over the long term, which for stocks could be 5–10 years or more, higher-risk investments should outperform, but this cannot be guaranteed.

Secondly, most investors conclude that it is vital to diversify if the objective is to preserve and grow wealth. The important point is that the investor who wants to see his portfolio grow over time and with the minimum volatility needs to be in a wide range of stocks and a wide range of asset classes.

Thirdly, the efficient markets theory suggests that the best strategy, at least for the bulk of a portfolio, may be to buy and hold rather than to trade frequently. Frequent trading costs money and may not improve returns unless the investor is convinced that he has some information or analytical skills not available to the whole market.

Fourthly, professional investors usually assess their performance in comparison to a market index, e.g. the MSCI World index or a particular country index. For a mixed portfolio they might take (say) 60% of an equity index and 40% of a bond index. Choosing the right index or combination of indices is arguably the single most important part of the investment process since, over time, this will be a key driver of performance.

Fifthly, one of the key conclusions of behavioural finance is that markets can move out of line with fundamental factors for long periods, as bubbles and crashes develop or overshoots occur. This can complicate investment choices and means that, even if an investor identifies an opportunity, he may have to wait a long time until other investors see it and push the price up.

Finally, however, there is evidence of 'mean reversion' over the long term, i.e over time markets do return to their mean or average level based on fundamentals. In other words, if a market has been outperforming over a period, there is a good chance that it will underperform at some point in the future. This is a result that follows from both conventional finance theory and behavioural finance.

INVESTMENT STYLES AND APPROACHES

The following is an overview of some of the main approaches used by investors in practice and how the assessment of economic fundamentals is incorporated.

Market Timing

Despite the scepticism of finance academics most investors attempt some degree of market timing. For example, they may try to buy stocks just before economic recovery begins and move out near the top of the upswing, and into bonds just as the downswing begins, gaining with the rise in the stock market and then gaining again with the rise in the bond market! If investors can also time things internationally, it is then theoretically possible to move in and out of different countries and always enjoy the best performing markets around the world!

The reality of course is that this is much more difficult than it sounds because of the huge uncertainties at every stage of the business cycle. Even if investors correctly judge the business cycle, markets sometimes seem to behave perversely, moving up when they might be expected to go down and vice versa! The danger is not just the obvious one of being overweight on a market when it is going down but also of being underweight on a market when it goes up.

For example, the S&P 500 index in the USA rose 68% in the five years to 1 January 1994. The clever (or lucky) investor who moved into cash for the whole of 1990, the recession year when the S&P moved down 8%, would have enjoyed an increased return of around 90%. But the nervous investor who was *out* of the market in *either* 1989 or 1991, both years when the

S&P surged 28%, would have seen a five-year return of only about 35% instead of 68% — no better than the return on deposits over that period.

Understanding economic cycles is a key component of market timing. Another is predicting the response of central banks to changes in the economy. Some investors also spend a considerable amount of time comparing their view of the fundamentals with their assessment of the consensus view. For example, suppose the investor's view is that the economy is moving into a late upswing phase and that the central bank will raise interest rates. If he also thinks that this is the consensus view he will anticipate that these expectations are all in the market already and there is no gain to be had from, for example, selling bonds. If, however, the investor reckons that this view is *not* the consensus view and therefore not yet discounted in the market, then selling bonds will be a good move if he is proved to be correct. As data emerge showing that the economy is indeed overheating and the central bank starts to move rates up, bond prices will decline.

Some investors completely disdain any type of market timing (see below). However, most professional investors do practice a degree of market timing but often only within a certain range. In other words, they are very unlikely to sell *all* their stocks if they think a market is due to fall but they will go underweight that market. And similarly if they think a market will rise they will go overweight.

Indexed Investing

Investing in an index of a stock market or a bond market is increasingly popular for two reasons. First it eliminates the danger of a poor performance relative to that index since indexed funds will normally perform at or just below the index performance. Returns are often just below because of the effect of fees and transactions costs. Studies of actively managed funds show that only a relatively small proportion of active funds, much less than half, persistently outperform index funds. Secondly, index funds typically have much lower fees than active funds.

Indexed investing tends to be recommended by believers in efficient market theory and many investment managers now suggest that it should be used at least for a significant core of an investor's portfolio. However, there are some conceptual and practical difficulties. One is that the weights for companies within an index rise when those companies' share prices rise. This means that if those companies are becoming more highly valued, index investors buy more of them and vice versa. Indexed investment can therefore resemble momentum investing. For example, in the late 1990s the weighting of technology stocks became greater and greater in most stock indices requiring index managers to buy more and more. When technology stocks fell in 2000–1 indexed investors were selling all the way down.

Another problem with stock indices is that the components change frequently and index funds, in a sense, lose out. When it is announced that a stock will drop out of the index, its price usually falls before the index fund manager sells, and vice versa. However, the onus on active managers is still to prove that they can do better overall and the evidence generally is thin.

There is also the question of which index or indices to use, particularly for a global portfolio. In some countries market indices are very biased towards particular sectors just because those are sectors in which large companies are quoted on the stock exchange. Or if we look at world bond markets, an index of world bond markets weighted by size would give a huge weight to Japanese government bonds, but simply because there are so many of them. The fact that Japan has a large and increasingly worrying government debt implies that investors should consider having very low weights in that market, but an indexed approach implies a high weight.

Economic fundamentals can therefore play a key role in the initial choice of indices, particularly if the investor is looking at his complete portfolio or a wide range of asset classes. In other words, while economic fundamentals will not play much role in choosing (say) between indices of the UK stock market, they can play a role in considering how much weight to give to emerging markets in a global portfolio or how much weight to put in property.

Contrarian Approaches

This means buying when everybody else is gloomy and pessimistic and selling when people are optimistic or euphoric. Followers of this approach are naturally believers in behavioural theories of markets rather than the efficient market theory. The biggest problem for contrarian investors is being too early. For example, some investors sold or went underweight in the US stock market in 1996 or 1997, arguing that the market was overvalued, and missed out on one of the biggest bull markets in history. Selling the S&P 500 index in early 1997 at around 800 did not seem a very clever move when it rose to 1,500 three years later. If the money were transferred to bonds it would have been worth the equivalent of only about 1,000 in early 2000. Fast forward to early 2002 with the S&P 500 index at 1,150 and money invested in bonds would now be worth about 1,120 and the decision does not look so terrible. (The reader will know what happened next!).

The contrarian investor has two further problems. First, after selling a market, if it continues to rise, the investor may decide he was wrong and seek to go back in. A professional manager may hold out against this temptation but might also lose the funds as the client moves the money elsewhere. If he does go back in to the market he will have missed out on part of the rise and also, in a sense, face higher risk at the higher level. Secondly, if he is out of the market he has missed out on the possibility of selling nearer the top. The successful market-timer who sold at 1,500 in early 2000 and bought bonds would have the equivalent of over 1,730 in early 2002.

Contrarian investors often rely heavily on fundamental analysis. When they see a hugely bullish market or a deeply pessimistic market they then look at the fundamentals to try to determine where the market should be. In the 1990s there was a major debate on where the US stock market should be valued, with some investors convinced that the market was entering a bubble and losing touch with fundamentals while others were convinced that the fundamentals had changed, and this debate is likely to continue (see Chapter 20).

Limited Bets around Benchmarks

Most professional investors are very careful not to use market timing to put all their eggs in one basket but, instead, use it to change their portfolio weightings in a small way. They start with a benchmark, usually a widely quoted index, e.g. MSCI stock indices or the Salomon brothers bond indices, but it could be a specially constructed one. Then they make departures from the benchmark weighting according to their view of the markets. For example, suppose that the benchmark weighting for US stocks is 40% of the portfolio. If the investor believes that the US economy is approaching a recession and therefore US stock prices are likely to fall, then they may go down to 30% or perhaps lower. But only a very aggressive fund would go down to near zero.

With this kind of approach the choice of the right benchmark is as important as the choice of stocks within the portfolio. For example, using the Dow Jones stock index as a benchmark would imply that the stocks picked are likely to be large blue-chip companies. Or if the portfolio is to be 'balanced', i.e. include both stocks and bonds, then the proportions of stocks and bonds in the benchmark will be a key determinant of the portfolio's risk and return, unless the manager departs from the benchmark in substantial ways. The willingness to take risk will therefore be reflected both in the benchmark used (e.g. more stocks in a high-risk portfolio) and also in the size of the departures from that benchmark.

Economic fundamentals enter into this approach in two distinct ways. First, there is the choice of indices; then there is the use of economics in market timing. As with all market timing, the investor needs to consider both the expected direction of the market and the risk of being wrong. The latter will help to determine the *extent* of the departure from the benchmark.

Fixed Weight Portfolios with Rebalancing

This approach is to decide on weights for each asset class on a one-time basis. These weights can be decided by using a model, which plugs in the historical risk/return pattern and recommends a portfolio, or it may be determined by the investor's own views of the fundamentals of different asset classes. Economic fundamentals may play a role here, but having decided on the weights the investor then stays with them and 'rebalances' the portfolio periodically, perhaps every month, quarter or even year. This investor would have been selling stocks and buying bonds throughout the late 1990s and doing the reverse in 2000 and 2001. In a sense this approach takes profits on rising markets and increases holdings in falling markets, thereby building in a degree of contrarianism. Clearly this approach will give an inferior performance to the successful market-timer, but will be superior if the market-timer gets it wrong. This approach works best, the more rapidly a 'mean reversion' takes hold.

Value Investing

Value investors search for company stocks, fixed income securities or country stock markets which are underrated by the markets or where the investor feels the market may not be anticipating fully the potential for that company, industry or country. For individual stocks or corporate bonds this requires a disciplined approach to the fundamentals including both a careful analysis of the financials of that company and a close understanding of the company's management and business. For a country the emphasis is on economic (and political) fundamentals, insofar as they relate to the country risk outlook, potential economic/profits growth and domestic interest rates. The emphasis is on whether the stock, bond or overall market is properly valued by the markets, given its fundamentals.

Growth Investing

Investors using this approach focus on companies or countries that are likely to grow rapidly and therefore should see their stock price or stock market move up rapidly. Growth-based investing was very fashionable and very successful in the late 1990s bull market, focusing mainly on technology stocks. When the market fell, value investing came back into its own. However, the distinction between the two is not as clear-cut as is sometimes suggested. For example, a value investor could also buy a stock on a high price/earnings multiple (usually regarded as a growth stock) if he thought that it was undervalued.

Many growth investors focus entirely on individual stocks and ignore economic fundamentals. They argue that growth stocks will do well whatever the economic environment and it is not worth taking account of that. Some growth investors do use a top-down country approach in addition to the bottom-up stocks analysis. And emerging market stock funds often rely heavily on economic fundamentals to choose growth countries.

Technical Analysis

In its purest form this approach ignores economic fundamentals and focuses on the technical behaviour of the market, i.e. trends, volumes and chart patterns. Some investors using technical analysis prefer not to even think about the fundamentals of the market, because they fear that such knowledge might confuse them. Others combine technical analysis with fundamental analysis.

Technical analysis offers a rich variety of approaches to markets (beyond the scope of this book) but broadly it divides into two types. First, there are forms of trend following or momentum investing, for example buying when a market has been rising and selling when it has been falling. Many investors do seem to approach markets in this way and there is evidence of markets overshooting in both directions. The investor who jumps on a trend early and closes his position before it reverses can do well. Obviously this works best when there is a persistent trend and less well in trendless and especially very 'choppy' markets. Many short-term traders follow this approach, making use of technical analysis. Most argue that the crucial requirement is to 'cut losses and run with profits'. This means using stop-losses (i.e. automatically selling if the market moves against you rather than waiting for it to recover) or option techniques to protect the downside or lock in profits. However, plenty of traders lose money and most professional investors use the approach cautiously.

The second approach is to look for turning points or 'break-outs'. These are believed to occur when the direction of the market is changing. Technical analysts look for chart patterns such as trend-line breaks, 'head and shoulders' formations and 'double-tops'. Technical analysts of course often combine these two approaches. Overall, technical analysis can be quite complicated and, in practice, just as among fundamental analysts, technical analysts frequently disagree on the interpretation of a market.

Many investors combine technical analysis with a fundamental approach. One common combination is to use the fundamental view for long-term decisions but rely on technical analysis for the short-term timing of buy/sell executions. Another approach is to buy or sell only when both fundamental and technical analyses point in the same direction. A third approach is to use technical analysis to suggest when to close a position. This is based on the idea that fundamental analysis can give an idea of the direction of a market but technical analysis is more useful for assessing the strength and extent of any move.

Arbitrage Investing

This is an approach based on looking for unjustified differences in prices between similar assets. To take a simple example, suppose that the yield on a 9-year bond is not in between the yield of an 8-year bond and a 10-year bond from the same issuer, as you would expect. This may occur because the market is relatively illiquid and there is simply not enough buying, selling or market-making. If the investor spots this discrepancy he may be able to make money by buying one and selling the other. In recent years there has been a substantial amount of money, particularly from hedge funds, going into this investment approach, but this of course means that there may be diminishing opportunities because the market is more liquid and prices move more quickly.

However, there is always an element of risk because the securities are different. The more different they are, the more likely it will be that there is some element of fundamentals in the difference. For example, a 10-year euro bond issued by the French government is now a relatively close substitute to one issued by the German government, but there could be circumstances where fundamentals do matter, for example if any element of doubt creeps into the continuance of EMU.

Hedge Funds

The original concept of hedge funds is a relatively low risk style of investment, based on going long on one security and short on a similar one. For example, the manager might be long on one oil company and short on another in equal measure, calculating that the first company's share price will outperform the second's. This approach is hedged because, even if the market overall falls, it can still generate good returns. With pessimism about the potential for a strong upward trend in markets in recent years this approach (now called 'hedged equity') has been attractive to many investors.

Hedge funds now cover a wide range of different approaches from low risk to very high risk. Arbitrage funds (see above) have been very popular in recent years with the concept of 'similar assets' considerably stretched. Investing in 'distressed securities', i.e. those close to bankruptcy, is another common approach and is really an extreme form of value investing or contrarianism. Another approach is called 'event driven' and aims at buying or selling securities where events such as mergers or macro-economic developments such as policy announcements are expected to bring price changes. The so-called 'macro funds' approach is less in favour now, following the high-profile difficulties of some famous examples in the late 1990s, notably George Soros' fund. However, they still exist.

Although hedge funds are so diverse they share several important characteristics. First, they rely on managers being clever at spotting profitable opportunities. This is in contrast to a typical long equity fund which will tend to move broadly with the overall asset class. If stocks generally are up, most funds will also be up, and vice versa, even if the manager does not outperform the index itself. Hedge funds' lack of an underlying asset class is both a strength and a weakness. For the believer in efficient markets it is definitely a reason for caution since hedge funds do not have the long-run market trend on their side and, moreover, fees tend to be high. However, it is often seen as a strength because it means that hedge funds can do well in a poor market environment and also will not be correlated with long market positions. The latter point makes them an attractive diversification, provided that they perform.

Secondly, hedge funds frequently go short on securities as well as long. Again, this can be a plus in a falling market. It also opens up many more alternative strategies. Thirdly, and linked to this, hedge funds frequently use leverage, i.e. borrowings. Sometimes this leverage implies substantial risks but often, because of the hedged nature of investments, the actual risk is smaller than it appears. Finally, most hedge funds are very actively managed with a high turnover of assets.

Economic fundamentals may enter into the investment process of some hedge funds although, as already mentioned, 'macro funds' based purely on economic fundamentals are rarer now. Many funds deliberately aim to hedge out any macro events, by being market neutral, interest rate neutral or even industry neutral if they are investing in stocks. Some funds are computer driven, looking for arbitrage opportunities or other patterns in securities. However, most hedge fund managers are very aware of the macro environment, even if their main motivation is to hedge away any risks arising.

CONCLUSION: COMBINING DIFFERENT APPROACHES

As we have seen, some investment approaches rely heavily on the assessment of economic fundamentals, others consciously ignore them and others try to hedge away the fundamental risks. And while some investors follow the pure approaches outlined above, in practice most investors combine several of these approaches. For example, pension fund managers deliberately select several different managers with different styles. This provides diversification and also means that, over time, they can study different approaches and perhaps come to better-informed decisions on which ones to retain. Increasingly they use indexed investments for a core part of their assets because fees are lower. But they also select various other managers with a particular 'active' approach to complement this core, providing exposure to other asset classes and different investment styles.

Individual managers may also combine different elements of these styles in their overall approach. For example, some use a combination of 'bottom-up' analysis of stocks (value or growth) with 'top-down' analysis of the economic fundamentals of markets. That way they hope to combine the best of both. Many also combine technical analysis with the fundamentals. In the end, very few investors ignore the economic fundamentals altogether, but while some rely heavily on assessing them correctly, others prefer to avoid being exposed to them.

20

Ten Years of Changing Fundamentals

In a simple world, fundamentals would stay fundamental and not change over time. And indeed to a large extent the fundamentals do persist. Many of the ideas on economic relationships and market behaviour in this book would be familiar to a mythical reader who had not read anything for 10 or even 50 years. However, some things do change, both in the markets and in how markets are analysed. New theories emerge, new understandings develop and economies and markets evolve. This chapter looks at the main changes over the last 10 years, following the order of chapters in this book.[1]

FASTER TREND GDP GROWTH?

One key area of change is an apparent acceleration in trend economic growth. In academic economics a new focus on economic growth (known as 'endogenous growth theory') surfaced more than 10 years ago and has attracted much attention. In the markets the key issue has been whether the trend rate of growth in the USA accelerated after about 1995 due to faster productivity growth linked to the technological revolution. If potential growth has increased, the implication is that the economy can grow faster without creating inflation. This means that interest rates will only be raised when the economy is growing at a much faster pace than before, profits can also expand more rapidly and higher valuations in the stock market may be justified.

This issue was analysed in depth in Chapter 4 of this book. The broad conclusion was that the USA may now be able to achieve a rate of growth in the 3–4% p.a. range, significantly above the average of the 1974–94 period of about 2.5%, though probably still lower than in the 1960s. Some of this improvement is due to changes in measurement technique, some may be due to faster technological progress (though this is still contentious) and some reflects the higher rates of investment of recent years.

Looking forward, provided that investment remains strong as a percentage of GDP and assuming that there are further gains in productivity to be made using the new technologies, economic growth should be able to continue at this elevated rate. However, whether investment will remain at the levels of the late 1990s is one of the key uncertainties over the next few years. Company profit margins and rates of return on capital declined sharply in 2000–1, which puts continuing high investment in doubt. On the other hand, stock market valuations remain substantially above the replacement value of capital (the ratio known as Tobin's Q). This gap is likely to be corrected over time and can be closed in two ways: either investment will remain very strong so that the capital stock increases, or stock market valuations will fall.

Outside the USA there is no evidence of a similar acceleration in productivity or GDP growth. While some analysts believe that it will come through in the next few years the majority are sceptical. Certainly the ECB proceeds on the basis that there has been no definite change in

---

[1] The basis of this chapter is a comparison of this book with the author's book, written 10 years earlier. J. Calverley (1995) *Pocket Guide to Economics for the Global Investor*. McGraw-Hill.

Euroland; nor, sofar, has the UK seen any improvement, but time will tell. Nevertheless, the success of the USA has reinforced the trend towards freeing up markets which began in the 1980s and received a major boost in 1989–90 with the collapse of the Soviet Union. This trend has continued despite the setback of the Asian crisis.

The 2001 recession conformed in many ways to the fundamentals of cycle theory (Chapter 2) but not all. Hopes that the new economy would banish the economic cycle proved false. However, the 2001 downturn in the USA and Europe did turn out to be very mild, probably because the Federal Reserve cut interest rates very quickly. The US inventory downturn in 2001 was severe, perhaps reflecting the greater transparency of inventory positions with the help of computer technology. Also the downturn in investment was sharp. But consumer spending held up remarkably well, with the help of buoyant house prices and lower interest rates.

INFLATION TARGETING HAS KEPT INFLATION LOW

The monetary area has changed profoundly over the last 10 years and, with a possible further fall in inflation rates to almost zero or even deflation, may change further. On the policy side the biggest shift in the last 10 years is the introduction of explicit inflation targeting in most countries with responsibility charged to independent central banks. This system started in New Zealand in 1990 but took a major leap forward when it was introduced in the UK in late 1992. It has since become very widespread, with the USA as the major exception, though the USA does have an independent central bank and probably follows an implicit inflation target of 1–3% p.a.

In terms of economic performance one of the key surprises in recent years has been the sluggish response of inflation to faster economic growth in many countries. The willingness of the Federal Reserve to cut interest rates very rapidly in 2001 reflected the low inflation in the USA at that time, despite 10 years of economic growth. Although the Fed had been raising interest rates in 1999–2000 in a conventional anti-inflation strategy to slow the economy, inflation actually showed only a very limited upward tendency. This was partly due to the strength of the dollar — a temporary benefit — but also reflected structural changes in the economy which have, to some extent, dampened inflationary tendencies. These structural changes include increased competition in product and labour markets, higher productivity growth, globalisation, which has exposed manufacturing and increasingly services to international competition, and the institutional independence of central banks which has lowered inflation expectations.

The UK also has shown a good performance of inflation. Again, the strong currency has helped. But in the UK an important structural change appears to have been a reduction in the so-called NAIRU (the non-accelerating-inflation-rate-of-unemployment). Euroland's inflation performance has been less encouraging. Inflation did rise well above the ECBs 2% limit in 2001, which accounted for the ECB's reluctance to cut interest rates until late in the year. The higher inflation response in Euroland partly reflected the weak currency. But also Euroland does not seem to have benefited much, if at all, from structural improvements.

Despite the improvements in the inflation performance, the basic connections between an overheating or overemployed economy and rising inflation remain intact. If the 2002 upswing proves robust, it is probable that central banks will again be trying to restrain their economies in 2003–4. On the other side, with inflation relatively low, the risks of deflation have increased and, if economic growth disappoints, central banks might have to face these perils.

THE SPECTRE OF DEFLATION

In some countries inflation has given way to deflation. In 1992 inflation in the OECD area (measured by the private consumption deflator) averaged 4.9% p.a., a significant improvement on rates from the 1970s or 1980s and well down on the 1990 peak (6.3%). But in 2002 inflation is projected to be only 2.1% p.a. and, in Asia, a number of countries have faced outright deflation for several years. In Japan inflation is likely to be −1.5% in 2002.

Deflation makes nonsense of interest rate policy. Whereas standard central bank procedure is to counteract recessions by pushing real interest rates to zero or even negative, deflation makes this impossible because nominal interest rates cannot be less than zero. The loss of central bank control over the economy is worrying especially if deflation is associated with weak asset prices, as it is in Japan. Japan's solution has been to boost the money supply through central bank purchases of securities in the market as well as increasing banks' reserves. However, with most banks effectively insolvent due to the burden of bad loans, and borrowers worried about the economic outlook, the benefits have been slow to come through.

If the world economy is weak in coming years, deflation will become a wider problem and is likely to place enormous pressure on the central banks. Their experience over the last 30 years has been in fighting inflation, yet this battle would become irrelevant. In the author's view the focus is likely to shift towards managing asset prices.

THE GROWING SIGNIFICANCE OF ASSET PRICES

In 1992 asset price effects were not high on the radar screens. The US stock market crash of 1987 had had surprisingly little impact on the economy and was easily offset by an easier monetary policy. And the recession of 1990 was due to a combination of tight monetary policy to combat rising inflation and the Gulf War. It was true that the Japanese stock market had crashed from its peak in 1990 but, in 1992, the full decade-long effects of Japanese asset price deflation were not yet clear.

In 2002 the importance of asset prices to the economy and markets is much more evident. Japan's experience is a major warning, as is the experience of some of the Asian crisis countries. But more attention is also being paid to the risks of bubbles such as the NASDAQ bubble in 1999–2000. Indeed some analysts believe that the wider stock market remains in a bubble and estimate that a fair value for the S&P 500 index, currently standing at 1,150, will be at least 20% lower.

Central banks have tended to react more when asset prices fall than when they rise, leading to the so-called 'Greenspan put'. While this is a great boon to investors it also carries the risk that markets move up to excessively high levels because of the floor provided by central banks. The danger is that eventually the central banks can no longer support asset prices by cutting interest rates and there is a major move down, with a consequently severe knock-on effect on spending in the economy, potentially bringing a severe recession.

The risk of asset price deflation combined with general price deflation has therefore emerged as one of the main 'nightmare scenarios' facing investors. This is in marked contrast to 10 years ago when the re-emergence of high inflation remained a major fear and deflation still seemed remote.

FISCAL POLICY MAKES A COMEBACK

Ten years ago the general view was that fiscal policy would be employed rarely if at all and was a much less useful tool than monetary policy. However, it has in fact played a major role in both economic developments and the markets. In 1992–3 Japan actively used fiscal policy to try to restimulate the economy. A series of budgets and supplementary budgets, particularly using public works projects, were implemented to kick-start the economy and seemed to have some temporary success. However, as economic growth did not become strong enough for the authorities to close the budget deficit, it continued to widen over the last 10 years. Increasing concerns over the growing size of debt have meant that an expansionary fiscal policy is no longer an option. The government now needs to reduce the deficit, though it is recognised that this will be more easily achieved in a growing economy than during a recession.

In Europe fiscal policy was sharply tightened from 1996 onwards as part of the qualification for entering EMU. One of the consequences was the relatively slow rate of GDP growth for the region during the second half of the 1990s. For the future the Growth and Stability Pact essentially precludes active fiscal policy by fixing the limit for deficits at 3% of GDP. In a recession the deficit is likely to swing naturally by several percentage points of GDP, which means that, unless countries start from a significant surplus, there is no room for activism. Germany and Portugal were caught in this trap in early 2002.

US fiscal policy has perhaps followed the most remarkable trajectory. After the 'supply-side' experiments of the 1980s led to large deficits, a popular backlash against fiscal deficits gathered force. In 1993 this bore fruit in President Clinton's decision to tighten fiscal policy at the beginning of his Presidency — a move which disappointed many of his supporters since it left less scope for popular left-wing spending programmes. However, bond yields duly fell and the economy embarked on a long period of strong growth, with this policy (correctly) given considerable credit. By the end of the 1990s the budget was in surplus and the issue became how to manage the expected pay-down of government debt.

However, in 2001 fiscal activism (Keynesianism) returned to the fore. President Bush had campaigned on tax cuts for supply-side reasons, but when he entered office the economy was weakening and the justification for tax cuts became the need to boost the economy. After 11 September a further stimulus was proposed, though this ran into opposition in early 2002 when the economy showed signs of improvement. The government's stimulus came through in the second half of 2001 and into 2002 and was broadly welcomed by economists because, partly through luck, the timing was good.

In the UK fiscal policy also provided the economy with a boost in 2001 and this was purely fortuitous. In 1997–8 the incoming Labour government had deliberately followed a tight fiscal policy, continuing the trend established by the outgoing government, with the result that deficits gave way to surpluses by 1998 and the economy performed well. However, starting in 1999, and accelerating sharply in 2000, the government began to shift, boosting government spending at a much faster rate and projecting for the budget to go into deficit. In effect fiscal policy became extremely expansionary. Fortunately the government was unable to implement the spending policy as quickly as it wanted so that several departments underspent their budgets and much of the stimulus was delayed until 2001, just when the private sector, particularly the manufacturing sector, had slowed with the global slowdown.

In 2001, 2002 and 2003 the OECD Secretariat calculates that the British government stimulus is equal to 0.7–0.9% of GDP each year, and that by 2003 the UK will return to a government deficit. With one of the lowest debt ratios of the OECD countries (and also a relatively low unfunded pension liability) this is not a threat to the government's solvency. It does, however, put pressure on monetary policy, which must restrain private sector demand if the economy is not to overheat. The situation would be exacerbated if the UK voted to join EMU since that would imply lower interest rates and, almost certainly, a lower currency. Fiscal policy ought to be tightened at that point, though this would mean higher taxes and would be unpopular.

Finally, fiscal policy has played a significant role in emerging markets in the last 10 years. In Asia persistent surpluses probably lulled investors into a false sense of security prior to the 1997 crisis but, after the crisis, low government debt did at least make it easier to recapitalise banking systems. However, in other developing countries, notably Turkey and Argentina, their crises revolved around unsustainable fiscal deficits combined with fixed exchange rates.

Three specific developments over the last 10 years are likely to keep fiscal policy at the forefront. First, in countries facing deflation, interest rate policy becomes much less useful in controlling the economy, thereby potentially giving more of a role to fiscal policy. Secondly, interest rate policy is also unavailable to the countries in EMU, which should mean that fiscal policy is given more of a role. Thirdly, there has been increased focus on the problem of off-balance sheet government liabilities which mean that government debts are actually much higher than they appear. In Europe and the USA a large part of this problem relates to pensions. In Asia, including Japan and China, the problem also involves the likely necessary recapitalisation of banking systems.

The conclusion on fiscal policy, as an instrument of macro-economic control, is broadly similar to the view of 10 years ago. Fiscal policy can provide a useful temporary boost to the economy but only if it is well timed. In practice, timing is usually very difficult, which is why interest rate activism is preferred. However, where interest rate activism is becoming more problematic, e.g. for countries suffering deflation or countries that are members of EMU, fiscal policy is potentially now more important. But countries will only be able to use it effectively to lift the economy out of recession if they achieve a surplus during the economic upswing phase and therefore avoid high overall levels of debt.

GLOBALISATION

Turning to trade and international relations, it is a cliché that the last 10 years has seen a surge in globalisation as trade, portfolio capital flows and foreign direct investment have all increased dramatically. Despite violent objectors and reluctant governments the process continues and is bringing enormous benefits in terms of specialisation and economic growth. However, capital flows remain volatile overall, which can contribute to economic instability.

As in the 1980s the largest net contributor to world capital flows has been Japan, and the largest recipient the USA. Some economists believe that the rising US current account deficit will again become a major issue (as it was in the late 1980s). Others argue that the increase in globalisation means that the current account deficit can be much more easily financed than before. The author's view is that the deficit will indeed become an issue at some point, primarily because the USA is now building up a large net liability to the rest of the world. In the 1980s the USA was still a net creditor.

However, there is little sign of increased macro-economic policy coordination. This perhaps reflects the failures of the past when the USA urged Germany in the 1970s and Japan in the 1980s to stimulate their economies to help the world economy, but proved to be a bad experience for both countries (inflation in Germany and a bubble in Japan). But a cynical view would suggest that it may also be due to the fact that the USA usually pushes for policy coordination at times when the dollar is weak, not strong.

The expansion in trade flows has been helped by technological change, which makes it much easier to outsource production, not just of manufactures but of services too. China is emerging as the new 'workshop of the world' helping to keep manufactures prices down and contributing to the weak rate of global inflation. Progress in freeing trade continues, backed by the Uruguay Round and establishment of the WTO, but remains vulnerable to political pressures, particularly in periods of higher unemployment.

BULL MARKET IN BONDS

Interest rate activism has retained its key role in economic policy over the last few years and therefore continues to drive the short-term bond markets. The markets have seen cycles of short rates of three years or so in the last decade, with an overall downward trend. Cycles have been broadly aligned in all the major countries, including the USA, the UK, Euroland and even Japan, with short rates peaking in 1995, 1998 and 2000. The exception is Japanese short rates, which have moved in a very narrow range since 1996, between zero and 0.5% (for 3-month rates) reflecting the deflationary environment. Overall, however, in the last 10 years, roughly since the last recession, the *level* of interest rates has fallen several percentage points in all countries, reflecting lower inflation.

Long-term bonds have also continued their trend to lower yields, thereby providing investors with substantial capital gains above the coupon. However, if central banks succeed in hitting their target of inflation at 1–2% p.a. in future, it is doubtful if the downward trend for yields has any further to go. Yields should be expected to cycle in the 4–6% range. If the central banks fail and economies underperform, taking inflation still lower, yields too could go lower. If deflation takes hold, yields have much further to go, potentially down to the Japanese level of only 1–2% p.a.

For investors one of the key trends of the last decade has been the increased interest in, and issuance of, higher risk bonds, ranging from good corporate credits to emerging country bonds and junk bonds. This represents partly a 'reach for yield' as investors look for higher returns. But it also reflects, for some investors, a switch away from equities, which have been seen as too high risk and, by some, as too highly valued.

HIGH EQUITY VALUATIONS

On any measure the US equity market reached unprecedented valuations at the high in 2000. The broadest measure of the market, the Wilshire 5000 index, then suffered a peak to trough decline of 40% between March 2000 and September 2001. At the time of writing this index stands just under 11,000, 25% below the peak. Nevertheless, compared with historical standards the current valuation remains high. Even on moderately optimistic forward earnings the p/e ratio is still more than 20-fold, compared with a long-term average of 14–15 while Tobin's Q (the ratio of market valuation to book capital at replacement cost) is also higher than average.

Only time will tell whether these valuations can be sustained. If US economic growth can maintain a 'new economy' trend rate of 3.5% p.a. or more, while inflation, interest rates and bond yields all stay moderate, the macro-economic conditions will remain favourable. If the geopolitical situation does not deteriorate, the background of world peace and increased glob-alisation will also continue. Then, providing investors are comfortable with lower rates of returns than those seen during the 1990s, valuations could hold high or descend gently without major disruption.

Nevertheless it is difficult to escape the conclusion that average returns will be lower in the coming years than during the 1980s and 1990s. That 20-year period saw a long-term rise in valuations in the USA and Europe (including the UK) from a price/earnings ratio of under 10 times at the low of 1982 to a ratio of over 30 times at the peak in the USA and 25 times in Europe. The p/e ratio would have to rise to 90 times over the next 20 years to generate the same returns, which almost nobody thinks is plausible. Also, if the p/e ratio shows a downward trend, then equity returns could be lower than the growth of profits. Generally, it has become a conventional view that market returns will probably be in single figures in coming years. This also fits with the concept of mean reversion which says that, in the long run, valuations return to average or, put another way, the fundamentals win out.

DOLLAR STRENGTH AND EURO WEAKNESS

There have been three major developments in the currency area. First, the Asian crisis followed by the devaluations in Russia, Brazil and Argentina have dramatically increased the number of floating currencies in the emerging world. Only a handful of countries now operate fixed exchange rate systems or currency boards. Secondly, moving in the opposite direction, 12 European countries have so far joined the Monetary Union and more are expected to follow. Thirdly, the dollar has swung to a level of strength while the euro has been unexpectedly weak.

Explanations for the euro's weakness centre on the size of capital flows going into the USA, which overwhelm even the large USA current account deficit. These inflows may reflect better economic prospects in the USA with higher rates of return. Or they may be due to better investment opportunities in the USA because of the large liquid capital markets and liberal takeover rules. Crucially, these long-term investments are not hedged (though they could be if the dollar threatened to move suddenly), and they overwhelm the positions of short-term speculators, many of whom have been long euros.

Large swings in the dollar versus European currencies are not a new phenomenon. Ten years ago the dollar was just emerging from a prolonged period of weakness, which in turn followed the dollar's strength in 1983–5. It is very possible, therefore, that the dollar will turn down again at some point, with a potential downward move of 20–30% or more if the currency substantially overshoots, as it usually does. However, currency cycles are long and difficult to predict so this move could still be a few years away.

For the USA a weak dollar will boost the economy as the current account deficit is gradually corrected. Since the most likely scenario for dollar weakness is one where the US economy itself is weak, the decline in the dollar is likely to be a welcome development and will not prompt the Fed to raise interest rates. Such a scenario is therefore likely to be good for the US stock market. For Europe, however, a weak dollar will hurt exports and lower inflation, prompting cuts in interest rates. Bonds are likely to gain, especially if the ECB is slow to cut interest rates, creating a flatter yield curve and a move down in long-term bond yields.

In the emerging markets the most shocking event of the decade was the Asian crisis. Other crises, including Russia's default, Brazil's devaluation and Argentina's melt-down, continued the pattern set by Mexico in 1994. But Asia's crisis had a profound impact on thinking about investing in emerging markets. At the straightforward level, fixed exchange rates are now viewed as a very high risk strategy for a country. More fundamentally the attractions of investing in many countries has been seriously called into question on grounds of performance, transparency, corporate governance and risk. The author's view is that this caution leaves many emerging markets underpriced as a result.

CHANGES IN INVESTMENT FUNDAMENTALS

There are perhaps three main areas where the fundamentals have changed in the last 10 years. First, the extraordinary bull market in the USA, particularly in technology stocks, has led to a surge of interest in 'behavioural finance'. The academic basis for this goes back 20 years or more, with the essential idea being that investors' actions to buy, sell or hold are often irrational. More recently behavioural finance has taken on a Darwinian tint, suggesting that people's attitudes to risk and return are motivated by aspects of human nature which probably have some survival value in a hunter-gatherer society, but which are not strictly rational from the point of view of an individualist investor. While these theories provide a ready explanation for bubbles and manias, they also provide a warning to those who believe that the markets are rational.

Secondly, the huge growth of derivatives, outside the scope of this book, has provided tremendous opportunities to reduce risk through sophisticated hedging techniques and to take increased risk through speculative positions. The performance of derivatives is linked to the performance of the underlying asset, but with the additional complication of changes in volatility. Of course volatility itself is subject to fundamental influences, including the stage of the cycle and changes in uncertainty over government policy, etc.

Finally, the higher valuations on most assets, in other words the reduction in yields, has led to a search for higher yields. Sometimes this search appears to be unwise. At least until 1998 in the high yield bond markets and 2001 in the stock markets, investors seemed too often to have an unrealistic attitude to risk. The shocks of recent years have made investors much more cautious and widened spreads considerably. But investors still may be underestimating the real returns available, even on lower risk assets. For example, government bond yields of over 5% p.a. currently and dividend yields on blue-chip companies of 2–3% p.a. may actually be quite good long-term investments in an era of low inflation.

For investors the markets are always changing and, over time, some of the fundamentals move on too. This is what makes the subject so fascinating. But most of the regularities in the economy do continue through time and the author remains convinced that, through a careful study of these patterns, there are always investment opportunities. These opportunities then need to be seized in a structured way and incorporated in a diversified portfolio. Good luck!

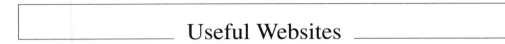

Useful Websites

There are a vast number of websites with economic data and information. However some of them are restricted to paying clients while others require payment on-line for some or all their publications. The following is a selected list of websites that the author has found useful and which can provide a starting point.

OFFICIAL ORGANISATIONS

www.imf.org is the website of the International Monetary Fund. It provides detailed data and information on all countries, including many IMF 'letters of intent' with emerging countries.
www.worldbank.org is the site of the World Bank. Again, data and information on countries is available.
www.oecd.org is the site for the OECD, the Organisation for Economic Co-operation and Development. It contains data, information and analysis for the major industrial nations.
www.federalreserve.gov is the site of the US Federal Reserve. Excellent research can also be obtained from the regional Federal Reserve banks, which can be accessed via this site.
www.ecb.int is the English site of the European Central Bank. Individual European central banks also publish a wide range of research.
www.bankofengland.co.uk is the site of the Bank of England.
www.boj.or.jp/en is the English site for the Bank of Japan.
www.bis.org is the site of the Bank for international settlements. Based in Basle this is the bank for central banks. It provides data and research on many topics in the financial markets.

OTHER USEFUL SITES

www.iijpm.com is the site of the *Journal of Portfolio Management.*
www.afajof.org is the site of the *Journal of Finance.*
www.iie.com is the site of the Institute of International Economics in Washington. Contains numerous papers and studies on international economic issues.
www.nber.org is the site of the National Bureau of Economic Research, the US organisation that dates business cycles. It contains useful data and research on past business cycles.
www.tutor2u.net is a site aimed at A-level students in the UK. It has a wealth of economics information, explaining concepts in a straightforward way, as well as very useful links to other sites.
www.bloomberg.co.uk provides information on bond markets.
www.bp.com is the site of BP Plc, the British oil company. Included is BP's annual energy review, one of the best sources of data on oil and other energy sources, with data in PDF and excel format.
www.iea.org is the site of the International Energy Agency, another good source of energy data.
www.freetheworld.com is the site for the Economic Freedom Index referred to in Chapter 10.
www.spglobal.com/earnings.html gives past data and analysts' expectations for stock earnings on the S&P 500 index.

www.stern.nyu.edu/globalmacro/simple_content_frame.html is a site run by Nouriel Roubini at the Stern School of Business in New York, containing useful articles and press cuttings on current major economic and financial topics.

www.wws.princeton.edu/~pkrugman/ is the new site of Paul Krugman, a famous US economist. It covers many topical issues as well as some more academic issues.

www.halifaxplc.com is a site belonging to HBOS, a UK bank, which provides UK house price data.

www.nabe.com is the site of the National Association of Business Economists (for the USA) and provides excellent links to information sources.

www.economomagic.com contains a vast array of US data going back to the 1950s for free.

www.sbe.co.uk is the site of the Society of Business Economists in the UK. Also contains useful links.

www.americanexpress.com/privatebank contains the Economics for Investment publications, produced by the author and his team.

www.dbresearch.com is the website of Deutsche Bank research. Contains forecasts and commentary.

www.bmo.com/economic/ is the website of the Bank of Montreal run by Chief Economist Tim O'Neill. Contains forecasts and commentary for the major countries.

Glossary

The chapters noted at the end of each entry indicate the principal chapter where the term is used.

Arbitrage investing Exploiting price differences between similar assets in anticipation that the difference will close. (*Chapter 19.*)

Bretton Woods system The name given to the post-war system of fixed exchange rates which lasted until the early 1970s before breaking down and being replaced with floating rates. It was named after the hotel in the USA where the Allies met in 1944. The IMF and World Bank were also set up following the Bretton Woods conference. (*Chapter 14.*)

Capacity utilisation An indicator of the extent to which existing capacity in the form of plant and machinery is in full use. In practice the 100% level is not in itself very meaningful because in Japan the economy is frequently reported as producing at more than 100% of estimated capacity while, for example, in the USA the economy rarely gets above 85%. The US authorities regard 82% as a critical level beyond which inflation will start to rise. (*Chapter 3.*)

Capital formation Economists use the word capital in different ways but the underlying concept is the same. The key is that it represents a store of value which is not immediately consumed, i.e. it is either money or a capital good. It cannot be a consumer good which is quickly used up. Capital flight typically means money flowing out of the country. Fixed capital means machinery, factories, etc. while fixed capital formation means investing, i.e. building factories or offices and buying machines to go in them. (*Chapter 1.*)

Coincident indicators Data releases which are regarded as normally coincident with the economic cycle. Typical components are industrial production, employment and personal income. This index is not much looked at by the markets (though its individual components are), with much more attention being given to leading indicators. (*Chapter 2.*)

Comparative advantage A term much liked by economists and much misunderstood by non-economists. A country is said to have a comparative advantage when it can produce one product comparatively more efficiently than another product. This has nothing to do with absolute advantage. For example, India can produce both cotton goods and cars, as can the USA. But in terms of efficiency (or absolute advantage) the USA is more efficient at both if one was simply to count the hours of work that go into producing one or the other, because the USA uses more machines. However, India has a comparative advantage in cotton goods because of lower wages and availability of raw cotton at cheap prices. The theory therefore says that India would do well to concentrate upon the good in which it has a comparative advantage rather than trying to produce everything. Then both countries will gain from trade. Note that anybody who says that some countries do not have a comparative advantage in anything is misunderstanding the concept. (*Chapter 8.*)

Competitiveness   An often mis-used term. Companies and industries in a particular country face increasing pressures to be competitive as trade increases and trade barriers fall. Economists talk of price competitiveness and non-price competitiveness, meaning that there is competition in both price and other factors such as quality and after sales service. For a country as a whole competitiveness is assured (at least in the long term) by changes in exchange rates and/or real wages. Politicians and others exhorting their countrymen to become more competitive really should use the words productive or efficient since it is improvements here which will raise living standards. (*Chapter 8.*)

Constant prices   Because of the prevalence of inflation in the last 30 years economists prefer to look at many measures of the economy in constant price terms (as opposed to current prices) to separate the real from the nominal economy. For example, in current price terms GDP may rise 5% but after allowing for inflation of 3% the real growth rate, i.e. in constant price terms, is 2%. The difficulty is that the calculation of prices is not always easy so that the calculation of the 'deflator' to be used is much less precise than statisticians like to pretend. (*Chapter 1.*)

Consumer confidence   A monthly measure of how confident consumers feel about the economy, based on survey data. (*Chapter 2.*)

Consumption   Economists distinguish consumption from other forms of spending in order to define it as goods which are actually consumed, as opposed to spending which is for investment in the form of fixed capital or stock building or machinery, etc. In the national accounts data, consumption also includes spending on cars and refrigerators, although technically, since cars last more than one year, the full spending is not all consumption. In balance sheet data some allowance is made for this by including cars and durable goods as a wealth factor. (*Chapter 1.*)

Convertibility   Governments make exchange rates convertible to varying extents. Prior to 1979, for example, many countries had what is called 'current account convertibility'. In other words, any transactions relating to the current account of the balance of payments, i.e. exports of goods and services or income on investments, was freely convertible by governments. However any investment abroad by a domestic resident or company was subject to some degree of exchange controls. During the 1980s the UK and Japan led many countries, including recently many developing countries such as Mexico and Egypt, to full convertibility. This means that any demand for foreign currency for whatever reason, including investment abroad or holding a foreign currency bank account at home, is freely available. This trend creates more difficulties for managing currencies but it is believed by the IMF and the World Bank and many others to promote foreign investment in the country and ultimately make for a better economic policy framework and stronger economic growth. (*Chapter 8.*)

Counter-cyclical   The economy goes through its economic cycle and at times governments want to counter the direction of the cycle. For example in the USA in 1988–9, in 1994 and in 1999–2000 the emphasis was on countering the boom and slowing the economy. The main policies that can be used are monetary policy, fiscal policy and exchange rate policy. (*Chapter 2.*)

Crowding out   The term used to indicate that government borrowing can crowd out other borrowing. Since the availability of credit in the markets is ultimately determined by the level of savings in the economy, the existence of too much government borrowing may prevent other borrowing from taking place. Crowding out normally works through interest rates, particularly long-term interest rates, remaining too high. (*Chapter 6.*)

Current account   The trade account of countries normally refers to trade in goods only. However US data now includes trade in services as well. Economists generally prefer to look at the current account of the balance of payments (as opposed to the capital account) which includes trade in goods and services plus interest payments and transfers. For most countries trade in services adds between 20 and 50% to trade in goods although this percentage is on the increase. The current account as measured must then be matched in the balance of payments by the capital account (plus any change in government foreign exchange reserves). As an accounting identity either the current account or the capital account shows the net capital inflow or outflow for the country. (*Chapter 8.*)

Deflation   This is a term which is used in two different ways. Sometimes it can be used to indicate simply a tightening of policy aimed at slowing the economy but its original meaning meant a decline in the price level. With inflation now only marginally above zero in many countries, the risk of deflation has become a real one. Japan, China, Hong Kong and Argentina have already experienced it. The particular danger of deflation is that, if people believe that prices will actually fall in the coming months, they will delay spending and that delay in spending can take the economy into a slump and of course take prices down further. This was the pattern in the USA in the early 1930s. (*Chapter 3.*)

Demand   A popular term used among economists to mean spending. An increase in demand therefore could come from consumers or business or government and would be seen and evidenced by a rise in sales. Demand is met by supply, sometimes known as output. (*Chapter 1.*)

Depression   This is the phase of the business cycle seen only every few decades where either the economy slumps sharply or, as in the so-called Great Depression of the 1870s, it goes through a long period of slow growth and weak profits. Most economists believe that depressions are now much less likely than in the past because of the larger role of government in the economy and tighter official control of the financial system. (*Chapter 2.*)

Diffusion index   The technical term for the way many leading indicator indices and survey-based composite indices are calculated. The overall index is arrived at by comparing the number of its components that are rising, falling or staying the same. In intuitive terms the idea is that the stronger the economic upswing the more components of the index are likely to be moving up. Approaching a turning point some will turn down before others so this measure should give some warning. (*Chapter 2.*)

Disinflation   The term used to indicate a policy or process where inflation is brought down. (*Chapter 3.*)

Disposable income   A technical term used by economists to indicate income after taxation. The difference between what is actually spent on goods and services and disposable income is called savings. Note that the amount spent may include borrowing and indeed during the 1980s saving rates fell mainly because borrowing increased. (*Chapter 1.*)

Econometrics   This is the branch of economics which produces economic forecasting models and also tests relationships between variables. For example, does higher unemployment lead to lower inflation? Essentially this is a mathematical treatment of history and therefore is not always a good guide to the future. Econometrics has become much more sophisticated in recent years, but econometric modelling of the economy is still far from a perfect science. In general models seem to be good at forecasting GDP in all the years except when it is important, because it is a turning point of the business cycle! (*Chapter 2.*)

Effective exchange rate   An index calculated by many central banks of the level of a country's exchange rate in relation to other currencies, on a trade-weighted basis. (*Chapter 14.*)

Efficient market hypothesis (EMH)   The theory that the market price of a stock, or any other asset, already takes into account all the known information and reasonable expectations about the future. (*Chapter 19.*)

Emerging markets   Term given to the stock markets of developing countries. There is no definitive way to distinguish which markets have yet to emerge, which are emerging and which have already emerged. For practical purposes analysts often use the International Finance Corporation (IFC) classifications. The IFC, part of the World Bank, is based in Washington. Emerging markets are attractive to investors for three reasons. First, they often show good long-term returns because of the fast underlying growth of GDP and profits. Secondly, their returns historically are often non-correlated, i.e. independent of returns in the major markets, so that they provide useful diversification. Thirdly, when a market first emerges, or suddenly improves, it can often provide truly spectacular returns. The big downside is that the volatility of emerging markets is much higher than for the developed markets. (*Chapters 10 and 16.*)

Equilibrium   Favourite term of economists, particularly academic economists, to discuss a point to which an economy will tend to move. In practice in the real world, investors will not really see equilibrium and indeed may be trying to take advantage of situations that are far from equilibrium.

Exchange controls (*see also* **Convertibility**)   Exchange controls are attempts by governments to control movements of capital either in or out of the country usually in order to protect an exchange rate. Countries are generally advised to remove exchange controls completely (i.e. make the currency fully convertible) because this is seen as a better way to promote investment. However, the Asian crisis showed the risks of combining full convertibility with a fixed exchange rate. (*Chapter 14.*)

Fiscal policy   The term used by economists to indicate the budgetary stance of the government. (*Chapter 6.*)

Flow of funds   This is a collection of accounts prepared by government statisticians which show the actual movements of money into different instruments during the course of a year. So, for example, they begin with savings of the household sector and show where those monies are put in terms of investment in house building and purchases of stocks and shares, etc.

Fundamentals   The forces in the economy which combine with events and market sentiment to determine markets. The opposite of 'technicals', though many investors see them as complements.

Gross domestic product (GDP)   A statistical calculation of the total flow of goods and services in the economy and as such can be seen as the sum of everybody's income or everybody's spending or everybody's production. Gross domestic product differs from gross national product in that GDP is what is produced in the domestic economy and GNP is what nationals of the country produce, including their income from overseas. (*Chapter 1.*)

GDP deflator   The inflation index which 'deflates' nominal GDP to real GDP. Announced at the same time as real GDP is released, it gives the best overall measure of inflation in the economy. (*Chapter 3.*)

Gross fixed capital formation   A technical term for investment, meaning spending on buildings, plant and machinery, plus spending on constructing residential property. It does not include spending on inventories (though inventories are included in the definition of investment). It is called 'gross' because it is calculated without any deduction for depreciation. (*Chapter 1.*)

High-powered money   In countries where banks are required to have a certain percentage of reserve assets in the form of deposits at the central bank, these, together with circulating currency, are described as high-powered money. Monetary base means the same thing. In principle the central bank can control high-powered money and if, given the reserve asset ratio, the authorities allow an increase, banks can lend out a multiple of this increase. In practice, the authorities in most countries do not use this approach because it leads to an extreme volatility in interest rates. The Volcker experiment during 1979 was an attempt to control high-powered money and let the interest rate go where it liked but was later abandoned for a far more flexible approach where interest rates are set at a particular level and then altered if the money supply appears to be expanding too quickly or too slowly. (*Chapter 5.*)

Hyperinflation   A situation of rapidly accelerating inflation. Some countries have inflation of 50–100% p.a. but generally hyperinflation is the term used for much higher inflation than this. The reason for hyperinflation is also well understood. It can always be traced directly to governments printing money to finance budget deficit. The key to the solution, straightforward in theory, but more difficult in practice, is to close the budget deficit. (*Chapter 3.*)

Industrial countries   The term applied to the developed countries of Europe, the USA, Canada, Australia, New Zealand and Japan. The usual definition is the OECD group (Organisation for Economic Cooperation and Development based in Paris), though Mexico, Korea and some central European countries are now members even though they are not usually seen as industrial countries.

Inventory cycle   A crucial element of the business cycle, also known as the stock cycle. At the beginning of the upswing, businesses decide that sales are likely to grow in future and therefore they start producing for inventory in order to be able to meet that demand when it comes. This extra production can be an important factor in generating the recovery itself. Similarly, as recession approaches and businesses suddenly becomes less confident about future sales, they will try suddenly to reduce inventory by cutting production. However, in so doing, they reduce overtime and earnings and often employment and thereby cut demand still more. Quite often inventory accumulation or inventory reduction can add or subtract as much as 1–2% growth in the economy in a particular year and thereby is a crucial factor in the economic cycle. (*Chapter 2.*)

Investment   Economists use the term investment (or capital formation) in a particular way. Investment is defined as spending on something newly produced which will directly provide a good or service later. Hence it includes spending on new buildings, plant and machinery by businesses, etc. which will be used to produce other goods or services later, e.g. factories, offices, machine tools, computers, etc. It also includes spending on inventories, i.e. goods that for the time being are stored, waiting to be used. It also includes the building of houses, which will provide accommodation in years to come. When an individual or company buys stocks and shares, this does not count as investment in economic terms but is described as 'accumulation of financial assets'. (*Chapter 1.*)

***J*-curve**   This is the path of the trade balance or current account balance in response to devaluation. It traces out the pattern of a *J*. At first the trade position gets worse primarily because imports cost more, the downward part of the *J*. After a while import volumes fall and exports rise because of the more competitive exchange rate, which makes the trade balance turn around and move up to a level above where it started. (*Chapter 8.*)

Keynesian   The term used to indicate a view of economics which tends to downplay the role of money and monetary policy and emphasise demand (i.e. spending) in the economy and the potential use of fiscal policy. In practice, this view of the economy would probably not be recognised by John Maynard Keynes himself, a British economist who died in 1946. Keynes was primarily a monetary economist and his three major economics books all included the word 'money' in the title. Keynesianism, emerging after his death was superficially based on Keynes' hugely influential 1936 book, *The General Theory of Employment Interest and Money*. But Keynesian economics ran into trouble in the 1970s when it became clear that the policy was leading to an increase in inflation and that the supposed trade-off between inflation and unemployment was simply not holding. However, the ascendancy of the alternative approach, monetarism, lasted only a few years. Equally there are few economists who would now claim to be unreconstructed Keynesians. (*Chapter 6.*)

Kondratieff cycle   The long cycle of 50 to 60 years first analysed in depth by Kondratieff, a Russian economist writing in the 1920s. (*Chapter 2.*)

Lags   A term beloved of economists to describe the time interval between one event and another. For example, inflation typically peaks some 6 months to a year after the economy peaks and then inflation starts to rise only a year or more into economic recovery. (*Chapter 2.*)

Leading indicators   Data releases which usually lead (predate) turning points in the economy. By taking a group of indicators the fluctuations in any one indicator are washed out. Typical indicators are average weekly hours, manufacturers inventories, new orders, stock prices, money supply and consumer confidence. Note, however, that the lead time between the leading indicators index and the economy varies considerably and can be as short as 1–2 months. Governments also compile indices of coincident indicators and lagging indicators. (*Chapter 2.*)

Liquidity trap   This was a term invented by Keynes to indicate a situation where, despite interest rates being very low, nobody wants to borrow to get the economy moving. He identified it in the context of the 1930s when the price level was actually falling and therefore, although interest rates were down at 1%, real interest rates were at 3–4% or more, reflecting the declining price level or deflation of the time. Japan has been in a liquidity trap for the last few years. (*Chapter 5.*)

Macro-economics   Economists divide into macro-economists and micro-economists. The macro-economy is how the overall economy operates and deals with inflation, unemployment, GDP growth, etc., the main subject matter of this book. Micro- economics is concerned with such questions as how companies operate and how to deal with public monopolies.

Monetarism   The view that money growth is closely linked to inflation. The idea goes back to the eighteenth century at least. The key proponents of monetarism were Irving Fisher who formalised the quantity theory of money early in the twentieth century and Milton Friedman who promoted monetarism throughout the 1960s and 1970s and who wrote, with Anna Schwarz, *The Monetary History of the United States*. (*Chapter 5.*)

Money illusion   This was the term used particularly in the 1970s to indicate people's unawareness of inflation. By focusing on nominal values people often seemed not to be aware that the real levels were not what they seemed. (*Chapter 3.*)

Output gap   A gap which opens out in times of recession between the trend growth path of the economy (as calculated) and the actual path. While the output gap is open inflation tends to decline. Once it closes and especially if the economy starts to overheat and go above its trend path, sometimes called an inflationary gap, inflation tends to rise. (*Chapter 3.*)

Overheating   When the economy grows fast and in particular when it approaches full capacity it is said to exhibit signs of overheating, notably rising inflation, shortages of skilled labour and increasing wages. Also there may be sharp rises in asset prices and in commodity prices. Signs of overheating usually receive a sharp response from the monetary authorities who raise interest rates to slow the economy down. (*Chapter 2.*)

Phillips curve   A simple scatter chart measuring unemployment on one axis against inflation on the other. Prior to the 1970s at least it seemed to show that high unemployment goes with low inflation and vice versa. (*Chapter 3.*)

Price/earnings ratio   The ratio of a stock price to company earnings per share. Usually the p/e ratio will use historical earnings, i.e. actual earnings in the latest year, but sometimes it will be quoted using prospective earnings, i.e. analysts' forecasts for the coming year. (*Chapter 13.*)

Productivity   Defined as output per unit of input employed. The most useful measure is labour productivity, i.e. the amount of output per man-hour. It can be measured as, for example, the number of cars produced per worker in a year. More commonly it will be measured as the value of output per man-hour. Provided that a good meausure of inflation is used over time, then changes in productivity can be measured. Clearly the income levels of a country depend crucially on labour productivity. Poor countries have relatively low productivity while the rich countries have high levels. Ultimately what determines productivity is the amount of machinery available to support labour, the effectiveness of the organisation of production (i.e. how efficient is it) and the skills of the workforce. (*Chapter 1.*)

Recession   A period of declining GDP. In the USA the National Bureau of Economic Research uses a complex variety of indicators to define turning points. Often recessions are simply defined as two consecutive quarters of declining GDP though this is only a rule of thumb and can be misleading. Other countries do not use such a precise definition. Sometimes the term growth recession is used to describe a period of slower growth than normal. Recessions are distinguished from depressions by the extent of the downturn. A depression is associated with the experience of the 1930s when output slumped by 10% or more in most countries. (*Chapter 2.*)

Recovery   The term used for the end of a recession. The US National Bureau of Economic Research defines the trough as the lowest month in the recession, i.e. just before output turns around and begins to rise again. The recovery therefore starts the month after the trough. It ends when the economy regains the same level of output it had immediately prior to the recession. This normally takes a year or more of increased output. (*Chapter 2.*)

Savings   Defined by economists as the difference between current income and current spending. Note that it could be negative if people borrow. (*Chapter 1.*)

Supply-side   The supply-side of the economy comprises the decisions to produce, how much and at what price. The emergence of supply-side economics in the 1980s was a reminder that the key determinant of incomes, especially in the longer run, is the efficient use and allocation of labour and capital in the economy. Supply-siders emphasised the importance of low taxation and reduced regulation to encourage increased productivity and output. This can be contrasted with demand-side economics which focuses on spending decisions. Both Keynesian economics and monetarism are primarily focused on the demand-side. (*Chapter 1.*)

Taylor rule   A suggested 'rule' to help central banks to decide on the correct level of short-term interest rates. Central banks have generally operated more-or-less in line with the rule although they do not follow it slavishly, particularly in conditions of asset price instability. The formula is as follows:

$$R = R_{trend} + \tfrac{1}{2}(G_{expected} - G_{trend}) + \tfrac{1}{2}(I_{expected} - I_{target})$$

where: R is the best level for the short-term interest rate (e.g. Fed Funds rate).
   R_{trend} is the trend or 'neutral' rate of interest in the economy, likely to be equal to trend growth plus target inflation. In Europe this is about 4% while in the USA and the UK it is about 5%.
   $G_{expected}$ is forecast GDP growth over the next year.
   G_{trend} is the central bank's view of trend economic growth. In Europe and the UK this is about 2.5% while in the USA it is about 3.5%.
   $I_{expected}$ is the expected rate of inflation.
   I_{target} is the central bank's inflation target. In the UK this is 2.5% on RPIX while in the USA it is generally seen as 2% p.a. (*Chapter 5.*)

Trade cycle   An alternative word for business cycle. (*Chapter 2.*)

Trend growth rate   A concept beloved of economists which aims to show the average growth rate that the economy can attain for a long period, 5–10 years or more, even though the actual economy may cycle around this trend. The components of the trend growth rate can be broken down into labour force growth rate and the rate of growth of labour productivity. Also sometimes called potential growth rate or underlying growth rate. It is believed to have risen in the USA in the late 1990s. (*Chapter 1.*)

Underlying growth rate   *See* Trend growth rate. (*Chapter 1.*)

Unit labour costs   Wage costs per unit of output. In effect, if wages are rising by 4% and productivity growth by 3% then unit labour costs rise by 1%. (*Chapter 1.*)

Velocity of money   The speed at which money flows around the economy. (*Chapter 4.*)

Volatility   Describes the size of fluctuations in the market price of a security. High volatility is associated with high risk. A crucial part of option pricing. (*Chapter 19.*)

Yield curve   The range of interest rates from overnight rates to 30-year bonds or more. (*Chapter 12.*)

Index

Index compiled by Annette Musker